THE NATURE OF HUMAN SOCIETY
HONOUR AND SHAME

THE NATURE OF HUMAN SOCIETY SERIES

Editors: Julian Pitt-Rivers and Ernest Gellner

HONOUR AND SHAME

The Values of Mediterranean Society

Edited by
J. G. Peristiany

THE UNIVERSITY OF CHICAGO PRESS

THE UNIVERSITY OF CHICAGO PRESS, CHICAGO 60637
WEIDENFELD AND NICOLSON LTD., LONDON W.1
Introduction © 1966 by George Weidenfeld and Nicolson Ltd
Honour and Social Status © 1966 by Julian Pitt-Rivers
Honour and Shame: A Historical Account of Several Conflicts
© 1966 by Julio Caro Baroja
English translation © 1966 by George Weidenfeld and Nicolson Ltd
Honour and the Devil © 1966 by J. K. Campbell
Honour and Shame in a Cypriot Highland Village © 1966 by
J. G. Peristiany
The Sentiment of Honour in Kabyle Society © 1966 by Pierre Bourdieu
English translation © 1966 by George Weidenfeld and Nicolson Ltd
Honour and Shame among the Bedouins of Egypt
© 1966 by Ahmed Abou-Zeid

Published 1966

Library of Congress Catalog Card Number: 66-11886

Printed in Great Britain

CONTENTS

J. G. Peristiany

INTRODUCTION

Introduction

Mediterranean honour and shame were first discussed by the present group of authors in 1959 at Burg Wartenstein, the European Headquarters of the Wenner-Gren Foundation.[1] Most members of this group continued their discussions in Athens in 1961 and in 1963 during conferences convened by the editor for the Social Sciences Centre, Athens,[2] and sponsored by the Greek Ministry to the Prime Minister's Office – Press and Information Department – and the 1963 conference also received a subsidy from Unesco.

More convincingly, perhaps, than any recourse to past history, the essays contained in this volume reveal the continuity and persistence of Mediterranean modes of thought. At the same time the very frequency of the analogies encountered make it easier to set aside the superficial similarities of form and to centre our investigations on an analysis of the content. The fact that, on being provoked, a Greek Cypriot, a Bedouin and a Berber may answer 'I also have a moustache' as the least common denominator of equality between all males, does not necessarily point to affinities between their cultures. In this context it is the comparison of the male-female relationship and that of the roles of the sexes within these societies that points both to the significant analogies and to the equally significant differences.

All societies have rules of conduct, indeed the terms 'society' and 'social regulations' are coterminous. All societies sanction their rules of conduct, rewarding those who conform and punishing those who disobey. Honour and shame are social evaluations and thus participate of the nature of social sanctions, the more monolithic the jury, the more trenchant the judgement. Honour and shame are two poles of an evaluation. They are the reflection of the social personality in the mirror of social ideals. What is particular to these evaluations is that they use as standard of measurement the type of personality considered as representative and exemplary of a certain society. Whoever is measured by its standards and is not found wanting may, without falling from grace, break a number of rules considered minor in relation to those of honour. Thus, in a number of instances, one may take another person's property, life and even honour, while retaining his own honour. The reverse is also true. The man who never endangers the property, limb and honour of his fellows[3] may neither be considered as having honour of his own nor gain honour through his passive acquiescence to social regulations. Honour is at the apex of the pyramid of temporal social values and it conditions their hierarchical order. Cutting across all other social classifications it divides social beings into two fundamental categories, those endowed with honour and those deprived of it.

It is true that in evaluating a person's conduct his social standing is taken into consideration. It is also true that no person is acceptable, whatever his position and achievements, if he lacks the components of honour. Excellence in these qualities pertains to the ideal type of man, deficiency in them opens the way to social destitution. The ideal and the respected man are on different steps of the same value ladder. A study of the value judgements concerning honour and shame involves the study of the supreme temporal[4] ideals of a society and of their embodiment in the ideal type of man. It is also a study of the basic mould of social personality.

This way of reasoning can only lead to the conclusion that as all societies evaluate conduct by comparing it to ideal standards of action, all societies have their own forms of honour and shame. Indeed, they have. Why, then, do some societies make more constant reference than others to these forms of social evaluation? Do they protest too much? It is an interesting, if unoriginal, thought, since peoples under foreign domination have been saying much the same thing about fair play, sportsmanship, religious and social equality, the white man's burden and all the other virtues peddled by their alien rulers. The anthropologist cannot ignore the constant preoccupations of the society he is studying. The Mediterranean peoples discussed in these papers are constantly called upon to use the concepts of honour and shame in order to assess their own conduct and that of their fellows.

If honour and shame are universal aspects of social evaluations, the polarity of the sacred and the profane is equally common. But our concern is not with the universal causality or logic of these phenomena but with their relevance to a particular social system and to the search for correlations which might provide an index to the classification of these social systems.

It is not possible to read about honour and shame in these six Mediterranean societies without making frequent mental excursions and involuntary comparisons with the *gesta* of chivalry, with school gangs, with street corner societies, etc. What do these groups have in common? This, it seems to me, is the crux of the problem. The papers collected here may allow the formulation of a *tentative*, an exploratory, answer. Honour and shame are the constant preoccupation of individuals in small scale, exclusive societies where face to face personal, as opposed to anonymous, relations are of paramount importance and where the social personality of the actor is as significant as his office. Within the minimal solidary groups of these societies, be they small or large families or clans, spheres of action are well defined, non-overlapping and non-competitive. The opposite is true outside these groups. What is significant in this wider context is the insecurity and instability of the honour-shame ranking. Even when honour is inherited with the family name it has to be asserted and vindicated. To accept this is to accept the all-powerfulness of public opinion rather than that of a hierarchical superior. When the individual is encapsulated in a social group an aspersion on his honour is an aspersion on the honour of his group. In this type of situation the behaviour of the individual reflects that of his group to such an extent that, in his relations with other groups, the individual is forcibly cast in the role of his group's protagonist. When the individual emerges with a full social personality of his own, his honour is in his sole keeping. In this insecure, individualist, world where nothing is accepted on credit, the individual is constantly forced to prove and assert himself. Whether as the protagonist of his group or as a self-seeking individualist, he is constantly 'on show', he is forever courting the public opinion of his 'equals' so that they may pronounce him worthy.

The fragmentation of contemporary Western society, the multiplicity of models put forward for imitation, the lack of a clear hierarchical order of preference between these models, are deeply puzzling for modern youth.[5] With what group do we identify ourselves? Should one belong to many interlocking groups? Is the primary identification with one of them constant? In the final analysis which is the court of peers sitting in judgment over our conduct? Indeed, *who* are our peers and for how long? A Greek *choros* and a contemporary traditionalist Mediterranean society would have thought of these questions as being so many riddles. Social mobility and urbanization have completely altered our outlook. The essays collected in this volume concern a perennial social phenomenon studied within the social framework with which it has been traditionally associated.

The first essay is that of Professor Julian Pitt-Rivers, who introduces the theme through his discussion of the general structure of the notion of honour in the literature of Western Europe. In the second section of his essay the meaning of honour and social status is seen through his examination of the semantic range of the notion of honour in Andalusian society where he carried out intensive field work. He points out that reputation is not only a matter of pride but of practical utility, and that different social groups have different systems of evaluation, so that a study of these evaluations is at the same time a study of the position of these groups in the social structure. It is a study of leadership. In analysing the moral sanctions of the *pueblo*, Pitt-Rivers points out that these have only a limited importance for the middle class and none for the upper. Here a most interesting question is asked: why do the families who claim honour accompanying lineal descent appear to be so careless of their sexual honour? It is, says the author, not only because they are free of the sanctions enforcing the plebeian code of honour, but also because their honour is impregnable. Women in the uppermost social class, when behaving in a manner which would seem unfeminine to the plebeian, do not forfeit their femininity, as femininity, in the higher class, is not a passive, a negative reflection of male dominance. The honour of a woman of high society does not have to lean on a male for protection.

The studies of Professors Pitt-Rivers and Caro Baroja are complementary. Caro Baroja's essay, based on both field work and literary texts, is mainly the outcome of a thoroughgoing analysis of legal, theological and historical Spanish documents.

His analysis and articulation of the data collected by various disciplines of the social sciences provide us with an object lesson not only of their mutual interdependence but also of the fact that social anthropology and sociology are particular ways of looking at social phenomena.

Professor Caro Baroja examines the political, economic and religious reasons for changes in the conception of honour. His coupling of collective honour with patrilineality which we find also in the case of Bedouins, Cypriots and Kabyles poses the problem, apparent in the case of Cyprus, whether 'collective honour' is not one of the main cements of the patrilineal family. Professor Caro examines the relations between 'social context' and ideas concerning prestige. In so doing he discusses the influence of the Inquisition on the concept of 'purity of blood' and thus of hereditary claims to honour, until he comes to the modern epoch when, with the help of political writings, the idea is propagated that 'only the poor have honour'. At the same time the idea that honour is menaced by money problems weighs heavily upon all classes in Spain.

During his analysis of Spanish honour and shame Caro Baroja seeks for an answer to the question why the personality of Don Juan exercises such deep fascination. His answer is that Don Juan is the 'literary result of a society in which personal prestige' or disgrace has come to exercise 'an obsessive influence'. Don Juan follows through his actions to extremity and 'since the honour or shame of the female sex was a matter of such concern to their families, the demonstration of personal supremacy' in their seduction, 'constituted one of the most remarkable triumphs'.

Early in his essay Professor Caro quotes Fray Luis de Granada: 'the deeds most admired in man are those that demand effort and courage and a disdain of death'. He ends with the statement that, today, wealth, and almost 'nothing else', seems an almost physical force against which there is no means of fighting.

These ideas seem to coexist not only in the Homeric world but also in that of the Greek Cypriot highlander described by the editor and in that of the Sarakatsani, the northern Greek transhumant shepherds, studied by Dr John Campbell.

Speaking mainly for the Greek Cypriot, I find in him a predilection for his own conception of 'men of honour' – that is, for the exemplification of absolute values, consistent with, and as distant as, his Byzantine heritage. He endows things Greek with magic, from music to epic poetry, as he finds in these an echo of his conceptions of a world where honour is an active value. At the same time his conception of equality spurs him on not only in his struggle against almost all and every man but also against Janus-like Fate-Nature. He cannot rest until he has asserted himself against them – but at the same time he yearns for someone with whom he can be at peace. In heaven it is the Mother of God, on earth this would be the figure of the Grandfather-King, of which his most recent experience once again goes back to Byzantine times. Between idealized King and people this Greek world brooks no intermediaries.

The Greek Cypriot sees himself in his dealings with fellow-villagers as the protagonist of a family and – outside his village – as the protagonist of his village, his province (or island) or his nation. The family I describe as a *social isolate*[6] intent on defending both its worldly interests and its honour. This isolate moves with other similar units in a field of social relations which is regulated by the Greek Cypriot conception of honour. One's honour is involved only in particularized relations in which each actor is a well-defined social *persona*. When the actors are anonymous, honour is not involved.

This is a society without clearly defined spheres of competence in which each male individual constantly asserts his basic equality with all others. The Greek Cypriot highlander is not antagonistic but *agonistic*. There is a prestige hierarchy, but this hierarchy does not correspond to social classes. Again, prestige which is hard to gain can be easily lost so that a true man is always on the alert, constantly prepared to prove himself, a man who, actually and metaphorically, is prepared to stake his 'all' on the throw of a dice.

Dr Campbell has carried out, as indeed have most of the authors with respect to their area, the first full-scale social anthropological study of a Greek community. The Sarakatsani, the transhumant shepherds of northern Greece, are a sight to warm a romantic heart as they move up with their flocks to the summer pastures of the Zagori district of Epirus. Feared and resented by the villagers as all pastoralists are everywhere by sedentary people, they form a closed world within which the family is the most important unit. A number of related families form a *parea*, a company, numbering between fifteen and fifty individuals dominated by a group of brothers. The key regulations of life are simple. Kinsmen are loved and trusted. Unrelated Sarakatsani are considered almost as enemies. One of the main ways of expressing hostility to 'others' is to denigrate them, while seeking honour for oneself and, through self, for one's family. Both the natural and the social aspects of the Sarakatsan world are hostile; theirs is a world in which, speaking from the viewpoint of body, soul, well-being or honour, one may get easily 'lost'. The entire society watches for the young shepherd's first quarrel, that is for his first chance to prove himself. Young men use every opportunity to assert themselves until they become heads of families, when age and increased responsibilities induce them to compete on another plane – that of 'cleverness'.

Dr Campbell analyses the different notions of honour and honourability and their various shades of emphasis in different social situations, and discusses both the formal relationship of the Sarakatsani with the Orthodox Church and their conception of sin. The Sarakatsani, in contradistinction to the 'Puritan', accept sensuality as part of the human condition, but struggle to contain and to discipline it. The struggle for survival and competition for honour breed envy, and this leads to deceit and cunning. Envy is so pervasive that all that an honourable man can do is to control it, especially as envy was the sin of the devil when he rebelled against God.

Just as man fights an unending battle to survive in his physical envelope and his social personality, God fights the devil to save the souls of men. It is interesting to note that it is not the struggle for honour but the struggle for material possessions which breeds envy and temptations which endanger a man's soul.

The agonistic quality of honour appears at its clearest in Professor Bourdieu's analysis of honour in Kabyle society. Kinship imposes its pattern on personal relations within clan or village in the sense that all such relations are conceived on the kinship pattern. It is for this reason that values of honour constitute the basis of the Kabyle political order.

Fights, war between the political and warlike leagues (*eçffuf*) and wars between tribes are strictly regulated games. In this context they do not undermine social order but safeguard it.

Great battles are rare. Even firearms often remained silent and the contest assumed the form of a ritual. This ritual of conflict, claims Bourdieu, constitutes a perfect expression of the logic of honour as it provides society with a well-regulated social setting in which to display, in symbolic form, the values and beliefs it prizes. A man plays the game with intensity as he tries to be faithful to his public image and as his actions reflect on the group he represents. At the same time the struggle, the *agon*, is so well-regulated that a 'state of war' could last for years.

Professor Ahmed Abou-Zeid discusses the same values amongst the Bedouins of the western desert of Egypt, not in their individual, but in their communal connotations. Here the basic social unit is the *beit* (the people of one tent). Up to thirty tents, inhabited by cousins descended from a common ancestor three or four generations back, are grouped in one camp. It is round this kinship group and round its stock that a Bedouin's values revolve. A man takes pride in the number of his offspring, an indication of his virility, in the size of his lineage, which affords him protection, in the honour of his kinsmen, an honour indivisible which affords him protection, pride and security.

One of the most important ways of displaying the honour of the *beit* is by granting the 'right of refuge', so that a man pursued by his enemies may find here asylum. By granting asylum a man publicizes his honour and that of his kinsmen. The highest grade of honour, writes Abou-Zeid, is attained when the ideal is realized at the expense of the performer himself. The best example of this is the obligation of honour to grant sanctuary to an enemy. At the same time the sacrifices made for the attainment and upholding of honour should not exceed certain socially recognized limits. Professor Abou-Zeid says clearly that even the honour-breeding virtues of generosity and hospitality become factors of shame when carried to extremes.

All contributors have noted this phenomenon in their chosen societies. The crime of *hubris* in Ancient Greece consisted in so over-emphasizing one's virtue that one competed, through this over-statement, for honours beyond man's reach. *Hubris*, in our context, is a negation of one's social condition. 'Over-reaching', shames one's fellows and sets standards which cannot be maintained without disputing the social order. Social life is made of compromises. The stress on different social values varies with the phases of social life while the ideal, the fixed star, helps us to steer a relatively consistent course. For any one man to embody the ideal, to pursue a rigid and uncompromising course, generates social reactions from which most truly outstanding men have suffered.

I wish to thank the contributors not only for generously presenting in this volume an analysis of, in many instances, the most important data that they have collected in the field and during their studies of the literature, but for their patience with editorial delays. Special thanks are due to Professor Pitt-Rivers who carried with selflessness a major burden in the editing of this volume. We are all equally indebted both to the sponsors and the staff of our three Mediterranean meetings: to the late Dr Paul Fejos and Mrs Fejos in 1959 and, more especially during the 1961 meeting to the Social Science Centre's secretary, Miss Helen Ghini, and during the 1963 conference to the Centre's graduate research assistant, Miss Helen Argyriades, who shouldered most of the organizational difficulties.

NOTES

1 A collection of essays deriving from this conference has been edited by Professor Pitt-Rivers under the title *Mediterranean Countrymen, Essays in the Social Anthropology of the Mediterranean*, (Mouton & Co., Paris and la Haye, 1963).

2 The acts of the Mediterranean sociological conference will be published by Mouton in 1965, under the title *Contributions to Mediterranean Sociology* ed. J. G. Peristiany.

3 It is true that an action cannot be socially measured when reference is made only to its content. The social distance between the actors and the context of the action have to be considered, unless one is dealing with values rooted not in a social order but in universal ideals. If the referent of these examples had been a particular society, the fellow, the *socius*, would have had to be carefully defined.

4 I use the term 'temporal' to show my recognition of the fact that in all societies there is another ideal, that of saintliness, which transcends that of honour. The road to attainment of any ideal is the same in the sense that one has to *sacrifice* the lower for the higher. The definition

of saintliness might be that saintliness is above honour and that there is nothing above saintliness.

5 For example, young manual workers gain such a large measure of financial independence at a time when students and technical apprentices lead an economically restricted life, that the working youths propose fashions and models of behaviour which are copied by their cultural superiors. At the same time knowledge retains its importance as an element of social ranking. The resulting ambiguities of value orientation and of clearcut social identification are important elements in the assessment of our cultural trends.

6 I first used this term, borrowed from Henry Maine and also that of *sex-linked characteristics*, borrowed from genetics, in my Frazer Lecture delivered in Glasgow in 1959.

Julian Pitt-Rivers

HONOUR AND SOCIAL STATUS

Chapter One

The theme of honour invites the moralist more often than the social scientist. An honour, a man of honour or the epithet honourable can be applied appropriately in any society, since they are evaluatory terms, but this fact has tended to conceal from the moralists that not only what is honourable but what honour *is* have varied within Europe from one period to another, from one region to another and above all from one class to another. The notion of honour is something more than a means of expressing approval or disapproval. It possesses a general structure which is seen in the institutions and customary evaluations which are particular to a given culture. We might liken it to the concept of magic in the sense that, while its principles can be detected anywhere, they are clothed in conceptions which are not exactly equivalent from one place to another. Like magic also, it validates itself by an appeal to the facts (on which it imposes its own interpretations) and becomes thereby involved in contradictions which reflect the conflicts of the social structure and which this essay will attempt to unravel. In the first part I shall examine this general structure as it is found in Western Europe without much concern for the local and temporal variations. In the second part I shall examine the semantic range of the notion of honour in modern Andalusian society.

The Concept of Honour

Honour is the value of a person in his own eyes, but also in the eyes of his society. It is his estimation of his own worth, his *claim* to pride, but it is also the acknowledgement of that claim, his excellence recognized by society, his *right* to pride. Students of the minutiae of personal relations have observed that they are much concerned with the ways in which people extort from others

the validation of the image which they cherish of themselves[1]
and the two aspects of honour may be reconciled in those terms.
Honour, therefore, provides a nexus between the ideals of a
society and their reproduction in the individual through his
aspiration to personify them. As such, it implies not merely an
habitual preference for a given mode of conduct, but the entitle-
ment to a certain treatment in return. The right to pride is the
right to status (in the popular as well as the anthropological
sense of the word), and status is established through the recognition of a certain social identity. When the English girl claims to
be 'not that kind of a girl' she is talking about her honour, and
in Calderón's plays the heroes invoke their honour with a
standard phrase, *Soy quién soy*, I am who I am.

The claimant to honour must get himself accepted at his own
evaluation, must be granted reputation, or else the claim becomes
mere vanity, an object of ridicule or contempt – but granted by
whom? The moralist retains the right to arbitrate the claims to
honour in accordance with his own values (and many of the
treatises on honour are, in fact, tirades against the mores of the
day[2]), but the social scientist is concerned with the facts and processes of recognition: how, on what grounds and by whom is the
claim to honour recognized?

Every political authority displays the pretention to incarnate
the moral values of the society which it governs, to 'command
what is right and prohibit what is wrong'; it therefore claims the
right to bestow 'honours' and it follows that those whom it
honours are, so it maintains, honourable. When this is accepted
by the whole population then the problem of honour presents no
quandary. The argument goes like this: the sentiment of honour
inspires conduct which is honourable, the conduct receives
recognition and establishes reputation, and reputation is finally
sanctified by the bestowal of honours. Honour felt becomes
honour claimed and honour claimed becomes honour paid. But
this argument is not always justified in a complex society where
consensus is not uniform. The individual's worth is not the same
in the view of one group as in that of another, while the political
authorities may view him in a different light again. Moreover, it
is not only a question of differing evaluations of the same person.
The qualities needed to exert leadership in a rural community
are not those needed to please at court. Honour as a sentiment

and mode of conduct becomes separated from honour as a qualification for the Honours List. The two conceptions might be placed at the poles between which common usage fluctuates: at one pole we might put the notion of honour derived from conduct in the sense in which 'All is lost save honour', and at the other, the titles which are piled by the usurper upon the traitors who helped him to power. Adherence to the code of honour is thus juxtaposed to the possession of honours.[3]

If honour establishes status, the converse is also true, and where status is ascribed by birth, honour derives not only from individual reputation but from antecedence.[4] The two conceptions can conflict. The theme of the story of the Cid is the triumph of honour derived from excellence over honour derived from birth, a theme which remains as popular today as ever. The well-born are assumed to possess by inheritance the appropriate character and sentiments which will be seen in their conduct, but when it is asserted they do not, as in the case of the Cid's antagonists, the heirs of Carrión, the concept of honour faces an ambiguity which can only be resolved by an appeal to some tribunal, the 'fount of honour': public opinion, the monarch, or the ordeal of the judicial combat which implied a direct appeal to God. Once the monarchy no longer allowed direct access to the Deity in this matter, but took on the entire responsibility of arbitrating the claims to honour, the court incurred the criticisms which arose from the conflict inherent in the notion, such as the popular opinion which regarded the honour of rustics as more worthy than that of courtiers[5], or the wry comment of Voltaire who maintained, in answer to Montesquieu, that it is precisely at court that there is always least honour.[6]

The claim to excellence is relative. It is always implicitly the claim to excel over others. Hence honour is the basis of precedence. Hobbes, sternly ignoring the views of the moralists from Aristotle onwards discusses honour in terms of this and formulates what I would call 'the pecking-order theory of honour'.[7] In a society of equals, such as a community of peasants, to attain the respect of one's fellows may be as high as honour can point, but where we approach the pole where honour is established through the bestowal of honours, there must needs be competition for them. Where there is a hierarchy of honour, the person who submits to the precedence of others recognizes his inferior status.

He is dishonoured in the sense that he has disavowed his claim to the higher status to which he aspired. The superb mottos of the aristocracy of Europe rub in the point: *Roi ne puis, duc ne daigne, Rohan suis*, or prouder still: *Después de Dios, la Casa de Quiros*. We can see the hierarchy of honour stretching from its source in God, through a King whose legitimacy depends upon divine sanction, through the ranks of the social structure down to those who had no honour at all, the heretics and the infamous. It is not only among the aristocracies, however, that honour has a competitive aspect, though the struggle for precedence may be more acute among them. The victor in any competition for honour finds his reputation enhanced by the humiliation of the vanquished. This is as true on the street-corner as in the lists. It was believed at one time in Italy by the common people that one who gave an insult thereby took to himself the reputation of which he deprived the other.[8] The Church of England hymn puts the point succinctly:

> Conquering Kings their titles take
> From the foes they captive make

but the hymn goes on to contrast this principle of honour with the Christian ethic. Since the treatises on honour first began to appear in the sixteenth century, Churchmen have stressed the basis of true honour in virtue and supported their thesis with the authority of Aristotle, yet they seem never to have convinced the protagonists in the struggle for honour, nor even for that matter all the writers on the subject. Nor do they appear to have persuaded the monarchs in whose gift honour lay who, in dispensing it, followed more often their personal whims or considerations of political expediency; honours have often been for sale by a sovereign with empty coffers. Yet if sovereigns have fallen short of the ideal of bestowing honour only on the virtuous, the same can be said of the *vox populi*. Respect and precedence are paid to those who claim it and are sufficiently powerful to enforce their claim. Just as possession is said to be nine-tenths of the law, so the *de facto* achievement of honour depends upon the ability to silence anyone who would dispute the title. The reputation of a dangerous man is liable to assure him precedence over a virtuous man; he may not be thought privately to be honourable, but while no one is prepared to question the matter, he is treated as though he were and granted the precedence which he claims. On the field of honour might is right.

There are reasons in the nature of honour itself which submit it to the shifts of power, and these will become clear if we examine how honour is recognized or impugned, and by whom. We should start by noting the intimate relation between honour and the physical person. The rituals by which honour is formally bestowed involve a ceremony which commonly centres upon the head of the protagonist whether it is the crowning of a monarch or the touch on the head with a book which confers academic degrees in the University of Oxford. As much may be said of many rites of passage and in fact we should regard honorific rituals as rites of passage. The payment of honour in daily life is accorded through the offering of precedence (so often expressed through an analogy with the head), and through the demonstrations of respect which are commonly associated with the head whether it is bowed, touched, uncovered or covered; while, again, the head of the person honoured is used to demonstrate his status whether it is adorned, dressed in a distinctive way, prohibited to be touched or even if it is chopped off.[9] It is worth observing in the latter case that the right to be executed in this way, even though the execution itself is a dishonour, preserves a recognition of the honourable status of the victim which derives from his birth and which the dishonourable personal conduct he was condemned for does not suffice to obliterate, since it is the concern not only of the individual but of his lineage. Decapitation recognized that there was something worth chopping off. Even where polite society has outlawed physical violence it retains the ritual slap on the face as a challenge to settle an affair of honour,[10] and it was commonly admitted that offences to honour could only be redeemed through blood. 'La lessive de l'honneur ne se coule qu'au sang.'[11]

Any form of physical affront implies an affront to honour since the 'ideal sphere' surrounding a person's honour of which Simmel speaks is defiled.[12] Moreover, the significance of the presence of a person is highly relevant to his honour. That which is an affront if said to his face may not dishonour if said behind his back. That which, if done in his presence, is offensive may not be so if he is not there to resent it. What is offensive is not the action in itself but the act of obliging the offended one to witness it. Thus in the villages of rural Andalusia a father cannot admit the presence of his daughter's suitor – custom imposes an avoidance between the two – yet he would be dishonoured if his daughter were to marry without being courted, not the contrary. In all these instances we can see that honour is exalted or desecrated through the physical person and through actions related to it which are not merely symbolic representations of a moral state of affairs, but *are* what we might otherwise infer they represent, that is to say, they are transactions of honour – not the bill of goods, but the goods themselves. Therefore, the act of resentment is the touchstone of honour, for a physical affront is a dishonour, regardless of the moral issues involved, and creates a situation in which the honour of the affronted person is in jeopardy and requires 'satisfaction' if it is to return to its normal condition.[13] This satisfaction may be acquired through an apology which is a verbal act of self-humiliation or it may require, and if the apology is not forthcoming does require, avenging. To leave an affront unavenged is to leave one's honour in a state of desecration and this is therefore equivalent to cowardice. Hence the popularity among the mottos of the aristocracy of the theme of *nemo me impune lacessit* (no man may harm me with impunity). The equation of honour with valour and cowardice with dishonour, apparent in this, derives directly from the structure of the notion, quite regardless of the historical explanations which have been offered of this fact.

We have not so far considered the question of intention at all, and have implied that it is subsidiary in cases of physical affront. Intentions are, however, all important to the establishment of honour since they demonstrate the sentiment and character from which honour *qua* conduct derives. To show dishonourable intentions is to be dishonoured regardless of the result. To desire to run away in battle is dishonouring whether one succeeds in doing so or not, while honour – and in this case honour through the conduct which gives proof of proper sentiments is clearly meant – can still be saved when all else is lost. Moreover, intention is a necessary component of the competition for honour expressed in the challenge; the essence of an affront is that another should dare to affront one. Therefore, when apologies are offered they normally take the form of a denial of the intention to cause offence. By proclaiming it to be unintentional the offender reduces the gravity of the affront; it makes the apology easier to accept while it also reduces the humiliation of the apologizer and therefore makes it easier to give. Thus, one can see that while honour is established or impugned by physical behaviour this is because certain intentions are made manifest in it, are, as it were, necessarily implicit. To maintain that one did not intend what one did is to require a certain indulgence on the part of the listener – an indulgence which may not be granted if he has been seriously affronted; for actions speak plainer than words where honour is concerned. Yet words also have their value as actions and in this field the way things are said is more important than the substance of what is said. The apology which does not sound sincere aggravates the offence.

To sum up, both words and actions are significant within the code of honour because they are expressions of attitude which claim, accord or deny honour. Honour, however, is only irre-vocably committed by attitudes expressed in the presence of witnesses, the representatives of public opinion. The problem of public knowledge as an essential ingredient of an affront has been stressed by various authors, and it has even been doubted that honour could be committed by words uttered in the absence of witnesses. On the other hand, a person can *feel* himself to be dis-honoured even if the dishonour is not known. Yet there is no disagreement that the extent of the damage to reputation relates to the range of public opinion within which the damage is broadcast. This is the basis of the dilemma which faces the hero of Calderón's, 'A secreto agravio, secreta venganza'; how to cleanse without publicizing his dishonour. Public opinion forms therefore a tribunal before which the claims to honour are brought, 'the court of reputation' as it has been called, and against its judgements there is no redress. For this reason it is said that public ridicule kills.

Given that a man's honour is committed by his estimation of the intention of others, everything depends upon how an action is interpreted. Certain actions have a ritual significance which is conventionally recognized, others depend for their interpretation upon the nuances of manners. To affront ambiguously enables a man to attain his ends without perhaps having to face the response to his affront; he can at least put his antagonist to the test in such a way as to avoid the responsibility for the breach of the peace which ensues. The opening scene of *Romeo and Juliet* provides an illustration:

'Do you bite your thumb at us, sir?'
'No sir, I do not bite my thumb at you, sir, but I bite my thumb.'

The intention, though denied, was plain enough to provoke a scrap. The ambiguous affront has the advantage also that it places the antagonist in a dilemma: if he responds, the affront can be denied and he can be declared touchy, quarrelsome and therefore ridiculous; if he does not respond, he can be made to appear cowardly and therefore dishonoured. If a man sees no insult and can be justified in seeing none, then his honour is not jeopardized. Hence the possibility of 'turning a blind eye'. But if he realizes that he has been insulted (and others will usually help him to realize it), yet does nothing about it, then he is dishonoured. The ambiguous affront which provokes no reaction is therefore commonly followed by a more explicit one, if the intention is indeed to challenge. The victim of an affront is dishonoured only at the point where he is forced to recognize that he has been. A man is therefore always the guardian and arbiter of his own honour, since it relates to his own consciousness and is too closely allied to his physical being, his will, and his judgement for anyone else to take responsibility for it.

When a person reacts to a slight upon the honour of another, it can only be because his own is involved. Thus, according to ancient French law,[14] a member of a slighted man's family or lineage could pick up the glove, or a man bound in liege to him, but no one else. The pact of brotherhood between knights referred to by Caro Baroja (p. 95) created such a lien and, in *Romeo and Juliet*, Mercutio considered his friendship with Romeo a sufficient justification. The possibility of being represented by a champion in the judicial combat was restricted to those who were judged unable to defend their honour personally: women,[15] the aged or infirm, or persons of a social status which prohibited them from responding to a challenge, in particular, churchmen and, of course, royalty. It must otherwise always be an individual's own choice whether to maintain or abandon his claim to honour, whether to react to a slight and vindicate himself or to accept it and the dishonour which accompanies it. Thus a man is dishonoured if, when he is able to do so for himself, he allows another to pick up the glove for him. This remains true even though at certain periods the seconds were expected also to fight.

The ultimate vindication of honour lies in physical violence and when other means fail the obligation exists, not only in the formal code of honour but in social milieux which admit no such code, to revert to it. This is congruent with what has been said already about the relation between honour and the physical person. Within the formal code the duel displays the principles involved: the offended party, judging that his honour was impugned, issued a challenge by which he invoked the honour of his offender and demanded satisfaction. The offender was obliged then either to retract and offer apologies (a course of action which was incompatible with the conception which many men had of their own honour) or to accept. Yet 'satisfaction' is not synonymous with triumph, only with the opportunity to achieve it under conventionally defined conditions which imply a judgement of destiny. In this sense the duel shares with the judicial combat the nature of an ordeal, though the implication was manifest only in the case of the judicial combat which was ordained by the magistrates as a means of validating an oath. God would surely not protect a perjuror who had taken his name in vain. In this way the realities of power, be they no more than the hazards of the field of honour, were endowed with divine sanction. The fact of victory in the judicial combat was something more than hazard for it implied validation, and the satisfaction by which honour was restored was something more than personal satisfaction, for it was accorded by the appeal to the test of courage regardless of the outcome. The duel finished the matter; the quarrel could not honourably be prosecuted thereafter, either by the contestants or their partisans. On this account the duel and the judicial combat are to be distinguished from the feud which, even though it is inspired by similar sentiments, requires none of the formal equality of the duel nor its ceremonial setting and claims no judicial character for its outcome. Thus, unlike the jousting lists which promoted the competition for honour, the duel is rather the means of settling disputes with regard to it. It is not surprising then that it has tended to be frowned upon by the state which has frequently forbidden it, even during epochs when it remained the accepted custom of the aristocracy. (The Church, in keeping with its commitment in this regard, also prohibited it at the Council of Trent.)

The appeal to a private ordeal cuts out the 'fount of honour' from its role in determining the honourable status of its subjects. Like Richard II, the state prefers to have the last word in such matters rather than remit them to the unpredictable hand of destiny. Yet seen from the individual's point of view, to have recourse to justice is to abnegate one's claim to settle one's debts of honour for oneself, the only way in which they can be settled. When challenged to fight, it is not honourable to demand police protection. Therefore, while the sovereign is the 'fount of honour' in one sense, he is also the enemy of honour in another, since he claims to arbitrate in regard to it. He takes over the functions of the Divinity thanks to his sacred character. The change from the period when the law prescribed the judicial combat to that when the duel was made illegal corresponds to an extension of the competence of the state in judicial matters. Yet no man of honour, least of all an aristocrat, was prepared to remit to the courts the settlement of his affairs of honour. Hence the inefficacy of the legislation against duelling.

The conflict between honour and legality is a fundamental one which persists to this day. For to go to law for redress is to confess publicly that you have been wronged and the demonstration of your vulnerability places your honour in jeopardy, a jeopardy from which the 'satisfaction' of legal compensation at the hands of a secular authority hardly redeems it. Moreover, it gives your offender the chance to humiliate you further by his attitude during all the delays of court procedure, which in fact can do nothing to restore your honour but merely advertises its plight. To request compensation or even to invite apologies are courses of action which involve risk to honour if they are not adopted with the implication that they cloak a demand for satisfaction. If someone steps on your toe inadvertently while getting on to a bus, you humiliate yourself by complaining, even if apologies are proffered. The man of honour=precedence says nothing at the time, but catches his offender a sharp one on the shin as he gets off; his honour is revealed to have been jeopardized only by the action which restores it to grace and he has circumvented the risks of placing it in foreign keeping. *Nemo me impune lacessit* therefore is not only a favourite motto of the aristocracy but of any group which values this conception of honour. The resemblance between the mores of the street-corner society and those of the aristocracy, both contemptuous of legality, derives from this: the aristocracy claims the right to honour=precedence by the tradition which makes them the leaders of society, arbiters rather than 'arbitrated' and therefore 'a law unto themselves'. The sacred quality of high status is demonstrated in freedom from the sanctions which apply to ordinary mortals. (The same principle explains the incest of the Gods.) On the other hand, street-corner society claims also to be a law unto itself, not because it is above the law but because it is outside it and because the concept of honour=virtue has no claim upon its aspirations.

When honour is impugned it can be vindicated. Yet the power to impugn the honour of another man depends also on the relative status of the contestants. An inferior is not deemed to possess sufficient honour to resent the affront of a superior. A superior can ignore the affront of an inferior, since his honour is not committed by it – though he may choose to punish an impudence. The combatants in a duel must recognize equality since they stand on equal terms in it. Montesquieu refers to the mediaeval laws[16] according to which a judicial combat could take place between a gentleman and a villein. Yet the former was bound to appear, then, without the symbols of his rank and to fight as a villein on foot. This disposition disappears from the code of honour of a later age. When Voltaire answered provocatively a discourtesy from the Chevalier de Rohan, the latter had his henchmen beat him and Voltaire's noble friends declined to take up his cause. In addition to his hurt he was covered in ridicule. He did not forgive the Duc de Sully at whose house the incident occurred. Yet the Chevalier was not apparently dishonoured in the eyes of his peers, even though he evaded the duel to which Voltaire attempted to challenge him by procuring his imprisonment and exile. A man is answerable for his honour only to his social equals, that is to say, to those with whom he can conceptually compete.

The intention of a person, we have said, is paramount in relation to his honour, but it is the intention evident in his actions rather than that expressed in his words. A man commits his honour only through his *sincere* intentions. Giving his word of honour, he asserts sincerity and stakes his honour upon the issue, be it a promise regarding the future or an assurance regarding past events. If his true will was not behind the promise or the assertion, then he is not dishonoured if he fails to fulfil the promise or turns out to have lied. If he intended to deceive, he is not dishonoured by the revelation that he did so, since he 'did not mean it', he 'had his fingers crossed', that is to say, he meant the opposite of what he said. Yet according to the rules of this puerile device for disengaging honour, the fingers must be held crossed while the words are spoken; they cannot be crossed afterwards. This fact demonstrates the essential truth that it is lack of steadfastness in intentions which is dishonouring, not misrepresentation of them.

We can explain now something which appears anomalous in the literature of honour: on the one hand honour demands keeping faith and to break one's word or to lie is the most dishonourable conduct, yet in fact a man is permitted to lie and to deceive without forfeiting his honour.[17] The formal vocabulary of challenges commonly bears the implication of oath-breaker or liar. The judicial combat was a means of proving which of the two contestants was a liar, while, later, the word *mentita* (giving the lie) figures in the Italian codes of honour as the formal provocation which cannot easily be refused. In the Spanish drama *mentís* carried the same significance. On the other hand, King Ferdinand of Aragon boasted of the nine times he deceived the King of France, and Don Juan, in the play of Tirso de Molina, in spite of the deceptions he had perpetrated, declared himself a man of honour as he gripped the stone hand of the Comendador and gave this as his reason for accepting the predictable consequences.[18] It appears to me that critics of recent times like the dramatists who took up the theme have neglected to consider the fact that Don Juan is a man of honour. He is a rascal by their standards and indeed an offender against loyalty, hospitality, friendship and religion, as Professor Parker has noted.[19] But such a view neglects to examine the concept of honour which is displayed in the play and to say, like Professor Parker, that Don Juan is the negation of 'Caballerosidad' in every respect is to beg the question. Don Juan is a protagonist of the 'pecking-order theory of honour'. He is an affronter of other men, a humiliator and deceiver by design of both men and women, a scoffer at the moral and social orders and, in his sexual relations, a 'scalp-hunter', but not a voluptuary and not, be it noted, an adulterer; his four female victims are presumed virgins; he is not a man to grant precedence to another even in this.

To take an example from contemporary ethnography, the Greek peasants whose concern for their honour is very great, regard deception involving a lie as perfectly legitimate and honourable behaviour.[20]

The anomaly is therefore this: while to lie in order to deceive is quite honourable, to be called a liar in public is a grave affront. The explanation lies in the ambiguity as to whether the word given did in fact commit the honour of the liar, and this can only be established by a knowledge of his true intentions. If it did not, that is to say, if his intentions were misrepresented but not rescinded, then the person deceived, not the deceiver, is humiliated. If, however, the lie was told or the promise made because the liar did not dare to affront his antagonist, or if, having committed his honour to another man, he lacks stead-fastness, then the liar is dishonoured. He has desecrated that which is sacred to him, his true self. The whole question hinges therefore on the moral commitment of the liar. To lie is to deny the truth to someone who has the right to be told it and this right exists only where respect is due. Children are taught to tell the truth to their elders who are under no reciprocal obligation, since it is they who decide what the children should be told. The duty to tell the truth curtails the personal autonomy of the man who may otherwise feel himself entitled, on account of his social pre-eminence, to represent reality as he pleases and offer no justification. The moral commitment to tell the truth derives then from the social commitment to persons to whom it is due. This is the meaning of the story of the emperor's cloak. At the same time, a man may not question the truth of an assertion made by one who does not owe it to him. The right to the truth and the right to withhold it both attach to honour and to contest these rights is to place honour in jeopardy.

A man of honour may not lie to someone whom he is not prepared to affront, for to deceive a person intentionally is to humiliate him, and this amounts to an insult to which the norms of the community define the modes of honourable response. Given the ambiguity of the interpretation of his action, the person thus offended is entitled to interpret the lie as an act of cowardice and to declare the liar dishonoured by it. The *mentita* therefore represents a counter insult which demands of the person accused as a liar that he demonstrate by his response that he did in fact intend to affront, under pain of being proved otherwise a coward. Yet if he responds to the challenge, he is not dishonoured (for it is not dishonouring to affront another man): he is only dishonoured as a liar if he fails to do so.[21]

Hence the importance of the oath in relation to honour. It commits the honour of the swearer just as 'crossed fingers' liberate it and aims to eliminate the ambiguity as to his true intentions. By invoking that which is sacred to him – his God, the bones of saints, his loyalty to his sovereign, the health of his mother or simply his own honour – he activates an implicit curse against himself in the eventuality of his failure to implement his oath or, at least, he assures that public opinion is entitled to judge him dishonoured. Moreover, he cannot attain the honour of the person to whom he is bound by oath by deceiving him. The latter is untouched by his deceit. If he proves false, the dishonour is his alone; retribution can be left to public opinion or to the Gods.

Yet even an oath which is not made freely is not binding, nor is a word of honour which is not intended as such. The attempt to use ritual to commit the honour of a man comes up against the difficulty that no man *can* commit his honour against his will, since his honour is what he wills and the attempt to oblige him to do so invites him to 'cross his fingers'. The ritual of the oath, like the rites of the church, is invalid without the intention of the participant.

I have used the word 'sacred' in a colloquial sense which may well raise objections from anthropologists. Yet in saying that a man's honour is sacred to him I do no more than repeat what is stated in a host of contexts (including the American Declaration of Independence). It is literally more exact to say that a man's true self is blended with the sacred. In the oath, the sacred is invoked in order to commit honour in ways which indicate something more than a conditional curse: 'I swear by all that is sacred to me' presupposes such a close connection. We have noted also that the same forms of conduct demonstrate respect for persons of superior honour as for religious objects, while the position of the monarch as both the fount of human honour and appointed by the Grace of God brings a divine sanction to the social system. His honour, in addition to connecting a man to others within the hierarchy of his society, connects him to his sovereign and to the Deity: 'A traitor to my God, my King and me' was the form of the indictment which expressed the challenge in *Richard II* (Act I, Scene 3).

Moreover, the notion, common in all the languages of Europe, that honour is susceptible of 'defilement' or 'stains' of which it requires to be purified entitles us to mark a resemblance to the customs of primitive societies whose chiefs are the object of prohibitions similar to those which circumscribe the man of honour. The early anthropologists might well, in fact, have translated the word *mana* as *honour*,[22] at least in the contexts in which it referred to persons, and noted that the Polynesian victor who acquired the *mana* of his slain foe by taking his name was behaving rather like the conquering kings of the hymn. But they became interested in the subject while studying magic and the 'primitive mind', and they therefore stressed the differences rather than the resemblances between the customs which they studied and their own. They could with difficulty envisage the 'savage' as having honour such as they themselves possessed and the age in which they wrote was disinclined to perceive the 'irrationality' of the primitive mind in its own attitudes to social status. However, this is not the place to pursue the analogy, which would confront us with other problems.

We have so far discussed honour as a purely individual attribute. Now we must examine how it is related to social solidarities. Social groups possess a collective honour in which their members participate; the dishonourable conduct of one reflects upon the honour of all, while a member shares in the honour of his group. 'I am who I am' subsumes 'whom I am associated with'. 'Dime con quién andas y te diré quién eres' says the Spanish proverb (Tell me whom you associate with and I will tell you who you are). Honour pertains to social groups of any size, from the nuclear family whose head is responsible for the honour of all its members to the nation whose members' honour is bound up with their fidelity to their sovereign. In both the family and the monarchy a single person symbolizes the group whose collective honour is vested in his person. The members owe obedience and respect of a kind which commits their individual honour without redress. Here intentions are irrelevant to the identity of the essential being, for the individual is born a son and a subject, he does not compete or contract in order to become so. Thus parricide and regicide are sacrilegious acts which homicide is not.

The idea that the honour of the group resides in its head was fundamental to the conception of aristocracy and assured the fidelity through the oath of the liegeman to his lord; the inferior in such a relationship participated in the honour of his chief and was therefore interested in defending it. Yet the principle holds beyond the ties of the feudal system; the system of patronage depends upon it, also. Hence the hubris of the tyrant's minion, the vicarious glory of the noble's servant.

Yet there exist other social groups whose leader is an elected representative and whose person, as opposed to his post, possesses none of this sacred quality. Here the tribunal of public opinion is sovereign: in trade-guilds, municipalities or republics.

This observation provided Montesquieu with his basic dichotomy: a distinction between the monarchy whose operative principle is honour, and the republic whose operative principle is virtue, by which he meant civic virtue, something rather like what is meant today by 'citizenship'. He encountered difficulty in making himself understood to those who showed themselves unwilling to adopt his usage.[23] The distinction was criticized by those who maintained that there was honour in a republic, by those who maintained that there was virtue in a monarchy, and by Voltaire whose opinion has already been given.

The difficulty of distinguishing between the two terms, honour and virtue, was responsible for those confusions which were neither the first nor the last of their kind, which centre on the meanings of the word honour: honour which derives from virtuous conduct and that honour which situates an individual socially and determines his right to precedence. The two senses appear to be so far removed from one another that one may ask why they were, and still are, expressed by the same word, why the languages of Europe are so determined to avoid clarity in this matter.

The political significance of the sacred is that it arbitrates questions of value, lays the limits to what can be done or maintained without sacrilege and defines the unconditional allegiances of the members of a society. Authority as political power claims always to be moral authority, and the word therefore enjoys the same duality as honour from the moment that the legitimacy of the use of force is disputed. It cannot admit that its actions are devoid of legitimacy. In the same vein, no man of honour ever admits that his honour=precedence is not synonymous with his honour=virtue. To do so would be to admit himself dishonoured. For him there is only one concept, his honour. However far apart the abstract notions of precedence and virtue may be, they come together in the individual at the level of behaviour. Therefore, as we have seen in the instance of the lie, an action *may* be potentially dishonourable, but it is only when this action is publicly condemned that it dishonours. Hence, just as capital assures credit, so the possession of honour guarantees against dishonour, for the simple reason that it places a man (if he has enough of it) in a position in which he cannot be challenged or judged. The king cannot be dishonoured. What he *is* guarantees the evaluation of his actions. He is above criticism. This is what I call the principle of *Honi soit qui mal y pense*.'[24] It is incorporated in the jurisprudence of honour in a provision, implicit throughout, which is expressed by Bryson in the following terms: 'Just as honouring one who was undeserving was a kind of contempt, and true honour dwelled rather in him who honoured, so an offence given to an honourable man stained only the offender. As for the offended party, he was still more worthy of honour if he bore the offence magnanimously.'[25]

At the level of political action, the concept of authority partakes of the same nature; the king can do no wrong because he is the king and therefore the arbiter of right. Reference to authority takes precedence over reference to privately reasoned evaluations. What God, King, Country, or Party says is right. *Lèse-majesté* is the sister of rebellion and criticism of established authority, beyond the limits which convention allows, is an act of disloyalty. In this sense, therefore, the respect felt for the monarch possesses something of the same power to render sacred as the reverence felt for the Divine: in paying this respect, we abnegate our right to question and bind ourselves to accept what might otherwise appear to us wrong. The arbitrary nature of sacred power extends beyond the frontiers of religion.[26]

The ritual and ceremonial aspects of honour assure not only the opportunity for those who feel respect to pay it, but they commit those who pay it even if they do not feel it. Regardless of private feelings they serve to establish the consensus of the society with regard to the order of precedence; they demonstrate what is acceptable by reference to what is accepted. If the honour felt by the individual becomes honour paid by the society, it is equally the case that the honour which is paid by the society sets the standards for what the individual should feel. Transactions of honour therefore serve these purposes: they not only provide, on the psychological side, a nexus between the ideals of society and their reproduction in the actions of individuals – honour commits men to act as they should (even if opinions differ as to how they should act) – but, on the social side, between the ideal order and the terrestrial order, validating the realities of power and making the sanctified order of precedence correspond to them. Thus, thanks to its duality, honour does something which the philosophers say they cannot do: derive an *ought* from an *is*; whatever *is* becomes *right*, the *de facto* is made *de jure*, the victor is crowned with laurels, the war-profiteer is knighted, the tyrant becomes the monarch, the bully, a chief. The reconciliation between the social order as we find it and the social order which we revere is accomplished thanks to the confusion which hinges upon the duality of honour and its associated concepts. It is a confusion which fulfils the function of social integration by ensuring the legitimation of established power.

I have attempted to discover the general structure of the notion of honour in the literature of Western Europe and have therefore overlooked the very considerable differences between countries and epochs; I did not attempt to explain the variations in the frequency of duelling or the particular emphases which different periods placed upon the constituents of honour, religious, political, financial or sexual. However, such variations are also found within the culture of a single region and epoch and, while this has sometimes been taken to reflect differences between classes or factions in their struggles to impose their own evalua-

ERRATUM

The sentence beginning in line 14 on page 39 should read: Like tropical fish whose radiant colours fade once they are taken from the water, the concepts which compose such a system retain their exact significance only within the environment of the society which nurtures them and which resolves, thanks to its internal structuring, their conflicts with each other.

tions upon their society,[27] it must be pointed out that this is not merely due to the emergence of new social forces which require the rules to be altered, as it were, if they are to gain power, but to the fact that different elements of a society behave in different ways and think in different ways, albeit within the framework of a common language.

A system of values is never a homogeneous code of abstract principles obeyed by all the participants in a given culture and able to be extracted from an informant with the aid of a set of hypothetical questions, but a collection of concepts which are related to one another and applied differentially by the different status-groups defined by age, sex, class, occupation, etc. in the different social (not merely linguistic) contexts in which they find their meanings. Like tropical fish whose radiant colours fade once they are taken from the water, the concepts which compose such a system environment of the society which nurtures them and which resolves, thanks to its internal structuring, their conflicts with each other. The variations in the components of the notion of honour in Andalusia reflect, in this way, the articulation of the social structure, and can only be studied in terms of it. This is what we shall now try to do.

Honour and Social Status in Andalusia

A certain bashfulness disguises the expression of attitudes concerning honour in our own society (perhaps because the word has acquired archaic overtones), but this is not so in the small town in the Sierra de Cádiz where I first investigated this theme.[1] Here questions of honour can be debated without causing embarrassment, and they loom large both in theoretical discussions regarding the proprietory of conduct and also in the daily idiom of social intercourse: indeed, the honourable status of the members of the community is a matter of continual comment. Reputation is not only a matter of pride, but also of practical utility. Where free associations of a contractual kind govern the forms of co-operation and enterprise, a good name is the most valuable of assets. Moreover, the honour of a man has a legal status in Spanish, which it does not have in Anglo-Saxon, law.[2] The value attached to honour can also be seen in the custom of bargaining where intermediaries, reminiscent of seconds in a duel, are required for the successful negotiation. Attempts to damage reputation are constantly made and every quarrel which gains flame leads to imputations of acts and intentions which are totally dishonourable and which may well have nothing to do with the subject of the quarrel. The discussions of honour are not restricted to literal expression; circumlocutions are frequently used and the reputation of a person is more commonly attained by implications than by direct statements.

The girl who discussed in literal terms whether or not it was dishonouring to recognize one's own nickname[3] was in no way exceptional in her preoccupation to reach a clear distinction between the conduct which dishonoured and that which did not, though in maintaining that she could without dishonour respond when it was mentioned in the street, she was going counter to the general opinion of the community. She herself admitted that it depended upon the nature of the nickname, since, while some nicknames, such as hers, derive from the surname of an ancestor or from a place of origin, others are unflatteringly personal. I put her thesis to the test when challenged one dark night upon the road and earned, first of all some astonished comments that I should announce myself as 'the Englishman', and when I asked why I should not do so, a homily on 'how we behave here'. The customs of the bullring and the music-hall whose heroes present themselves under the rubric of their nickname are not those of the *pueblo*. I had, in any case, overstated her thesis, for the girl denied that she would go so far as to announce herself by her nickname, and she held more conventional views regarding the other ways in which honour could be forfeited. These, as she saw them, were concerned entirely with the possibility of imputing an improper relationship with a member of the male sex.

Criticizing people behind their back is one thing and treating them with contempt to their face is quite another. This society lays great emphasis on courtesy, and when people have quarrelled to the point that they are not prepared to behave with courtesy to one another, then they avoid entering each other's presence; it is recognized that the two 'do not speak', and others connive in avoiding situations where they might be forced to do so. There is, however, a certain class of person to whom courtesy is commonly denied, the 'shameless ones' (*los sin vergüenza*). These are people whose dishonourable reputation is established beyond all doubt through their habitual indulgence in conduct which is shameful: petty thieving, begging and promiscuity in the case of women. They are considered to be outside the moral pale, and, in this way, are associated with the gypsies who are thought to be, by nature, devoid of shame. Such persons are often addressed directly by their nickname without the Christian name and treated with open disdain (though fear of the magical power of gypsies usually affords them a certain respect from the unsophisticated). The fact that these people are prepared to put up with such treatment confirms their status as shameless.

The mores of Andalusia, like those of peasant Greece[4] are indulgent towards conduct which we might regard as boastful, and the example is not lacking of one, Manuel 'el Conde', who, even by their light, was regarded as somewhat overbearing. A man of short stature and unimposing physique, he was a recognized agricultural expert (*perito*), that is to say, one whose opinion could be called upon by the syndical organization. His opinion was given in fact, in not unforceful terms, upon any occasion when he thought it relevant. He was accustomed to boast of his ugliness, as though it were an embellishment to his other qualities, and to stake his claim to honour without quibbling:

'I have not much fortune,' he would say, and then, tapping his breast, 'but I have within me that which is worth more than fortune, my honour.'

He was also fond of interjecting a pun into the conversation when the subject of partridges was mentioned:

'La perdí' dice Usted? No, señor, no la perdí!'
('The partridge, you say? No, sir, I have not lost it!')

That which he has not lost is his shame, for it is common practice to allude to this word by the pronoun without pronouncing it; to 'lose it' means to lose one's shame.

From Manuel's vainglorious pronouncements two points are to be gleaned: first, the close association between the notions of honour and shame, which appear synonymous in many contexts as in these, and secondly, that this quality, once lost, is irrecoverable.

The word which I have translated as 'shame' is *vergüenza*, but it both carries a heavier emphasis and covers a wider range of meaning than the English equivalent. In a previous discussion of the subject[5] I have defined it as a concern for repute, both as a sentiment and also as the public recognition of that sentiment. It is what makes a person sensitive to the pressure exerted by public opinion. In these senses it is synonymous with honour, but the sentiment also finds expression in ways which are no longer so, such as shyness, blushing and the restraints which derive from emotional inhibition, the fear of exposing oneself to comment and criticism.

As the basis of repute, honour and shame are synonymous, since shamelessness is dishonourable; a person of good repute is taken to have both, one of evil repute is credited with neither. (This is so at least at the plebeian level which is all we are concerned with for the moment.) As such, they are the constituents of virtue. Yet while certain virtues are common to both sexes, such as honesty, loyalty, a concern for reputation which involves avoidance of moral turpitude in general, they are not all so. For the conduct which establishes repute depends upon the status of the person referred to. This is particularly evident in the differentiation of the sexes. The honour of a man and of a woman therefore imply quite different modes of conduct. This is so in any society.[6] A woman is dishonoured, loses her *vergüenza*, with the tainting of her sexual purity, but a man does not. While certain conduct is honourable for both sexes, honour=shame requires conduct in other spheres, which is exclusively a virtue of one sex or the other. It obliges a man to defend his honour and that of his family, a woman to conserve her purity. Yet the concepts of honour and shame also extend to the point where they are no longer synonymous, and at this point they lose their ethical value. Shame, no longer equivalent to honour, as shyness, blushing and timidity is thought to be proper to women, even though it no longer constitutes virtue, while honour, no longer equivalent to shame, becomes an exclusively male attribute as the concern for precedence and the willingness to offend another man. At this point also these modes of conduct become dishonouring for the inappropriate sex: for a man, to show timidity or blush is likely to make him an object of ridicule, while a woman who takes to physical violence or attempts to usurp the male prerogative of authority or, very much more so, sexual freedom, forfeits her shame. Thus honour and shame, when they are not equivalent, are linked exclusively to one sex or the other and are opposed to one another.

There is however one further usage of the word *vergüenza* which is common to both sexes and this is in the sense of 'to put to shame', literally 'to give shame' (*darle vergüenza*), or speaking about oneself, to feel shame, literally, 'to be given it'. It derives from the concern for repute, since one who is thus concerned is more easily put to shame than one who is not, but it is, so to speak, its negative counterpart. A person who *has vergüenza* is sensitive to his repute and therefore honourable, but if he *is given it*, he is humiliated, stripped of honour. By implication, if he had it already he would not have to be given it; and this is made clear in the usage of *darle vergüenza* to mean: to punish a child. A person who possesses *vergüenza* already does not expose himself to the risk of humiliation. In accordance with the general structure of the notion of honour explained in the first part of this essay, he is shamed (*avergonzado*) only at the point when he is forced to recognize that he has accepted humiliation. In this sense, as that which is not inherent in the person but is imposed from outside, shame is equivalent to dishonour. This explains the usage in the law of an earlier period (of which Caro Baroja speaks) of the punishment of *vergüenza pública*, the public dishonouring. Honour is the aspiration to status and the validation of status, while *vergüenza*, opposed to honour, is the restraint of such an aspiration (timidity) and also the recognition of the loss of status. Thus, just as honour is at the same time honour felt, honour claimed and honour paid, so *vergüenza* is dishonour imposed, accepted and finally felt. Honour originates in the individual breast and comes to triumph in the social realm, *vergüenza* in this sense originates in the actions of others as the denial of honour, and is borne home in the individual. The concepts of honour or shame are therefore either, according to context, synonymous as virtue or contraries as precedence or humiliation.

We might express the relationship between the two concepts in a diagram (*see overleaf*).

It will be noted that the ethically neutral qualities which are exclusively honour or shame are at the same time necessary ingredients of the qualities, linked to one sex or the other, which are ethically valued and are equivalent to both honour and shame.

43

HONOUR — Ethically neutral	HONOUR=SHAME — Ethically valued		SHAME — Ethically neutral	SHAME=DIS-HONOUR (ie, Shamelessness) Ethically negative
Masculinity = desire for precedence · Willingness to defend reputation · Refusal to submit to humiliation	Honesty · Loyalty · Concern for repute	Sexual purity · Pudeur · Discretion	Shyness · Restraint	Acceptance of humiliation · Failure to defend reputation
Authority over family = Manliness			= Timidity	
=				
Deriving from natural qualities	Deriving from education	Deriving from natural qualities		Deriving from absence of natural qualities
Behaviour appropriate to: ♂	← Both sexes →	♀		Inappropriate to both sexes

NB All the terms shown on this chart are either translations from the Spanish of the pueblo or summaries which represent recognized categories of behaviour, expressed in the evaluations which people make in the course of living. Thus, while 'manliness' is a literal translation of *hombría*, 'concern for repute' is derived from statements regarding *fama* and equally from expressions of concern regarding the *quedirán*, critical gossip. Female sexual purity is expressed by either *honra* or *vergüenza*. The implication of honourability or shamelessness associated with such statements is also made clear in a great variety of ways which include gesture. An established vocabulary of gesture exists in order to convey the meanings: 'hard face' (*cara dura*), which is a way of saying shameless, financial dishonesty, homosexuality, cuckoldry; and of course that great desecratory gesture known as the *corte de manga* (cut of the sleeve) is used to dishonour another man entirely.

This is so because they derive from natural qualities. Thus restraint is the natural basis of sexual purity, just as masculinity is the natural basis of authority and the defence of familial honour. The ideal of the honourable man is expressed by the word *hombría*, 'manliness'. It subsumes both shame and masculinity, yet it is possible to possess masculinity without shame as well, for which reason it is placed under the title of ethical neutrality. Masculinity means courage whether it is employed for moral or immoral ends. It is a term which is constantly heard in the *pueblo*, and the concept is expressed as the physical sexual quintessence of the male (*cojones*). The contrary notion is conveyed by the adjective *manso* which means both tame and also castrated. Lacking the physiological basis, the weaker sex cannot obviously be expected to possess it, and it is excluded from the demands of female honour. On the other hand, female honour is not entirely without a physiological basis also (although this is not expressed with the same linguistic clarity), in that sexual purity relates to the maidenhead. The male, therefore, both lacks the physiological basis of sexual purity and risks the implication that his masculinity is in doubt if he maintains it; it comes to mean for him, despite the teachings of religion, an, as it were, self-imposed tameness=castration, and is therefore excluded from the popular concept of male honour. The natural qualities of sexual potency or purity and the moral qualities associated with them provide the conceptual framework on which the system is constructed.

This division of labour in the aspects of honour corresponds, as the reader would guess, to the division of roles within the nuclear family. It delegates the virtue expressed in sexual purity to the females and the duty of defending female virtue to the males. The honour of a man is involved therefore in the sexual purity of his mother, wife and daughters, and sisters, not in his own. *La mujer honrada, la pierna quebrada y en casa* (the honourable woman: locked in the house with a broken leg), the ancient and still popular saying goes, indicating the difficulties which male honour faces in this connection, for once the responsibility in this matter has been delegated, the woman remains with her own responsibility alleviated. The frailty of women is the inevitable correlate of this conceptualization,[7] and the notion is not, perhaps, displeasing to the male who may see in it an

45

encouragement for his hopes of sexual conquest. Thus, an honourable woman, born with the proper sentiment of shame strives to avoid the human contacts which might expose her to dishonour; she cannot be expected to succeed in this ambition, unsupported by male authority. This fact gives justification to the usage which makes the deceived husband, not the adulterer, the object of ridicule and opprobrium according to the customs of southern Europe (and formerly, England and the whole of Europe).

I have described the symbolism of cuckoldry previously[8] which I summarize now as follows: the cuckold, *cabrón*, literally the billy-goat, is said to 'have horns'. The horns, a phallic symbol, are also the insignia of the Devil, the enemy of virtue, whose associates possess other symbols of a phallic nature, such as the broomstick upon which witches ride. Yet male sexuality is essential to the foundation of the family, as well as necessary, in its associated aspect as courage, to its defence. As well as potentially evil, it is also, when combined with shame as manliness, good. The manliness of a husband must be exerted above all in the defence of the honour of his wife on which his own depends. Therefore her adultery represents not only an infringement of his rights but the demonstration of his failure in his duty. He has betrayed the values of the family, bringing dishonour to all the social groups who are involved reciprocally in his honour: his family and his community. His manliness is defiled, for he has fallen under the domination of the Devil and must wear his symbol as the stigma of his betrayal. The responsibility is his, not the adulterer's, for the latter was only acting in accordance with his male nature. The pander, not the libertine, is the prototype of male dishonour,[9] for the latter may be assumed to defend these values when he is called upon to do so, that is to say, when *his* honour is at stake. The transfer of the horns from the adulterer to the victim of the adultery concords with the moral indeterminacy of the quality of masculinity and the positive value of manliness.

The adulterer may not be regarded as dishonourable – and we shall see that opinions vary in this regard according to social status – but this does not save him from committing a sin in the eyes of the Church. The idea that the punishment for a breach of rights should be visited by custom on the victim not the perpetrator may still perhaps strike us as anomalous, but this is only if we view this as an instance of a legal mechanism, a punitive sanction, and this is not in fact the framework within which it is to be interpreted.

The code of honour derives, as has been said, from a sacred quality of persons, not from ethical or juridical provisions, and we have seen how in European history it has conflicted with the law of the Church and the law of the land. If we view the adulterer and the cuckold, not in terms of right and wrong, but in terms of sanctity or defilement, we can see why the latter, the defiled one, should be the object of contempt, not the defiler. Through his defilement he becomes ritually dangerous and the horns represent not a punishment but a state of desecration.[10] In contrast, the adulterer is a sinner and, technically, in Spanish law, a criminal.

We have pointed out that where the concepts of shame and honour overlap they are equivalent to virtue, but the ethics of the community are not exhausted by this category. There remain the fields of conduct which contribute little or nothing to reputation but face only the individual conscience which, again, may not respond to all the injunctions of Catholic teaching. It is noteworthy that religion does not define adultery in the same way as urban custom nor the penal code, which exonerates *discreet* male marital infidelity by defining a husband's dalliance as adultery only if it takes place in the conjugal home or with notoriety.

Though the penal code of Spain defines offences against honour, proceedings are instituted only at the demand of the injured party. Other than as an ideological statement, the legal provisions serve also to validate the rights of individuals whose conduct, indicted in other ways, may be justified by reference to their honour. The sanctions which maintain the code of honour in the *pueblo* are popular and are based upon the idea of ridicule, *burla*. *Burla* is the destroyer of reputation, whether it is employed by one individual against another in an act of defiance (as the Burlador de Sevilla employed it against the men and women whom it amused him to dishonour), or as a sanction exercised by the collectivity in the form of public ridicule. I have previously given a description of the institutions which exert the collective sanctions: the giving of a nickname which refers to a specific incident or to a particularity of conduct, the popular ballads, especially those which were formerly sung by the masked figures of the Carnival, or the institution of the *vito* (elsewhere referred to as the *cencerrada*, the charivari), with its cow-horns, bells, strings of tins, catcalls and obscene songs.

If we examine the incidents which provoked these sanctions we may divide them according to the nature of the transgression. Of the damaging nicknames, a few relate to economic behaviour and a few to sexual behaviour, though the majority ridicule a person on account of a specific incident which appealed to the collective imagination or of a physical or cultural deficiency. Some songs of Carnival publicized acts of dishonesty, but many were concerned with sexual offences and in particular, infidelity to husband or fiancé. The marital misfortunes of shepherds, those 'sailors of the wavy sierras', as Gerald Brenan has called them,[11] whose long spans of absence from the *pueblo* make their wives subject to suspicion, were high among them. The justification given for singing these songs was that it was necessary to warn the husband or prospective husband of the condition of his honour, though the nature of the rhymes themselves show that this duty was undertaken with glee rather than compassion for the victim of such a betrayal. The *vitos* were aimed at publicizing scandalously, and thereby prohibiting, a living scandal.

The folklore has defined the traditional occasion for the charivari as the remarriage of a widowed person. There had once been such a *vito* in the distant past. Since the *vito* is against the law, it no longer takes place within any *pueblo* where there is a detachment of civil guards. There was one more recent case involving a young widow who had gone to live with a widower upon his parent's farm, but the majority of cases recorded, and the most violent ones, were provoked by the action of a man who was not widowed but had abandoned his wife in order to take up with another woman (and such a woman was necessarily shameless in the popular view). He was not, that is to say, a cuckold, but an unfaithful husband. However, the nature of the proceedings and the words of the songs left no doubt that he was endowed with the symbols of the cuckold, and this fact is reinforced by the usage of the *pueblo* which applies to such a person the word *cabrón*, which to the educated means only a cuckold. In the same vein, it is significant that, following the quarrel between Manuel el Conde and the carpenter,[12] the latter should have attacked his reputation by saying that he was cruel to his daughter, his only child, and that he intended to abandon his wife and go off with another woman, not that *his wife* had unfaithful intentions.

It would appear then that the theory of cuckoldry which we have outlined requires further explanation in order to cover this extended sense. This can be given without doing violence to that already offered.

To begin with, the *vito* is concerned uniquely with the behaviour of married persons. For the plebeians, in contrast to the middle classes, the rites of the Church are not essential to marriage and many common law marriages exist. The Anarchist movement which formerly had great influence here rejected all religious teaching and ceremonies, and in spite of a certain amount of proselytizing by the Catholic Action committee, the poorer people very often do not marry until they have a child. Therefore when unmarried people set up house together they are regarded as a young married couple by the community, and it is in fact quite likely that they will get married within a year or two. On the other hand if a person who is already considered to be married goes to live with another, not his spouse, this is, by the same logic, equivalent to bigamy, since the fact of cohabitation rather than the Church rite is the criterion of marriage.

It is accepted that young people who face opposition to their marriage from the girl's father may force the father's hand by running away to spend the night together. After this, their recognition as a married couple, their marriage for preference, is the only way in which his honour can be retrieved. There were no fewer than six such escapades during a single year. But in one of these cases the father failed to react in the expected fashion. His daughter was a minor and had fine prospects of inheritance since he was a well-to-do farmer. The young man had been employed upon the farm and hoped, so it was thought, to become through marriage its heir. The father's immediate reaction, in this case, was to have him arrested and thrown into jail on the charge of violation of a minor.

In no instance recorded in this town was the *vito* put on for a married woman who had left her husband to live with another man, though there have been cases elsewhere. It seems most improbable in a town of this size, three thousand inhabitants, that such a couple would remain in the place. Women who 'go off the rails' go off them elsewhere, and thereby they justify the country-man's cherished belief in the iniquity of the city. There are, nevertheless, a number of unmarried or abandoned mothers who remain in the *pueblo* with their family.[13] Their disgrace is clearly recognized, but they are not treated as shameless. Their status is somewhat similar to that of a young widow. Their prospects of remarriage are very poor, since the man who wished to marry such a girl would be dishonoured – honour requires that one marry a virgin, since otherwise one becomes a retroactive cuckold – yet if their conduct gives no cause for scandal, they are distinguished from the loose women who come within the category of the shameless and who are sometimes designated by the word *deshonradas*, dishonoured.

It is said that the *vito* would formerly have been put on for any marital infidelity in the *pueblo*, though in fact the transient adventure and the discreetly-conducted affair always appear to have escaped. This may be due, in part, to reasons of practical organization: the assemblage of young men with the equipment of horns and cowbells and the composition of the songs, all take time – and the *vito* must catch the couple together. Unlike the songs of Carnival which recount past events, the *vito* cannot relate to what is no longer happening.

There are however two categories of person who escape the *vito* altogether. These are the shameless ones and the *señoritos*, the upper class of the town. The shameless escape for the obvious reason that people who have no honour cannot be stripped of it. The *señoritos* escape because they are not part of the plebeian community, and their actions do not therefore affront its stan-dards of conduct in the same way. It is recognized that they are different. The elderly lawyer who maintained a widow as his mistress was not thought to be a candidate for the *vito*, even though her daughter was also subsequently credited with that title, nor was a *vito* ever put on for the sake of that rich man who took as mistress the wife of a plebeian, though the latter was celebrated by the nickname of 'the horn of gold'. The *señoritos* did not, however, escape mention in the popular ballads. Given that the desecration symbolized by the horns relates to the dishonour of a man through his failure as a defender of his family, it follows that this carries different implications whether he is plebeian or *señorito*. The upper class husband can maintain two establishments and divide his time between them, but this is not possible for the plebeian who has neither the time nor the resources; if he takes a mistress to live with him this can only mean a rejection of his family. Therefore the word *cabrón* carries a different connotation in the plebeian community; the implications of conduct are different. The plebeian adulterer desecrates his family by taking a mistress, the *señorito* demonstrates his superior masculinity by doing so. In fact it is common to find men of the wealthier class in the cities who maintain a second household, and though this is resented by their wives, they are not subject to general opprobrium. This was not found in any of the towns where I studied, all of them of a few thousand inhabitants only. Nevertheless the case was reported to me, from a town of no more than sixteen thousand inhabitants, of a man of wealth and high consideration who, childless in his marriage, maintained no fewer than three illegitimate families within the precincts of the town. His relations with these households were conducted with great discretion, though the facts were widely known, and he was never seen entering the house of one of his mistresses during the daytime. He gave his numerous sons a professional education and for this reason was regarded as a very good father and a good man.

The association of male honour with the family and the qualities necessary to defend it, rather than with the morality, religious or not, of sexual conduct does not mean that the latter has no hold upon the men of Andalusia. Yet it is curious that this aspect of Christian morality is given more weight by the plebeians (who are mostly anti-clerical and rather irreligious), than by the middle and upper classes who are pillars of the Church and often profoundly religious. There is, in fact, a plebeian preoccupation with the notion of vice which is freely applied to any form of sensual over-indulgence, in particular women and wine, and this is thought of as something approaching a monopoly of the outside world and of the rich who maintain connections with it. This view of 'vice' expresses a social reality: it is only possible to escape the sanctions of popular opinion by going away. The shame which is bound up with the collective honour of the *pueblo* is juxtaposed to the shamelessness of the cities, since vice implies shamelessness. Such a view also implies that the rich are shameless, and this is quite often said. This conception of honour, associated with shame as we have seen, is similar to that of the Christian moralists whose criticism of the code of honour has been mentioned. Indeed, and in more ways than in this, the views of the *pueblo* echo those of the moralists of an earlier age.

I have defined shame in its social aspect as a sensitivity to the opinion of others and this includes, even for the *señoritos*, a consciousness of the public opinion and judgement of the whole community. One finds therefore a rather different attitude towards sexual promiscuity among the *señoritos* of the small town than among those of the cities, an attitude which expresses itself in the idea that male marital infidelity is dishonourable because it is an act of disrespect towards the wife. The husband who respects his wife is not promiscuous. I have the impression that this notion is less important in more sophisticated places.

Yet if the judgement of the *pueblo* brings its weight to bear upon the mores of its upper class, it is equally true that the influences of the outside world pervade the *pueblo*. Moreover, the 'puritanism' of the *pueblo* does not suffice to obliterate a consciousness of the value of sexual conquest as a justification of masculinity. A conflict of values is therefore implicit between the male pride which expresses itself in gallantry towards the female sex, and that which reposes upon a firm attachment to the duties of the family man. Manuel el Conde, the protagonist of honour, furnishes an illustration. At a fiesta held in the valley one of the local belles walked past him with her head high, ignoring his presence. Manuel was piqued.

'If it were not,' he said, 'for the ring upon this finger, I would not let that girl pass by me as she has.' Manuel thus recoups upon the hypothetical level the masculinity which he sacrifices in reality to his familial honour. He eats his cake and has it, albeit in fantasy.

There is another way in which plebeian honour departs from that of the upper classes. Honour is an hereditary quality; the shame of the mother is transmitted to the children and a person's lack of it may be attributed to his birth, hence the power of the insults, the most powerful of all, which relate to the purity of the mother. After this, the greatest dishonour of a man derives from the impurity of his wife. On the other hand, if his own conduct is recognized as dishonourable, then the honour of his family has no protector. Therefore, in its aspect as equivalent to shame, the nuclear family shares a common honour. The children not only inherit their shame, their own actions reflect upon that of their parents. The purity of the daughter reflects that of her mother, and thereby, the honour of her father. Her brothers, participants in a common heritage, are equally attainted by the dishonour of any member of their elementary family.

Social status is inherited primarily from the father whose patrilineal first surname a son inherits and will transmit to his descendants. The economic status of the family depends upon the father's ability to maintain or to improve its wealth. Therefore, in its aspect as right to precedence, honour derives predominantly from the father, whereas in its aspect of shame it derives predominantly from the mother. The distinction concords with the fact that precedence is something which can be gained through action – male enterprise, whereas shame cannot be gained, can only be maintained through avoiding the conduct which would destroy it – female restraint. An earlier period of Spanish history conceptualized these notions with more clarity than today as we learn from Caro Baroja's discussion of the descent of rank and purity of blood, concepts which represent quite clearly the notions of honour as precedence, and shame, respectively.[14]

The *pueblo* is envisaged as a community of equals amongst whom economic differences do not amount to differences of social class, even though they are considerable. All address their age-mates in the second person, even the employee his plebeian employer. From this community the *señoritos* are excluded; they are accorded, as a title of respect, the prefix 'Don' to their Christian name which indicates their superior status, in contrast to the title 'Señor' which is given to the respected members of the *pueblo* who have reached the age of retirement. The status of respected elder in a community of conceptual equals is as high as any member of the *pueblo* can normally aspire. Such positions of authority as exist between members of the *pueblo* derive from power delegated from the upper classes in a particular post, not from the quality of the person. Therefore there are no occasions when an order of precedence is ever required. The rule of 'first come, first served' governs all the contexts of ordering persons whether in the market or at the town-hall. This is not so among the *señoritos* who possess a concept of social status which differentiates them from the plebeians and involves an order of ranking, however unclear the ranking order may be, and however loath they are to make it explicit in their treatment of their fellows. There are, nevertheless, degrees of deference paid according to their relative status even in the context of the *pueblo*, and there is at least one family which conserves documents from the eighteenth century to prove its superior origins. Though they mix freely in everyday life, occasions arise when it is necessary to separate the sheep from the goats, and persons whose claim to status is well-established from those whose claim is less secure: the reunions with the summer visitors (who are persons of superior status to any in the *pueblo*), the visit of an important outsider or the marriage of a daughter of a leading family. On all these occasions personal attachments to the host cut across any objective criterion of ranking, yet the ranking is clearly implied.

A situation when a stratified order of precedence was required occurred when the image of Our Lady of Fatima visited the town and places were reserved in the church for the leading citizens and their wives. This gave rise to disputes, and for understandable reasons. First of all, seating in the church is normally quite informal and irregular; the men separate from the women and stand at the back, if indeed they attend the same mass as their wives. Other religious fiestas are organized by the church brotherhood of the particular cult, but there is no value attached to the order in which a procession is followed, and *señoritos* and plebeians attend in a haphazard manner. There was no precedent which could be followed in the order of seating. On this occasion, it was decided that, since the church was likely to be overcrowded, seats would be reserved. Proximity to the image therefore became a criterion of precedence in an entirely novel setting. But how was it to be accorded? The question of precedence could not be decided by the mayor on the basis of official posts, as on the occasion of the governor's visit, since the privileged were to include more than the officials and his authority was irrelevant since this was a religious occasion. The reception committee which had been specially formed for the event possessed no authority to enforce their ruling, and the priest wisely preferred to have nothing to do with such details. As a result, many felt that they had not been given the honour which was their due, and a series of quarrels ensued regarding their placing, which conflicted with the spirit of the occasion.

The nearer we move to the centre of national society and the higher in the hierarchy of status, the greater the importance of precedence, since the greater the number of contexts in which it is required and the greater the need for criteria by which it may be established. It follows therefore that the importance of honour=precedence increases with social status until we reach the aristocracy and the members of official organizations whose precedence is regulated by protocol, and among whom the concern for precedence is increasingly vital.

In the *pueblo* the ideal of equality in honour reigns and precedence deriving from birth and associated with status is missing. When conflicts threaten, the personal attribute of masculinity comes to the fore to determine the pre-eminence of one man over another and the word *cojones* is heard. It is a term which expresses unqualified admiration for the protagonist, quite regardless whether his behaviour is from other points of view admirable. It is to be noted that it is seldom used or understood in the literal sense.[15]

Physical violence is not thought to be a legitimate way to attain one's ends, yet when his rights are infringed, a man is forced to stand up for himself under pain of appearing a coward. So when violence occurs, it is characteristic that both parties believe themselves to be on the defensive, merely protecting their rightful pride. On festive occasions it is expected that people will forget their animosities and meet in a spirit of amity. Nevertheless, much wine is drunk then and fighting not uncommonly occurs among the young men, not so much as a defence of rights but as an expression of rivalry. Such an incident took place at a fiesta in the valley on the eve of St John. It was attended by the sons of El Cateto and also by those of La Castaña against whom the former had an antipathy of long standing. Before the end of the evening, Juan el Cateto was declaiming that he had more masculinity than all the Castaños put together. In the fight which ensued between the male youth of the two families, no damage was done since the combatants were on the whole more drunk than the public to whom it fell to hold back the assailants. Such incidents serve to show how the struggle for prestige is subdued in daily life by the conception of a community of equals which ordains that a man may not humiliate another. It is not dishonouring to avoid a person with whom one has quarrelled, but on the occasion of a fiesta each is entitled to think that it is the duty of the other to avoid him. This view of the town as a community of honourable men concords with the notion, expressed in the Fuero de los Españoles, that every individual has the right to honour. The competition for prestige finds its limits in the obligation to respect the pride of others, and this is true at any level of the social structure. Both the Catetos and the Castaños were criticized for their 'ugly' behaviour which spoiled the fiesta. There is no conception of sportsmanship which permits men to accept humiliation with dignity or to inflict it rightfully within the limits of a defined context. The existence of the sport of boxing in other countries and in Madrid, which is known thanks to the newspapers, is regarded as proof of the barbarity of foreigners and the corruption of the great city.

The collective honour of the *pueblo* is expressed in rivalry between *pueblos* which furnishes a body of rhymes in which each is epitomized by its neighbours in the most disobliging terms, implying dishonour in a rich variety of ways of which the most outspoken concern the purity of their women. The collections of folklore abound in examples. This collective honour is not usually expressed, however, in a hostile attitude towards individual outsiders. The individual stranger presents on the contrary an occasion to demonstrate the honourability of the *pueblo*, and every member becomes potentially a bearer of its honour. How the visitor is received depends upon the context in which he confronts the community. If he is recognized as a person of status, if he comes alone and with friendly intent it is important that he be received in accordance with the principle of hospitality towards strangers; they alone can validate the collective image. Yet in order to do so the visitor must be a person worthy of respect. The higher his status, the more important it is that he be favourably impressed, for he does honour to the *pueblo* by coming. It is above all to the visitor of the *señorito* class that the traditional courtesies of Andalusia are shown. The plebeian visitor still requires to be favourably impressed but more suspicion attaches to his visit. He may have come for reasons which do the *pueblo* no honour; those who come to seek work are potential blacklegs;

those who come for commercial reasons may have come to cheat. Both have come seeking their own interest and while they should be favourably impressed, they should also be watched. Boys who come from neighbouring towns to court a girl are treated traditionally with hostility, if not actually with violence, by the young men of the *pueblo* whose collective honour is challenged by their presence.

Visitors who come in large numbers during the fiesta offer a problem; by swelling the attendance at the fiesta they do the *pueblo* honour, for the number of people who attend gives a measure to its importance, yet it may transpire that they have come with the intention of inflicting humiliation. A visiting football team, for example, does honour only so long as it is defeated, but if it wins it inflicts humiliation. If it succeeds in imposing its superiority, then it is liable to be resisted as in Ubrique where the *pueblo* defended their honour against humiliation by a more expert team from Cortes de la Frontera which scored two goals in the first five minutes, yet failed to win the match. Unprepared to submit to such treatment, the infuriated public drove the visitors off the field and out of the town in a hailstorm of stones, and their bus was sent after them to pick them up and take them away.

In all situations of challenge a man's honour is what obliges him to respond by resenting the affront, yet a challenge is something which can only be given by a conceptual equal; the force of an affront lies in the fact that it is an attempt to establish superiority over the affronted person. If this is not the case then there is no challenge. This may be demonstrated by a fact that appeared to me at first sight curious. The farm of Pegujál has an only son and he is mentally deranged. He lives there with his widowed mother and keeps a small flock of sheep. These he takes out to pasture wherever he wishes, often beyond the frontiers of his land, in disregard of the land rights of the valley. The owners or lessees of pasture may find him any day encroaching upon their property, and if any reproach is made to him he merely utters oaths and throws rocks. Encroachment upon pasture is one of the causes of quarrels in which the honour of both parties becomes involved, but in this case it is not so. His lunacy places him outside the community of normal men and he is therefore unable to affront. People take no direct steps to restrain him and, if he turns up on their land, they shrug their shoulders. His actions cannot constitute a challenge, since he is mad.

Equally, if there is already a difference in social status between the two parties, then actions which might otherwise be an affront cease to be so. The man who has the right to authority over others does not affront them in exercising that right. It is not humiliating to obey the commands of a person entitled to give them. This fact is crucial to understanding how honour is effective in relations within the hierarchy of this society. To receive protection from someone not recognized as a superior is humiliating, but from the moment that protection is accepted superiority is admitted, and it is no longer humiliating to serve such a person. Service and protection are the reciprocal links which hold a system of patronage together. At the same time the patron increases his prestige through the possession of clients, while the client participates in the glory of his patron. The two are linked together by a personal tie which gives each diffuse rights over the other: service when it is required, assistance when it is needed. The system is reinforced through the institution of ritual kinship and expressed in its idiom. The terms *padrino*, *apadrinar*, *compadre* (godfather, to sponsor, co-parent) have extensions far beyond the literal sense. *El que tiene padrinos se bautiza*, the saying goes. (He who has godparents gets baptized.) In the struggle for life success depends in reality upon the ability, much less to defend one's rights against equals, than to attract the favour of the powerful.

The social class of the *señoritos* is defined by their way of life, but their prestige relates to their ability to operate a system of tacit reciprocities: to possess clients who owe them fidelity and respect, *compadres* with whom to exchange favours, and equally, patrons of whom they in their turn can demand favours, not only for themselves but for their clients. Thus they build up the reputation for beneficence which is an aspect of honour. Beneficence therefore transforms economic power into honour. Let us see, therefore, how the notion of honour relates to money.

Financial honesty (*honradez*) is associated with honour in the sense that it is dishonourable to defraud. Yet the circumstances need to be defined since to outwit is permissible, even mandatory in the context of bargaining. As one well-qualified to judge once warned me, 'In your country it may be different but here a bargain is not a bargain unless you have told forty lies.' Rather than a matter of abstract principle, the obligation to deal honestly is, in fact, a personal one. You owe honesty in defined situations, as loyalty to a particular person. To persons with whom you have or wish to form ties, to kin, friends, or to employers, particularly if they are also godparents; to abstract entities such as limited companies less, and to the state not at all, since these latter categories, not being persons, cannot offer the reciprocity required in the system of patronage. Within the community of the *pueblo* there is an obligation to honour one's undertakings, and complaints about those who have failed to do so both stress this as a norm of conduct and also demonstrate that it is not always obeyed. In fact, men learn whom they can trust little by little, testing each other as they go along. In the case of default they have at least recourse to the tribunal of public opinion before whom they can impugn the reputation of the other, as well as the more cumbrous and distrusted mechanisms of the law. The tribunal of public opinion is not of much use when dealing with people from another town or from the city, and the law is less effective also, so the distrust towards outsiders seems sensible enough. For the same reason the outsider has less control over the sanctions which enforce honesty towards him.

There is a tendency to presume upon the favour of a patron when he is the employer, and servants and bailiffs frequently regard it as their due to take financial advantage of their situation. For these reasons the absentee landowner, even though he turns up at harvest time, seldom avoids being cheated. *El ojo del amo engorda el caballo.* (It is the eye of the master which fattens the horse.) Moreover, persons of high social status tend to be lenient towards the peccadillos of their trusted employees as long as they 'don't go too far'. To be penny-pinching does not go with the ideal of aristocratic behaviour.

The ability to pay is an essential part of honorific behaviour, whether in the context of hospitality towards strangers, or in asserting pre-eminence among equals or bestowing protection upon inferiors. Paying is a privilege which goes to the man of precedence since to be paid for places a man in a situation of inferiority. Hence disputes about paying the bill which occur whenever there is no clearly defined superior who can claim the right to do so. (In such a situation a man must put up a good fight in order to defend his honour even though he may be delighted to lose.) There are barmen in establishments frequented by gentlemen of honour who have amassed a tidy fortune simply by giving way to all those who claimed the privilege of paying. The humiliation of being paid for is still very real, even though it may no longer go so far as in the days of George Borrow who tells of a nobleman who ran his friend through with his sword at the end of a drinking-bout, because the latter insisted on footing the bill.

The show of beneficence forbids one to appear grasping or concerned with money. Yet on the other hand, the man who takes no care to preserve or augment his resources may lack the wherewithal to validate his honour on the morrow. There are many spendthrifts in the cities to whom the attraction of honorific behaviour in the present outweighs their concern for the future. Such people are often more involved in display and competition with equals than in meeting their obligation to dependents.

There is no subject upon which more contradictory opinions have been put forward than 'the Spanish attitude to money'. They range from Don Ramón Menendez Pidal's assertion that 'it is a natural trait in the Spaniard not to allow any calculation of gains and losses to prevail over considerations of another order',[16] to the sly jibe of Cortés that he and his companions suffered from a disease of the heart which could be cured only with gold. Foreign observers have brought their testimony to bear at both extremes, some praising the disinterestedness of the Spanish character, others, perpetrators of the Black Legend in the Spanish view, asserting the opposite. Such a contradiction can only be reconciled through an appeal to context. By translating the ideal of beneficence into the reality of behaviour we can see that it implies a concern in acquisition, on the one hand, with a view to gaining honour through disposing generously of that which has been acquired, on the other. To give a thing away one must first of all get hold of it. The same concern is acquiring honour, through the act of beneficence rather than, as in the Anglo-Saxon countries, through the fact of possession, explains these extreme views. For honour derives from the domination of persons, rather than things, and this is the goal which distinguishes the acquisitive values of Andalusia. It is, needless to say, a goal which is inimical to capitalist accumulation.

The concept of honour presents itself in a different contextual framework to the individual according to his place in the social structure, and the differing value attached to it can be explained by this. Its relation to economic and political power is not seen in the same light by those who possess such power and by those who do not. Those who have no possibility of playing the role of patron do not compete with their equals in the same terms, while their prestige relates, as we have seen, to a public opinion which recognizes virtue rather than precedence as the basis of honour.

At the same time their lives are circumscribed by a community which is a territorial unit and proximity makes the moral sanctions of the *pueblo* effective. This is not the case with the upper classes whose social superiority places their honour in a sheltered position with regard to those sanctions. Their effectiveness varies with the size of the community, so that a distinction must be made not only between different classes but also between the community of a few thousand souls in which public opinion represents a homogeneous body of knowledge and comes to bear upon every member, and those where only the eminent are known to everyone. The urban parish possesses a certain social identity, a network of neighbourly relations through which social control is exerted which likens it to a limited extent to a rural community,[17] yet the possibility of a relative anonymity is open to the man who moves from one district to another, and the force of public opinion is diminished when it is no longer omniscient. The diminished concern with the ethical aspect of honour in the large towns must surely be related to this fact.

The situation of the *señoritos* is also different in the two environments. In the *pueblo* they form a small group who meet each other every day and whose every action is common knowledge to the entire community. They constitute its upper class. In the city this is no longer the case; people of equivalent occupation and wealth form a middle, not an upper, class, and they accept the leadership of persons of greater wealth and wider horizons. They are therefore simultaneously less subject to the sanctions of the *pueblo* and more subject to the influence of the upper class. The *señoritos* of the small town appear fine figures at home, but when they come into the city, they shrink in stature, and seem no more than the uncouth country cousins of the urban middle class. *Señorito de pueblo* is a term of denigration in the mouths of city folk.

We must consider the honour of the aristocracy. The Andalusian aristocracy is largely dependent upon landed estates in whose administration they take a varying interest. They maintain their ancient palaces in the cities of Andalusia though many spend much of their time in Madrid. They form the nucleus of so-called 'society' which includes persons of wealth or eminence who do not belong by birth to the aristocracy. This is what I refer to as the upper class. While its various elements mix freely and intermarry, a fundamental prestige attaches to birth which modifies, but does not obliterate, consideration of wealth.

The moral sanctions of the *pueblo* have only a limited importance for the middle class and none for the upper. It is no doubt a satisfaction to them to feel that they are appreciated by their dependents and admired by the populace, but their reputation looks to their equals for validation, not to their inferiors. Their lives possess far more privacy than the *pueblo*, and though they appear as public figures, their intimacy is confined to the circles of their dependents and their peer-group. Gossip indeed exists and tends to be relayed over a wide range, so that a person of the upper class possesses a public character, but his social position is a matter of birth and wealth, and it is therefore, in a sense, impregnable to gossip. If he is disliked by his peers he may be avoided, but his honour is very rarely publicly affronted. He is dishonoured only by being ostracized by his social equals.

The sanctions of honour=virtue therefore play a less conspicuous part than in the plebeian milieu, or for that matter in an earlier period of history. Those who have been ostracized have been so because of their political behaviour during the Civil War or their financial unreliability, rather than their sexual behaviour.[18] However, between plebeian and upper class honour there is, in addition to the difference already noted which was seen in the conception of the cuckold, a further difference. A man's sexual honour is attained not only through the purity of his womenfolk but through his commitment to any other woman in whom he has invested his pride. The infidelity of his mistress leaves him a cuckold also. Thus on one occasion a lady of the upper classes whom gossip had credited with a clandestine lover over a number of years transferred her favours to a fresh admirer. Shortly afterwards her abandoned lover was seen lunching with her husband and the comment was made: 'There go the two cuckolds!' The abandoned lover was equated with the infelicitous husband.

This usage no longer submits to the explanation which I have given of the symbolism of the horns in the plebeian community, that they stigmatize the failure to defend familial obligations. It is here the lover's honour=precedence, not his honour=shame which is at stake for he has no rights over the woman in question. He is humiliated only in that he has lost to another the 'right' to her favours,[19] the title of 'amant de titre'. The fact that this usage does not conform to the definition given above does not invalidate it. The point, precisely, was that the plebeian conception is not the same as that of the educated classes. The difference corresponds to the relative emphasis placed upon honour as deriving from virtue rather than from precedence. If the former meaning is taken as a basis, then this extended sense must be regarded as a figurative form. On the other hand, if the usage of the educated is adopted, as one who fails to assert his sexual claims, then the plebeian usage must be regarded as, in part, figurative. The two senses overlap, but they do not coincide. Both must be regarded as figurative from the point of view of the brief definition of the *Diccionario de la Academia* quoted above.[20]

The greater sexual freedom of men of the middle classes corresponds to the fact that they are less constrained by the social control of public opinion, due to their greater freedom of movement and material possibilities. But it is also influenced by the fact that, whereas in the plebeian class the woman is the financial administrator of the family – she remains in the *pueblo* when the man goes away to work and therefore she keeps the key to the family chest – in the middle class the woman has relatively less importance in the question of the financial resources of the family, since the husband is not a manual worker but an office worker, rentier, businessman, professional or administrator. She enjoys relatively less liberty of action since she has servants who perform the tasks which take the plebeian housewife out to the fountain or the market. She is seen in public much less, spends her day in her house, or in visiting hers or her husband's female relatives or in church or occupied by church affairs. Outside her family circle she spends little time in mixed company. Her husband goes alone to the casino or the *tertulia*, the group of friends who meet habitually for conversation. The middle class wife is noticeably more restrained in behaviour than the plebeian, her husband more authoritative and more jealous.

When we reach the upper classes, however, this tendency is reversed, and we find women enjoying much the same independence as in the upper classes of the other countries of Europe. They are subject to less, not more restraint. They smoke and drink in public places frequented by their class, attend social engagements with their husbands, drive automobiles, travel alone and exercise authority in ways which are not allowed the wives of the middle classes. All these activities imply, of course, a higher standard of living. Moreover, gossip credits them with a sexual freedom which is not attributed to the wives of the middle class, and since we are concerned with honour as reputation it is gossip rather than the truth which is relevant. Nevertheless, the number who live separated from their husbands is much greater than among the middle classes, where this is very rare.

If we take the paradigm of plebeian honour and shame shown on page 44 and compare it with the values of the upper class, we can see certain significant variations. Rather than variations in the structure of the concepts, it is a matter of emphases upon their different properties. Thus it appears that shame and honour are less often synonymous with one another. Shame is above all an emotional condition which relates to a given situation in which the individual is put to shame. It can even be experienced vicariously. The word is still used as a personal quality, and one who affronts public opinion is said to have lost it, but self-respect would be a more appropriate translation here; its aspect as hereditary and natural is no longer taken literally. Children are expected to resemble their parents in character, but the shamelessness of one person does not imply that of his family.

Physical courage for the male and unwillingness to accept humiliation for both sexes, are essentials of honour, and financial honesty also, since the contrary implies, apart from everything else, a base concern in money which is unaristocratic. Honour is a question of class honour and personal precedence rather than sex which dominates the honour of the *pueblo*. Sexual conduct is a matter of conscience and is the subject of religious sanctions. It exposes a person's self-esteem rather than his honour.

Therefore a paradox confronts us which the remainder of this essay will be devoted to clarifying: those whose claim to honour is greatest, and also most dependent upon lineal descent, are most careless of their sexual honour. It is the counterpart, in the sphere of sexual behaviour, of the paradox noted by Voltaire, that there is always least honour to be found surrounding the king. It is far from being particular to Spain; on the contrary, it is perhaps more marked in other countries. However, we shall restrict our consideration of it to the Spanish social scene.

An obvious explanation presents itself: the concept of honour varies from age to age and its importance appears much diminished in modern urban society. The disappearance of the duel in modern times is a testimony of this, though the existence of the duel far from sufficed to make aristocratic honour safe in the eighteenth century, and in the most recent period in which it was prevalent it was not much concerned with the defence of sexual honour.[21] An upper class is always more amenable to foreign influence, and thereby to change, and the ideas of the twentieth century have tended towards, not only a diminution of the concern for honour, but also a greater freedom of action for the married woman. Moreover, there has been a great change in the last three decades in Spain in this regard, not only among the upper class but among the urban middle class. The paradox might be regarded then simply as a fortuitous product of the folk-urban continuum[22]; sexual jealousy is going out of fashion and rustic society is behind the times – an assertion for which there is some evidence, as we shall see. It is also true that the aristocracy is much more subject to foreign influence: English nannies, German Fraüleins, foreign universities and visits to Paris to buy clothes.

However, it appears to me from an admittedly inadequate knowledge of the historical records that the greater independence of women of the aristocracy antedates by a long way the disappearance of the duel and the influence, such as it may have

c   65

been, of the movement for the emancipation of women, if indeed it is not rather a permanent feature of aristocratic society.

There is always a tendency to attribute that which one disapproves of to foreign influence and in this, Spanish critics have not been exceptional, whether Don Gregorio Marañon who attributed foreign origins to Don Juan,[23] or, two centuries earlier, Fray Joseph Haro who blamed the custom of the *Chichisveo* (*sic*)[24] on the Italians. Father Haro, writing at the beginning of the Bourbon period was certainly correct in attributing changes in custom to foreign influence. Yet his complaints regarding the looseness of morals, in particular of the upper classes, have a very traditional ring to them. Father Haro understood the word *chichisveo* in a rather different sense to the Italian (where it means simply the person of the *cavalière servente*) as the institution of chivalrous, he thought culpable, friendship between a married person and a member of the opposite sex. His explanation why the rich were the worst offenders was an economic one: that a gentleman is expected to make costly gifts in order to maintain such a friendship. Certain resources are perhaps necessary, but this does not explain why the lady's husband should accept that his wife should receive such an admirer. Economic reasons may be cited to explain why the poor did not indulge in the *chichisveo*, but not why the rich did.

If Father Haro gives a time-depth to the paradox he does not resolve it. There is no doubt that the customs of the aristocracy were changing in the early Bourbon period in this regard. Even though neither the theatre of honour nor the picaresque satires against honour can be taken as literal testimony, they at least indicate a popular preoccupation in the earlier period. Yet the desperation of the aristocratic heroes of the theatre of honour in defending their vulnerability through women implies, unless they are all to be taken as paranoids, that their womenfolk gave them reasons for anxiety. (The fact that the women were often innocent of any infidelity scarcely detracts from the point since that is what makes the plot a tragedy.) The behaviour of the protagonists implies that they were acting according to expectations which, over-optimistic or pessimistic as the case may be, had some foundation in reality: the husband that his wife might be seduced, the gallant that he might succeed in his suit. The existence of the institution of the Celestina alone implies that the danger to marital honour was a real one. Traffic-lights are not found where there are no automobiles. Lope de Vega's thesis[25] that the only security of a man's honour lies in the virtue of his womenfolk, which appeals to our modern standards by its reasonableness, suggests a new approach to the problem, not that the problem did not exist.

I conclude therefore that this is only partially a modern phenomenon to be attributed to foreign influence and will try to give a more fundamental explanation.

The paradox should be rephrased in accordance with the distinctions already made: the class which possesses by birthright most honour=precedence is most vulnerable in its honour=shame. When we say 'the upper class', we must distinguish between male and female honour, since the carelessness of women relates to their own reputation, while that of men to the steps which they take to cover their vulnerability through women. The obligation for men to avenge their sexual honour is what has varied, above all, from the age in which vengeance is represented as a duty to that in which such acts of vengeance are not only effectively punished by the law but regarded in sophisticated society as barbarous and atavistic. Since the conventions of modern upper class society repudiate any means of responding overtly to such an affront (save through legal action which only aggravates the dishonour by publicizing it), there is little that a man can do about his tarnished honour other than impose the best interpretation of events he can, or cut his losses and renounce his responsibility by an act of separation.

It has already been pointed out that the upper classes are hardly susceptible to plebeian sanctions and the development of modern urban society and the segregation of classes which goes with it makes them even less so. Just as the liar is only dishonoured when, impugned as a liar, he fails to vindicate his honour, so the cuckold is only dishonoured when public recognition is given to the fact that 'the horns have been put on him'. The *pueblo* does this, and the smaller the community the more effectively; the upper class does not. Therefore the situation tends to remain ambiguous and to allow alternative interpretations.

The alternative interpretations which can be placed upon the same behaviour are seen clearly in the ambiguity which surrounded the institution of the *cicisbeo*. The *cavalière servente* appears in the first instance as the guarantor of the husband's honour, who accompanies his wife on occasions when the husband is not able to do so. Since the husband allows it, *honi soit qui mal y pense*. But the sanctioned guarantee becomes, in the eyes of the sceptical, a cover-plan.[26] Whether or not this scepticism is allowed expression depends upon the status of those concerned and the social position of the critic. Father Haro, as a churchman, was in a position to voice his scepticism. In his view, the occasion is all that is needed and 'la carne hace su oficio' (the flesh knows its business); he ridiculed the idea that such a relationship could remain innocent. (He belongs to the school of thought which maintains that female honour is only safe if the lady is locked in with a broken leg.) Yet the idea that women not subjected to male authority are a danger is a fundamental one in the writing of the moralists from the Archpriest of Talavera to Padre Haro, and it is echoed in the modern Andalusian *pueblo*.[27] It is bound up with the fear of ungoverned female sexuality which has been an integral element of European folklore ever since prudent Odysseus lashed himself to the mast to escape the sirens. It is through their sex that women acquire power over men, and 'women have naturally the ambition to attain command and liberty, and they wish to invert the order of nature, attempting (even though it may involve the greatest cruelties) to dominate men'.[28] This then is the traditional way of thinking, but it is no longer that of the educated classes.

However, we must look at it from the woman's point of view. Status derived from birth is not uniquely a male attribute. A woman is granted the status of her husband, but she does not thereby forfeit that which she received by birth. Legally she retains her maiden name, merely adding her husband's to it, and she passes it on to her children as their second surname. Moreover, unlike English titles, Spanish titles pass through the female line in default of a male heir in the same degree of kinship. The result is that they frequently pass through women, changing from one patriline to another. A daughter, in default of sons, bears the title and her husband takes it by courtesy, as her consort. There is no lack of examples in the literature of anthropology of women who take on a social attribute of men, becoming substitutes for them, whether, for example, for the purpose of marrying a wife in the lineage systems of Africa, or of continuing a feud in Montenegro. Yet the point to be retained is that a Spanish woman of high birth is able to transmit her patrilineal status to her children.

Even though woman's shame in the plebeian sense is visualized as a positive attribute, something which can be lost, it cannot be won like precedence, nor is it inherent like status. It is preserved by refraining from actions which are proper to men, and this is possible and necessary, according to the division of labour, because women are under the tutelage of men. Legal independence is a male prerogative, and a woman acquires it only when she leaves the tutelage of her father (until recently at the age of twenty-three). If she has married before then, which is commonly the case, she has already passed under the tutelage of her husband. Had she already acquired legal independence, she would lose it on marriage. Only while she is of age and unmarried, or widowed, is a woman legally independent. Under such circumstances, she does not pass under the authority of her brother or sons, and the division of labour breaks down. She is obliged to take legal responsibility, to act for herself and for her children in legal matters or business, and she must support them; she adopts the social role of a man.

The life expectation of women is higher than that of men and their average age at marriage is some years younger, so that, even discounting the effects of the Civil War, a considerable number of women become widows at an age when they are still active. The Andalusian widow often takes on the duties of her independence with enthusiasm and makes up for the years she has spent in subservience to the male sex.

In the beliefs of the *pueblo*, the same association is made in this case between the male role and aggressive sexual activity, and this is seen in the fact that widows are commonly believed, even in cases of apparent implausibility, to be sexually predatory upon the young men. It follows from the basic premises of thought upon this matter that a woman whose shame is not in the keeping of a man is sexually aggressive and dangerous. The association reaches its extreme representation in the figure of the witch, the unsubjected female who rides upon a broomstick to subvert the social order sanctified by religion. She is a woman who has foregone the moral qualities of her sex and become the consort of the he-goat. Both in the beliefs regarding the sexuality of widows (whose remarriage it will be remembered, is given the same treatment as the *cabrón*), and regarding the supernatural practices of witches, the same assumption is displayed: once the sexual division of labour breaks down, women become men and where this occurs there can be neither honour nor shame.

Father Haro viewed the matter in these terms and attributed the deplorable state of sexual morality which he strove to reform to the fact that the sexes were abandoning their 'natural' roles in their dress and in their customs. Men were sitting on the floor like women, and women were getting up on to stools. Sodom and Gomorrah all over again! The inevitable result was the *chichisveo* in which all honour was irretrievably lost.

Another writer of the previous century had already demonstrated the thesis in a different way. La Pícara Justina tells the story of a girl who is robbed of her purity by a young man and left dishonoured.[29] She therefore disguises herself as a man and joins the criminal underworld. When finally she finds her betrayer and forces him to marry her (thereby restoring her honour), she reverts to female dress. The parable could not be clearer: a woman stripped of her honour becomes a man. Her honour restored, she reverts to her true sex.

The popular beliefs regarding widows and witches, the ancient churchmen, moralist and novelist, give us a clue to the interpretation of the conceptual chart, not an ethnography. It provides the moral basis for the oppositions associated with the division of labour, so that such a chart now enables us to see coherence in the judgements passed in situations in which *honra*, *hombría* and *vergüenza* are invoked, why the conduct which is honourable for one sex may be the opposite of that which is honourable for the other; why women who adopt male behaviour prejudice their shame, while those who have abandoned their claim to shame are no longer submitted to the sanctions which control the behaviour of honourable women. Such women can behave as men do, attend functions from which honourable women are excluded, and use their sexuality to dominate men, as Father Haro believed all women desired to do. Yet by the same token they also forfeit their hold upon the honour of men. It also entitles us to see the victim of the *vito* as an Odysseus who failed to make himself fast and succumbed to the sirens. It is the pollution of his status as a community member rather than his immorality which calls down the wrath of the excommunicatory rite.

We are now in a position to resolve the paradox regarding the women of the aristocracy. Not only are they free of the sanctions which enforce the plebeian code of honour, their status marks them off from the duty to respond to its precepts, not like the shameless whose failure to respond established their dishonourable status, but because by the principle of *honi soit* their honour is impregnable and does not therefore depend upon male protection. Thus the lady of the upper class can command men without inverting the social order, since her power derives from her rank, not from her sexuality. It is not humiliating for a male inferior to obey her orders. She escapes the restraints which weigh upon middle-class wives, since, whatever her conduct, she possesses a status which cannot be forfeited. Her religious duty and her conscience require her to be virtuous and obey her husband, but if she does not do so, she is wicked, she is not dishonoured. She cannot then be stripped of her honour and become a man in the sense in which the plebeian can, thereby threatening the 'natural order', for the natural order for the aristocracy does not depend upon the same conceptualization of the division of labour and the opposition of honour and shame associated with it, and it is not therefore threatened when women escape from the tutelage of men. It has been suggested that male slaves, on account of their inferior status, lack the social personality of men. By an analogous reasoning, women of high birth are accorded on that account a right to the kind of pride which is a male attribute, an element of masculine honour. They do not thereby forfeit their femininity, any more than the slave acquires a feminine status through being denied a masculine one; they acquire in addition some of the moral attributes of the male. Sexual and class status come together to qualify the rules of conduct which apply to their behaviour.

I have examined the conceptions of honour which are held by different classes in Andalusia, plebeian, *señorito* and aristocratic, and the ways in which these are modified by the fact of living in a small isolated township or a big city. Small-town plebeian honour stood at one extreme and aristocratic honour at the other. In the former, in many of its aspects, honour was allied to shame and equated with virtue; in the latter the yardstick of honour was precedence. The difference was explained, in the same manner as the difference within the *pueblo* between the honour of males or females, by the place of the individual within the social structure.

The dual nature of honour as honour aspired to and honour validated reflects the duality of the aspiration to a role and its attainment. To be dishonoured is to be rejected from the role to which one aspired. 'I am who I am' is answered: 'You are not who you think you are.' The search for identity expressed in these attitudes is the search for a role and the transactions of honour are the means whereby individuals find their role within the social organization. Yet, in a complex society, the structure of common understandings, like the structure of roles, is complex; the criteria of conduct vary, and with them, the meanings attached to the concept of honour. So we can see that, on the one hand, the need for common understandings and the mechanisms of social integration (such as the acceptance of the usage of the upper classes) tend to unify its conceptualization, on the other, the demands of the social structure promote differentiation.

It was suggested at the end of the first part of this essay that the confusion of the meanings honour = precedence and honour = virtue served the function of social integration by crediting the rulers with a claim to esteem and a charter to rule. But it is a function which is fulfilled only as long as the confusion is not recognized as such, and we have seen that this is far from being always the case. Once it is realized that 'honour has gone to the village', there is room for polemic, a polemic which has been carried on for centuries (particularly between the Church and the aristocracy) and of which the disagreement between Montesquieu and Voltaire is only one of a whole number, one which opposed the realism of the noble jurist to the moralism of the bourgeois poet, the 'is' view of honour to the 'ought' view.

The social struggle is visible behind the semantic battle; in a sense, the sense which Speier suggested, it is fought out in words. The rebellion of the agrarian masses of Andalusia was promoted by a concept which illustrates this, *'señoritismo'*; *señorito*, the term of respect towards a member of the ruling class became extended in *señoritismo* to mean the rule of corruption and social injustice. The vocabulary of honour was subverted by the failure of the *señoritos* to satisfy the claims upon their image. The confusion broke down. But the battle over words is fought out only perhaps to start afresh as the operative pressures of social organization impose themselves and the need resurges to sanctify a new established order. The 'is' becomes 'ought' once more and authority is re-endowed with *mana*.[30] Behind the new order of precedence and the redefined honour the same principles can be seen at work, for if, as Durkheim suggested, 'the idea of force is of religious origin',[31] it is also true that the reality of force possesses the power to sanctify itself.

The conceptual systems which relate to honour provide, when each is taken in its totality and in its varied contexts, a mechanism which distributes power and determines who shall fill the roles of command and dictate the ideal image which people hold of their society. At the ultimate level of analysis honour is the clearing-house for the conflicts in the social structure, the conciliatory nexus between the sacred and the secular, between the individual and society and between systems of ideology and systems of action.

NOTES

THE CONCEPT OF HONOUR

1 *eg* Erving Goffman *The presentation of self in everyday life* (Edinburgh 1956). Also: 'Deference and demeanour' *American Anthropologist* (1956).

2 An excellent example is T. Hooker *An essay on honour* (London 1741) but this was equally true of the Italian Renaissance literature on the subject.

3 Montesquieu ['Esprit des Lois' *Oeuvres* (Paris 1958) Vol. 2, p. 354] viewed this opposition as indicative of a corruption of the principle of monarchy: 'Il se corrompt encore plus lorsque l'honneur a été mis en contradiction avec les honneurs et que l'on peut être à la fois couvert d'infamie et de dignités.' (It is further corrupted when honour has been put in contradiction with honours and it is possible to be covered at the same time with infamy and with titles.)

4 The dual origin is reflected by the former meanings of the English word *valour* which was the leading qualification of honour: it referred both to social status and also to personal excellence.

5 Para Tirso, como para muchos otros autores, habia venido a ser lugar común literario que 'el honor se fué a la aldea'. Castro,

Americo: *Cinco ensayos sobre Don Juan*, Santiago de Chile, n.d.,
p. 22. (For Tirso, as for many other authors, it had become a
literary commonplace that 'honour has gone to the village'.)

6 *Questions sur l'Encyclopédie: Honneur* (Geneva 1774) Tome 3, p. 438.
He quotes the Regent, the Duke of Orleans, saying of a certain
gentleman: 'C'était un parfait courtisan; il n'avait ni humeur ni
honneur.' (He was a perfect courtier; he had no moods and no
honour.) 'Le misérable caractère des courtisans' had been discussed,
in fact, in *L'Esprit des Lois, op. cit.* p. 255.

7 Thomas Hobbes *Leviathan* Ch. 10.

8 *Cf.* F. R. Bryson *The point of honour in Sixteenth Century Italy: an
aspect of the life of a gentleman* (Chicago 1935) p. 84.

9 The rituals of dishonour also centre upon the head, of course, as the
prevalence of the custom of scalping testifies. Some psychological
theories regarding the significance of such customs are discussed
from the anthropological point of view by E. R. Leach 'Magical
hair' *Journal of the Royal Anthropological Institute* (1959).

10 Montesquieu suggests, following Beaumanoir, that since knights
disputed honour with their faces covered, in contrast to plebeians
the offence to the face carried the connotation of treating a knight as
if he were plebeian, that is, of denying his status.

11 'The laundry of honour is only bleached with blood.'

12 G. Simmel *Sociology of Simmel* translated by Kurt Wolf (Glencoe
1950) p. 321.

13 The language of the Spanish Theatre of the Golden Age treats
honour almost as if it were a good, something which can be taken
from one person by another and which may be owed and restituted.

14 Montesquieu, *op. cit.* p. 826.

15 It is true that there have been cases of duels between women,
particularly – and this seems to me highly significant – in the later
nineteenth century, but, like lady-bullfighters, these clearly involve
a travesty.

16 *op. cit.* p. 820.

17 *Cf.* Montesquieu *op. cit.* p. 262.

18 Tirso de Molina *El Burlador de Sevilla y Convidado de Piedra*
Jornada Tercera, lines 641–5

D. Juan: Honor	Honour
Tengo, y las palabras cumplo	I have and I keep my word
Porque caballero soy.	Because I am a gentleman.
D. Gonzalo: Dame esa mano	Give me that hand. Don't be
no temas.	afraid.
D. Juan: Eso dices? Yo temor?	What's that you say? Me afraid?
Si fueras el mismo infierno,	If you were hell itself
La mano te diera hoy.	I would give you my hand today.

19 *The approach to the Spanish drama of the Golden Age* (London 1957) p. 13.

20 Ernestine Friedl *Vasilika: a village in modern Greece* (New York 1962) pp. 80, 86.

21 The ambiguity which surrounds this problem is reflected in the discussions of the jurisprudence of duelling; an insult may be answered not by a challenge but by an indictment of lying (the Mentita) which throws on to the insulter the obligation to challenge. Since the challenger loses the choice of weapons there was every advantage in provoking rather than issuing a challenge. The function of the Mentita was to entitle the affronted party to gain the choice of weapons, but it also tended to enable the professional duellist 'to place a chip on his shoulder', provoke whom he pleased and stick to his preferred arms.

22 Marcel Mauss did in fact suggest such a translation. *The Gift* (London 1954) p. 36.

23 *Cf. Eclaircissements sur L'Esprit des Lois op. cit.* pp. 1169, 1180–3. Also, Emile Faguet *La Politique comparée de Montesquieu, Rousseau et Voltaire* (Paris 1902) p. 3.

24 The motto of the Order of the Garter, 'Fie on him who thinks ill of it.'

25 *Op. cit.* p. 36.

26 *Cf.* Meyer Fortes *Oedipus and Job in West African Religion* (Cambridge 1959).

27 Hans Speier 'Honour and social structure' in *Social Order and the Risks of War* (New York 1952) pp. 36–52.

HONOUR AND SOCIAL STATUS IN ANDALUSIA

1 J. A. Pitt-Rivers *The People of the Sierra* (Chicago 1961).

2 *Cf. Fuero de los Españoles* (1945) Article 4. *Cf.* also *El Código Penal* Articles 467–75 'Delicts against honour.' It is also implicit in the articles against duelling (439–47) and in the concept of adultery (448–52).

3 *Op. cit.* p. 168.

4 *Cf.* E. Friedl *op. cit.* p. 86.

5 *Op. cit.* p. 113.

6 Even in those which castigate with the epithet 'a double standard' the sexual mores of the Latin countries.

7 It was a commonplace of the theatre of honour, yet its aristocratic cuckolds appear not to be much concerned with questions of responsibility. Their unfortunate women get killed, not as punishment, but because they represent a living testimony to male dishonour.

8 *Op. cit.* p. 116.

9 *Cf.* the definition of *cabrón* in the *Diccionario de la Academia*: 'One who consents to his wife's adultery.'

10 For the Nuer of East Africa, adultery creates a state of pollution but 'it is not the adulterer but the injured husband who is likely to be sick' (E. E. Evans-Pritchard *Nuer Religion* (Oxford 1956) p. 189). A parallel can be found in South Africa in the first fruit ceremonies before which it is prohibited to touch the crops. 'In most South African tribes a breach of this taboo threatened ritual danger not to the transgressor, but to the leader whose right of precedence "was stolen".' Those who broke the taboo were nevertheless punished by the chief. (Max Gluckman *Rituals of Rebellion in South-East Africa* (Manchester 1954) p. 12.)

11 G. Brenan *South from Granada* (London 1957) p. 48.

12 *Op. cit.* Ch. 10.

13 Approximately 2% of the children born in the period of 1940–50 have no paternity.

14
'El honor	'The honour
que de mi padre heredé	which I inherited from my father
El patrimonio mejor	The best of patrimonies
Que en Valencia espejo fué	Which in Valencia was a mirror
De la nobleza y valor.'	Of nobility and valour.'

Tirso de Molina 'La Villana de Vallecas' *Obras Dramaticas* (Madrid 1952) Vol. 2, p. 792.

15 Thus, in place of the symbolism of the head 'standing for' the genitalia as in the Freudian interpretation, we have here a word for the genitalia being used to 'stand for' the quality which is commonly expressed by an analogy with the head.

16 *The Spaniards in their History* trs. Walter Starkie (New York 1950) p. 121.

17 *Cf.* Michael Kenny *A Spanish Tapestry* (Bloomington 1962).

18 In the cases of ostracism on account of sexual conduct of which I have heard, the victim was always a woman whose status was insecure from the point of view of birth.

19 This sense of the word cuckold is not, of course, unique to modern Spain. Anouilh, in *Ardèle ou la Marguerite* (Paris 1949, p. 81), ridicules the notion of honour contained in this conception of cuckoldry by making the lover challenge the husband to a duel on the suspicion that he has seduced his own wife.

20 Another figurative form produces the word *cabronada* which according to the *Diccionario de la Academia* means: 'an infamous action which is permitted against one's honour' and applies in fact to any shameful action. We might also point out that in Mexico the word *cabrón* has lost, in popular usage, all association with

cuckoldry and, with this, the symbolism of the horns which is not understood outside the circle of the educated. A comparison of the values and symbolism of honour in Spain and in the New World is badly needed.

21 Carl A. Thimm *Fencing and Duelling* (London 1896) gives statistics, only unfortunately for Italy, in the period of 1879–89. It is interesting however that he finds the causes distributed among politics, card-games, religious discussion and only eight per cent of 'serious insults' which may be taken to include sexual honour. I do not have the impression from the many duels cited by Thimm that Italy was exceptional in this regard.

22 Robert Redfield *The Folk Culture of Yucatán* (Chicago 1941).

23 *Don Juan* (Buenos Aires 1942). Marañon is another writer who fails to perceive that Don Juan is a man of honour=precedence and that the theme of the play is, precisely, a critique of this theory of honour – a fact which is surely congruent with the circumstance that the author was a priest.

24 *El Chichisveo impugnado por el R.P.* Fr. Joseph Haro (Seville 1729).

25 *El mayor imposible*. Lope makes clear in the last line of the play that he thought his thesis was unlikely to be put to the test.

26 *Cf.* Stendhal 'L'amour s'empara bien vite de l'usage des sigisbées.' *Promenades dans Rome* (Paris 1940) vol. 3, p. 88. Stendhal, incidentally, followed certain Italian authors in attributing the introduction of the *cicisbeo* in Italy to the Spaniards.

27 Pitt-Rivers *op. cit.* p. 175.

28 Haro *op. cit.* p. 12 'que las mugeres naturalmente son ambiciosas del mando y de la libertad y que quieren invertir el orden de la naturaleza, solicitando (aunque sea con la execución de las mayores crueldades) dominar a los hombres'. Father Haro's appeal to the order of nature must not be taken to be no more than the ranting of a baroque Sevillian priest. It bears some relation to those universal values which were examined, for example, by Robert Hertz in his great essay *The Pre-eminence of the Right Hand* in *Death and the Right Hand* (London 1960).

29 Andrés Pérez de León *La Pícara Justina* (Madrid 1912).

30 *Cf.* Luc de Heusch 'Pour une dialectique de la Sacralité du pouvoir' in Heusch (ed.) *Le Pouvoir et le Sacré* (Brussels 1962).

31 E. Durkheim *The Elementary Forms of the Religious Life* trs. J. W. Swain (London 1915) p. 204.

Julio Caro Baroja

HONOUR AND SHAME:
A Historical Account of Several Conflicts

Translated from the Spanish by Mrs R. Johnson

Chapter One

As is well known, the concepts of 'honour' and 'shame' exert a considerable influence in the societies of southern Europe, and in the past have exerted still more. However, in order to gauge the total extent of their importance several studies undertaken from different points of view would be needed. Thus, in the first place, no extensive historical research has so far been done which might reveal and illuminate the changes that these concepts have undergone, whether they have been sudden or gradual, nor any that might determine the part they have played in different sectors of those societies, at different times and in different regions. Secondly, there has been no investigation into how far they may have been rhetorical commonplaces, topics of discussion in a given community where, in fact, quite other interests predominate, so that these concepts may in the end have been no more than literary affectations. It has been frequently remarked from early times that those people who make most use of the words 'honour' and 'shame' and others associated with them in ordinary conversation, are not those whose lives are most strictly governed by the principles which those words express.

Thirdly, for a clear light to be shed upon the matter, there should be some subsidiary research into the nature of the actions in connection with which the ideas of 'honour' and 'shame' are most commonly invoked: it is well known that some people have tended to apply them to one type of action and others to another; so that it is frequently the case that a man who is not over-scrupulous financially is very strict in sexual matters, or vice versa . . .

Already in the seventeenth century, Don Francisco de Quevedo shows us in his satires on the underworld that in his day a woman convicted of thieving and prostitution might pride herself on never having been accused of witchcraft, regarding this as a greater honour, or the essence of honour itself.[1] Consideration of this might lead us to undertake some careful research into the question of 'honour' and 'reputation' among those who, in the general opinion, have none.

In the absence of such studies, I intend in these pages to offer some facts and ideas on the changes which the concepts of honour and shame have undergone in Spanish society at various periods, on the evidence of four sorts of documentation.

(a) Legal texts, which are extremely useful as guides for the solid foundation of any sociological research.

(b) Theological texts, which have never been thoroughly utilized, and are almost as important as the legal documents.

(c) Literary works, which, on the contrary, have in my opinion, been too freely used. By literary texts I mean, above all, the drama and the novel; and it is clear that, while plays and novels reflect points of view on moral questions, there is no doubt that, since they derive from the independent processes whereby literary ideas are transmitted internationally, they can only with extreme caution be adduced as evidence. It may be that the examples of the 'avenging of honour' which we find in some famous Spanish plays are nothing but imitations of those related by the Italian *novellieri* such as Bandello, etc. Even Calderón's idea of honour, on careful investigation of sources, may turn out to be something which in origin had little to do with Spain.[2]

(d) Strictly historical texts, such as memoirs, chronicles, letters, newspapers, etc, in which the facts are related without pretensions to style or any artistic manipulation, are for this very reason most valuable, and I shall have recourse to them as often as possible.

Finally I shall make some comments on the part played by the concepts of 'honour' and 'shame' in some present-day villages and rural communities, drawing upon direct observations – which did not, however, constitute systematic field-work.

2

The word 'honour' – *honos, honoris* – has many meanings in classical Latin. It is associated with the ideas of respect, esteem and prestige, and connected with the existence of public dignities and offices, and with rewards, ornaments and clothes which elevate their bearer above the rest of the community.[3] But there is something which, in the final analysis, separates the mass of honours or *honores* as they affected Roman life from the meaning they have among the modern peoples who make use of words derived from the Latin, such as the English *honour*, the French *honneur*, the Italian *onore*, or the Spanish *honor*. Our idea of honours among the Romans is exactly summed up in the *cursus honorum* which held sway for centuries where they ruled, while the expression *honestas* reminds us of the moral and philosophical speculations of such men as Cicero, who based their idea of an honoured and honourable life upon the thought of the Greek writers, of the Stoic and other schools. But these notions, whose clear juridical meaning belonged to the public realm and linked them with a powerful state (and even with a 'state philosophy') and whose conceptualization of the honourable life was based upon the cardinal virtues as defined by Aristotle and others of the founders of 'Ethics' as a branch of philosophy, gave way down the centuries to a state in which individuals and societies were governed by other ideals and other concepts; a whole system of moral and theological ideas developed through the middle ages, among which, I think, we should notice two in particular:

(a) The 'pride of blood', a sentiment much cultivated by the peoples we know as barbarians, such as the Visigoths, Ostrogoths, Franks, etc.

(b) The conviction that the righteous make up, first and foremost, a 'community of the faithful', an idea derived from Christian teaching, and which – as has on numerous occasions been observed – tends to restrict considerably the ethical principles current during the classical period, according to which the *community* was primarily one of *citizens*.

I shall try to show how the ideas of 'honour' and 'shame' develop from this triple root, furnished by the classical world, the Germanic or barbarian cultures, and Christianity. But first I must make a brief semantic investigation. *Honore*, *onor*, etc, are words which appear (in the feminine) in the earliest Castilian writing, during the eleventh to thirteenth centuries. After this the masculine gradually becomes general.

At this period the word was widely used as an equivalent of inheritance or patrimony, a sense which gradually gives way before other meanings. But besides this there is a point at which, according to philological authorities, *honor* yields to *honra*.[4]

In the *Diálogo de la Lengua* by Juan de Valdés, written in 1525, he includes *honor* in his discussion of obsolescent words, distinguishing it from *honra*, and considers that it could perfectly well be used in verse, but that it 'would look very bad in prose'.[5] This text – being the work of a man of great linguistic sensibility, even if on occasion he is somewhat arbitrary in his judgements – gives us an indication, apart from that of its date, which we ought not to overlook: *honor* is a word possessing poetic and social overtones which perhaps *honra* lacks, and its use is to be restricted to nobles, courtiers, etc, rather than ordinary persons.

This is a reason for studying the two words separately. Since it is in more general use we shall begin with *honra*.

It seems, in the first place, to be derived from the verb *honrar*; so that in its origin as in its use it would seem even more abstract, if possible, than *honor*.[6] According to a lexicographer of the early seventeenth century, a period at which Spanish life was more subject than today to the usage of these two words and the concepts they express, *honor* means the same as *honra*.[7] But we have already seen that before this time Valdés established a nuance of difference between them. Nor does the lexicographer I have quoted (Sebastián de Covarrubias) solve our difficulties by his definition of the words in question. Let us resort, then, to older and more helpful texts.

'*Honra* means preferment as a mark of praise, which a man gains by reason of the position he holds, or by doing some great deed, or by the goodness that is in him.' Such is the definition to be found in the Partidas,[8] which are a thirteenth century Castilian legal code whose importance is even greater from an ethical and philosophical point of view than from a purely legal one. *Honra* is here founded on personal virtue, and is created by the actions of the individual, or of those who engendered him in one place in society and not in any other.

'*Honra* rises by degrees, and he who can give the greatest honour in this world, that is, the king, should be the person to whom most honour is paid, not only in word but what is more important, in deed,' continues the same text,[9] possibly exaggerating royal authority and power in the matter, we may think, considering what we know of the life of Alfonso X (the author of this code), whose power was always extremely precarious.

The loss of honour is equated with the loss of life, 'for according to the Sages who made the ancient laws, two crimes are equal, to kill a man or to accuse him of wrong-doing; for a man once he is defamed, although he be innocent, is dead to the good and to the honour of the world; and besides, the slander may be such that death would be better for him than life . . .'[10]

For this reason a man guilty of destroying by calumny the reputation and honour of another should be severely sentenced, even to death, or if his life were spared his tongue was to be cut out,[11] according to the custom, at once cruel and symbolic, of punishing a man or woman in the organ with which the crime or sin was committed.

Honra finds its social expression in what is known as 'fame'; dishonour (*deshonra*) in 'infamy'. 'Fame' and 'infamy' were a matter for grave concern to the jurists and theologians of other ages, and as in many other instances, we may suspect that the attitude of people today to these two concepts comes less from their own elaboration of them than from a heritage transmitted since the middle ages through fables, exemplary tales, etc.

The Partidas also state that a bad reputation is worse than death,[12] so that from the definitions given there this diagram may be drawn up:

Honour	Dishonour
Fame	Infamy
Life	Death

'Honour' and 'dishonour' depend upon the consciousness of the individual; 'fame' and 'infamy' upon that of society. And both the individual and society are affected by the concepts of civil and moral 'life' and 'death', as well as by those of 'good' and 'evil'.

But the reasons why a person is or is not held in honour, has a good or bad reputation, besides being complex, were more various in medieval law and custom than in our own. Up to a point, too, they were different from those of the sixteenth and seventeenth centuries. We shall try to demonstrate this, starting from the same text of Alfonso X, and examining then the different social structures on which at different periods the concepts of honour and dishonour, fame and infamy operate. We have already seen the Partidas definition of honour. Let us now concern ourselves with what these say of dishonour.

3

The Partidas state, then, that there are 'infamies' which arise from *fact*, such as these:

(a) Being born out of wedlock.
(b) That one's father spoke ill of one in his will.
(c) That a king or judge spoke ill of one.
(d) That a man of good repute did so.
(e) Admitting to theft, making restitution after sentence.[13]

Other 'infamies' arise from *law*. Thus:

(a) The infamy of the woman taken in adultery.
(b) That of the woman who cohabits with a man less than a year after her widowhood.
(c) That of the father who remarries his daughter less than a year after his son-in-law's death.[14]

Finally, infamies of *common law* are those to which persons who live by certain trades are subject, and those who have certain vices. These classes of people, then, are 'infamous':

(a) Bawds and panders.
(b) Mountebanks and strolling minstrels.
(c) Those who fight with wild beasts for payment.
(d) Those who fight with other men for payment.
(e) Usurers.

Also sodomites, knights dishonourably discharged from the army, or whose spurs or sword-belt were struck off, and knights who took part in trade.[15] And, finally, those who commit other crimes and sins are infamous, whatever their rank: among them, traitors, forgers and adulterers, thieves and givers of bribes, swindlers and harbourers of criminals.[16]

'Infamy' is in itself a disqualification for such offices as those of judge, municipal or royal counsellor, spokesman, or for public office in general.[17]

This, then, is the system reflected in some medieval laws. The method of regulating the basis of honour is, in its simplicity, similar to that still in force in some other societies. According to it we have society (at least in theory) divided between people with 'honour' and those without it, between those of good repute and those of ill repute – the 'infamous'.

But what governs the actions which bring 'honour' or 'dishonour' as summarized by these laws?

In the first place a sentiment of which the laws themselves speak as if it had great importance as a creator of law: the sense of 'shame'.

The Spanish word *vergüenza* – shame – like the Italian *vergogna*, the French *vergogne* and the Portuguese *vergonça* derives from the Latin *verecundia*, and an examination of the last will help us to establish the sense of the others. *Verecundia* shows itself not only as chastity and modesty, as the blush which lewd speech or actions bring to the face, but also as respect for parents and elders, which prevents one from doing certain things in their presence, and as humility, reserve and respect for the laws and their representatives. *Verecundia* may border on timidity, and it is thus used at times, in a pejorative sense, although this is not usual.[18]

We should also note that *inverecundia* is not only immodesty in sexual matters, but equally disdain and lack of respect for laws and institutions. In this matter, in Spanish as in Roman life, everything from a mere blush at an indecorous word to respect for the king and the highest officials of the state, from sexual shame to a reverence for the law, including respect for parents, politeness in conversation, and personal neatness and dress, is regarded as a single whole. 'Shame' depicts for us the basis of an honourable life, and 'shamelessness' the road to infamy. The juridical texts support these assertions.

'*Shame*', as the Sages said, 'is the sign of timidity, which is born of true love.' Shame takes away men's boldness and makes them obedient to their duty. A bold people loses its shame even before its king, and comes to disobey him in important matters of peace and war. So a shameless community should be punished through its most rebellious members or ringleaders. So says Partida II, section XIII, law XVI.[19] This is an example in which the sense of shame is illustrated in the light of political behaviour.

But the Partidas themselves (I, section V, law XXXVIII) lay down that bishops should be 'chaste and shamefast', and here the idea of shame is given a sexual and repressive connotation: it is also what makes us avoid sin, and is a sign of good breeding, 'since through it the man of noble heart avoids doing or saying anything unbecoming to him'.[20]

This is to say, that in a typical medieval code of laws, moral and political ideas which today exist and affect society independently of one another, form an indivisible whole. Up to this point, however, we have not gone beyond an order of ideas which are well adjusted both to basic Christian morality and to the philosophical ethics of antiquity.

4

But at this point we witness a sort of somersault which leaves medieval man in an entirely different posture. In the Partidas again, even in laws dealing with what has already been analysed, another concept intervenes, a new factor which exerted an immense influence on the lives of many generations, even after the middle ages (though long before anyone had thought of establishing a sociology of values). I refer to the concept of *valer más* and to its opposite, *valer menos*. The words mean literally 'greater' or 'lesser worth' and they may be translated as 'prestige' or 'esteem' and 'disgrace' or 'disesteem'.

These two concepts introduce us to a type of action not strictly governed by pure virtue. It is true that 'disgrace' resulted from such acts as showing cowardice, breaking one's word or committing perjury: it was a kind of 'infamy', in a degree not greater or less but different, which could reduce persons of the highest lineage to a state of social ruin.[21] Yet 'prestige' seems only to have been won by force of arms, and scarcely ever with any regard for the principles of moderation and of serene and just courage.

During the latter part of the middle ages (from the thirteenth to the fifteenth centuries) there were many who considered that disputes over 'prestige' and 'disgrace' were, in fact, the mainspring of most human action. Lope García de Salazar, the historian of the lineages of Northern Spain and chronicler of the atrocities committed by them (atrocities which he nonetheless describes as 'successes and triumphs'), states at the beginning of Book 22 of his work that the wars of clans and families waged so bitterly by the Basques and inhabitants of the mountains of Santander sprang from the desire 'for greater worth (*mas valer*), as it was in ancient times throughout the whole world, among all the generations to this day, and those that are to come while the world endures'.[22]

This text gives us an essential key to understanding how from the ethical or purely Christian concept of 'honour' it is possible to reach another in which the moral laws founded on classical philosophy or on the precepts of the Christian religion are revoked, even at times absolutely. For this 'prestige' or '*mas valer*' is not attained by following the ideals of Christianity. In reality what moves men to aspire to it is not a matter of ideas at all, but an instinct arising in persons who live within social structures that are even older than Christianity or classical philosophy. 'Prestige', in fact, is connected with an idea of honour which is not individual but collective, and about which I must now say something.

The first point to be noted is that this collective honour is based on a system of patrilineal clans, like that which held sway among the Scots until the eighteenth century, among the Berbers of North Africa, the nomads of the Asian and African deserts, and other ancient and modern peoples, but which has particularly flourished in the Mediterranean area, in both town and country.[23]

Agnates, and even more distant categories of relatives, comprised in the lineage under various legal and religious titles, were regarded as solidary. The triumphs of one particular member of the lineage affected the whole of it, as did his disgraces also. All had their share in any honour, as in any dishonour. For this reason each lineage as a whole had pretensions to being 'worth more' than the rest. Therefore those defeated in this competition were equally 'worth less'. In a society formed on this basis there is obsessive competition for the possession of any existing public honours and offices, which then become hereditary within the lineage.

In each there is a senior kinsman, or chief, upon whom the greatest honours accumulate, and different branches or scions arising from a single stem. The genealogists' family trees spring from this principle, and in Spain they have given rise to as many fantasies in one age as to solidly erudite studies in another. As an example of the former those of Don Luis de Salazar y Castro (1657–1734) can be given.[24] It is not possible to examine here the question of the honours attained by various lineages at different times.

5

On the other hand we should emphasize the fact that this society is also obsessed by the dishonours which can fall upon lineages in the form of 'outrages', 'insults' and 'affronts'.

'Affront' (*afrenta*) is the name given to an action which dishonours a person even when it is done rightly and in the course of justice, as flogging or penance in the pillory. (In Spanish the verb 'to pillory' is, literally, 'to hold up to shame', *sacar a la vergüenza*.[25]) An 'insult' is an act dishonouring a person without plausible reason,[26] as also is an 'outrage' (*injuria* in Spanish), a Latinism which the Partidas translate, indeed, by *deshonra* – a concept to which, like later codes, they devote many laws.[27] Outrages – according to all these laws in synthesis – can be of several sorts.

(a) There are those of word, as when one man says something insulting to another in public.[28]

(b) They may also take the form of verses, *por cantigas e por rimos*, which may be written down. Thus, indeed, the early Galician-Portuguese collections of ballads contain a great number of satirical verses, known as *cantigas de maldecir* and *cantigas de escarnio*, some making use of maliciously veiled allusions, other containing quite open attacks.[29] Later, the Castilian collections contain similar satirical compositions under the name of *obras de burlas*, works in which the poets of the fifteenth century excelled – not always inspired, in truth, with the mere wish to amuse. Possibly the *Coplas del Provincial* of the time of Henry IV of Castile are the most defamatory ever written about any society. In these no one goes unscathed, and long afterwards they were doing harm to the descendants of those attacked in the scurrilous verses, which include every sort of insult.[30]

(c) Another form of outrage dealt with by the Partidas is that of ridiculing a person by mimicry (*remedijo*) or gesticulating in such a way as to provoke laughter.[31]

(d) Women are insulted or outraged by sending them bawds, making lewd proposals to them, and also by making them equivocal gifts or invitations of a certain sort.[32]

(e) A man may be insulted by deed, by a kick, or a blow of the hand, stick or stone, by pursuit with intent to wound, by tearing his clothes or by deliberate damage to his house or property.[33]

We may pass over the penalties that might be imposed for all these actions and the course of a suit for insult among the common people,[34] for during the middle ages those who piqued themselves on their 'worth' very frequently took justice into their own hands, without recourse to such laws, with the help of their lineage or kinsfolk, who took up their cause.

It was sufficient, in fact, especially in moments of tension, for a man who considered himself insulted, outraged or affronted to call upon his lineage (Spanish *apellidar*) as for example in Basque territory to shout 'Gamboa, Gamboa' or 'Oñaz, Oñaz', when all his relatives would rush to arms, to defend him or avenge the affront.[35] The chronicles are full of insults and affronts which resulted in bitter fighting between rival groups of kin and feuds lasting for centuries between lineages which might originally have been friends and allies, or even relatives.

6

It may be said that there were as many wars between lineages and factions over the possession of various honours as there were to avenge a dishonour or affront. I do not feel that it is necessary to amass examples, some of which would be melodramatic, others grotesque. Anyone who wishes to learn about some of the most typical should read the work of Lope García de Salazar already quoted or other texts of the same period concerning different regions.[36]

There are also some surviving fragments of poems in which families are mocked in connection with battles from which they emerged the losers, or in which 'vengeance' is demanded. Here is another concept of which we should take serious account. 'Avenging' or 'cleansing' affronts is an essential consideration in the social structure based on lineage. The most vindictive forms of revenge are to be found in various Mediterranean countries down to our own time; the Italian *vendetta* is an example. So, up to a point, was the so-called 'Catalan justice'. But more important and far-reaching than this is the fact, brought into relief by the historians of medieval literature, that vengeance is the basis of an infinity of epic poems. In the *Poema del Cid*, in the legend of the *Infantes de Lara*, in that of the *Conde Garci Fernández*, and many others, the avenging of an insult brings as much pressure to bear upon the protagonist as that exerted in Greek tragedy by the idea of Nemesis.[37]

Thus the concepts of 'prestige', 'honour' and 'revenge' are firmly united in the medieval consciousness. For this reason the medieval laws even accept the acts of defiance, or *reptos*, and challenges between nobles as a valid formula for settling their differences in affairs of honour. 'If a noble brings dishonour, or wrong, or harm upon another, he may be challenged for it in this way, by saying: I reject your friendship, and I challenge you, on account of such a dishonour, or wrong, or harm, that you did to me, or to So-and-so my relative, for I have the right to exact repayment for it.' So says one law in the Partidas,[38] while there is another in which it is made clear that a challenge is, essentially, *the rejection of the tacit friendship* which exists between nobles.[39] There are various attempts to regulate challenges by royal intervention, and there is a law, collected in the 'Royal Ordinances of Castile', dating from the year 1438, in the reign of Juan III, precisely when the great houses were feuding most bitterly, which sets a limit upon the reasons for which a challenge is permissible, and also upon the degree of relationship which allows a man to challenge another on account of the death of a relative. According to this law the right to challenge on such grounds would be restricted to the relatives shown in this diagram (*see opposite page*).

This law set out to restrict the principle of solidarity between agnates, which held sway in the societies of the period, especially in the great houses, whose leagues and alliances it was also hoped to limit then, and even earlier.[40] But the revenges and affronts went on for very much longer, no authority being able to cool the ardour of men's minds. Frequently the solidarity established by the lineage broke down because the various branches of it, each fixed in the idea of its own superiority or greater 'prestige', fought bitterly among themselves over the possession of honours and property. An enormous number of cases are recorded of

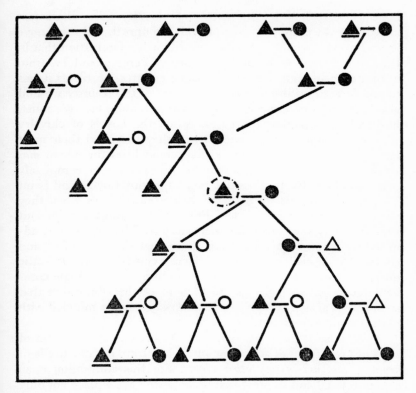

fighting between fathers and sons, brothers, etc. Apart from the examples to be found in the texts I have already quoted, I adduce those occurring in the life of Don Alonso de Monroy, Key-bearer and Master of the Order of Alcántara, written by Alonso de Maldonad, and which took place in the country of the Portuguese border.[41] A fierce individualism seems to have dominated men at the end of the middle ages. And this prepared the way for the breakdown of the lineage system, and of the basis of the morality founded upon that system. We should say something about this individualist tendency.

7

In the period under discussion, the ideal of society according to which *mas valer*, 'prestige', was the essential thing in life finds literary expression in the novels of chivalry. The characters created by the authors of these novels are unreal, and they move in an unreal world. But they exercised such a fascination that in the fifteenth century we find the names of Perceval and Tristram in use, even in regions like the Basque country, hostile as it was to any foreign tradition.[42] In other parts of the country we find also the names of Lancelot, Esplandian, Gawain, etc. We must, however, remark that the period when the novels of chivalry were most popular came later, when they exercised their most obvious influence over remarkable personalities for whom *mas valer* was no longer a question of lineage, but a completely personal affair. Even saints like Saint Ignatius Loyola and Saint Teresa went through a stage of their eventful lives when they were fascinated by them,[43] and Fray Luis de Granada points out very shrewdly the reason for their success. The deeds most admired by man – he says – are those that demand effort and courage and a disdain for death: 'Hence comes' – he adds – 'the flocking of people to see jousts and bull-fights and single combats and other such things, on account of the admiration that such things arouse, which admiration . . . is always mingled with pleasure and enjoyment.'

'And hence it happens, too, that the blasons and insignia of arms of great families are commonly taken from notable deeds of *bravery, and not of any other virtue*. For this admiration is so common to all and so great that it comes to have a place not only in real things, but also in fabulous and untrue ones, and from this comes the pleasure that many have in reading these novels of chivalry which are invented . . .'[44] Many other philosophers, moralists and theologians of the Renaissance agree with Fray Luis in condemning the novels of chivalry as immoral.[45] But today we should consider that their fictitious characters act under the guidance of a 'ruling class morality', as some German thinker would say, or by an ideal approaching the Nietzschean concept of the superman – which evidently has in its basis little connection with Christianity. And so these ideas of 'prestige' and 'honour', always in conjunction with more or less absurd battles and actions, also served as a guide to numerous adventurers of the sixteenth century, who were not saints nor anything approaching it, but men to be feared. When Lope de Aguirre ('the tyrant Aguirre', or 'Aguirre the traitor' and 'Aguirre the amazing' as he

called himself) had come out in open rebellion against Philip II
he wrote these words, in the midst of jibes and jokes, to a friar
who was that monarch's representative: 'because, after faith in
God, the man who is no better than another has not worth'.[46]
And writing to the king himself, in a letter full of terrible insults,
shrewd observations and savage satires against his representative
in the Indies, he informs him that he had crossed the ocean in his
youth, to Peru, *'to earn prestige (por valer mas) with my lance in
my hand*, and to do the duty incumbent on any gentleman'.[47]
Lope de Aguirre seems to have reached the point of madness in
his desire to win ever more prestige by violent means. On the
other hand we have cases like that of Don Alonso Enrique de
Guzmán who, also well into the sixteenth century, continued to
observe in his relationships with others, the principles and
customs of the middle ages and even earlier, such as the voluntary
choice of a knight as a *brother*, who is at one's side in danger and
in good fortune, and will defend one's honour in certain circumstances. This choice was marked by a ritual which recalls the
ceremonies of 'blood brotherhood' dating from primitive times,
which were studied by historians of ancient law, and are found
in fact in the novels of chivalry.[48]

Chapter Two

I

It may be said then that in the middle ages two systems of ideas concerning 'honour' existed, or coexisted; one, generally accepted, deriving from religious, philosophical and legal principles, the other deriving from factual situations, within the same social structure. The way in which the two systems adjusted to each other was indeed strange, and a clear demonstration that the principle of contradiction does not govern the life of society, but that the very essence of things is in the contradiction, as a Hegelian would claim.

But, in one form or another, the latent conflict existed, and in what terms we may see by reference to the expressive corpus of Spanish proverbs, whose corrosive force has never been sufficiently emphasized. It can be seen, then, that in discussing the honour which arises from possession of the classic virtues (prudence, justice, temperance . . .), from having done nothing shameful, the proverbs frequently extol it and regard its loss as something very much to be lamented: the ideas behind the proverb which says that 'glass and a man's honour shatter at the first blow' are repeated over and over again. There are also many which allude to the value of honour as a summary of virtues among ordinary simple people. By contrast, we find a lengthy series of sayings according to which *honours* are themselves of very doubtful value: 'the honour of this world is gone like a puff of smoke', 'honour, vanity and shadow', 'don't bother about honour, the king has plenty'; 'it is better to deserve honour than to have it'. Others emphasize the hardships to which honours are usually united ('most honour, most pain'). Others, finally, point out that honour alone is not worth a great deal: 'honour alone is a poor inheritance', 'honour without advantage, like a ring on the finger' 'between honour and wealth, the last is first',[1] this last being a statement in flat contradiction of all that is meant by the doctrine of 'prestige' whether knightly or of the lineage. There are some Spanish medieval texts in which it is roundly said that if money is not accompanied by nobility and fighting qualities it is a reason for 'disgrace'[2] or even, we might say, for 'infamy', since very often those who owned it were the Jews, considered infamous on two counts: by descent from the murderers of Christ – that is, by an inherited dishonour of a religious nature – and by being usurers, or, in other words, by a legal 'cause of infamy'.[3] But in opposition to the assertions of the aristocratic moralists there are already even in the middle ages shrewd minds which maintain that money is more than honour, since honours can only be obtained with it.

> '*Mucho fas el dinero, et mucho es de amar,*
> *Al torpe fase bueno, et omen de prestar.*
> *Fase correr al cojo, et al mudo fabrar.*
> *El que non tiene manos, dineros quiere tomar.*
> *Sea un ome nesçio e rudo labrador,*
> *Los dineros le fasen fidalgo é sabidor,*
> *Quanto más algo tiene, tanto más es de valor.*
> *El que non há dineros, non es de si señor.*
> *Si tovieres dineros, avrás consolación.*
> *Plaser e alegría, del papa ración,*
> *Comprarás paraiso, ganarás salvación.*
> *De son muchos dineros, es mucha bendición.'*[4]

(Wealth can do a great deal and is much to be loved. It makes the fool clever and worthy of respect. It makes the lame man run and the dumb man speak. The man without hands will find a way to take money. Let a man be a fool and a coarse rustic; money will make him a gentleman and wise, and the more money he has, the more respected he will be. The man who has no money is not his own master. If you have money you shall have enjoyment, pleasure and gaiety, the lot of the Pope; you shall buy heaven and earn your salvation; where great wealth is, there is great blessing.)

So begins the 'description of the properties of money' in *El libro de buen amor*, by the Archpriest of Hita, and it leaves us with nothing to add.

But two centuries later what the humorous Castilian poet had said was a commonplace topic repeated over and over again by the poets, on the basis of reasons which we must now examine at some length, together with other new ones which also make a decisive contribution to changes in the concept of 'honour' and 'prestige'. Some of these reasons were political in nature, others religious, yet others economic.

2

In the first place the violent campaign against the wars between lineages began in the reign of John II and continued in that of Henry IV of Castile. The persecution of the faction leaders by Ferdinand and Isabella, which was still going on long after, in the time of Charles V, destroyed many of the foundations of the old system of 'prestige', among others the strength of agnatic solidarity.[5] Many of the customs, accepted when the lineages were at the height of their power, and during the florescence of chivalry, fell more and more into disuse: above all those concerning ways of insulting, affronting or outraging, or of avenging insults on behalf of lineage or kin, by means of public combat and other actions of the kind. The struggle to impose a new political and social order which should overcome the old individualisms was long and hard, and, though numerous documents on it exist, it has not yet been thoroughly studied.

On the other hand, the Spanish monarchy in the sixteenth century was careful to habilitate or rehabilitate the honour of certain classes of persons, and to limit the power over it of the nobility and gentry. This 'new' tendency is to be found more or less clearly criticized in various passages of Don Diego Hurtado de Mendoza's classic work on the revolt of the Moriscos of Granada.[6] For centuries there were law-suits between the old nobles and the new municipalities, which were often resolved in favour of the latter.[7]

The monarchy also arranged for individual honours and those conferred from above to be more abundant. The creation of a court and of several great administrative organizations, the enterprises of discovery and conquest, and the endless wars in which the Spaniards were involved during the sixteenth century modified the forms of 'prestige'. But as the organizations created by the monarchy itself to provide it with support turned out later

98

to be very much stronger than had been foreseen, they came to exert very heavy pressure upon it, and even more upon the problems of 'honour', which in the sixteenth century, and to a greater extent in the seventeenth, became more acute and complex, until they made Spanish life something unique within European society. Now we shall try to give an idea of the social structure in which this different idea of honour develops, on the basis of the existence of an absolute monarchy with theocratic tendencies.

We remarked earlier that the right claimed by the medieval lineages of executing justice on their own account in matters of honour was gradually limited; in the same way the honours which had interested them most lost much of their significance in the face of others. Indeed, the patronage of ancient churches, the control of pious lay brotherhoods and of the councils and markets of different regions and towns, even of a few manors, was not very much compared with the honours which could be gained by *serving* the king, whether at court, in the army, or in the councils and tribunals of Spain or the New World, or even of various parts of Europe. With the new forms of employment, besides these honours great wealth might be obtained, and frequently very rapidly. The life of the period immediately preceding seemed rustic and provincial to many: taking the difference between 1480 and 1530, for example. But although society began to shape itself on new bases,[8] the conflicts produced by the concept of honour did not come to an end. Soon a punctilious noble hierarchy of a courtly character came into being, as prone as any other to disputing precedence in matters of etiquette and protocol.[9] The creation of the Spanish titled nobility appears to date from the early years of the reign of Charles V, when titles were increased in number and called 'Grandeza', importance.[10] Soon, too, struggles arose over points of honour and precedence between the monarchic institutions, such as the chancelleries, tribunals of the Holy Office, etc. As can easily be demonstrated, the Inquisition was one of those which carried on most lawsuits, quarrels and violent actions against councils, cathedral chapters, bishops, etc.[11]

By a fatal destiny the Holy Office, too, was by its very nature one of the organizations which most upset the lives of many families, precisely because of certain criteria which it set up relating to honours, reputation and shame, dishonours and ill-fame, and this from the moment it first began to function. The matter is of such importance in the history of the Spanish concept of honour that we must study it at some length.

3

The Iberian states during the middle ages had lived divided not only politically but religiously. But we can say that within each of them for a long time there existed a mutual tolerance of three confessions or religions: Christian, Muslim and Jewish. The relations between Christians, Muslims and Jews within each state were tenser at some times than at others, as has happened in modern times in the Turkish and Austro-Hungarian empires, for example. But as the Christians came to dominate more and more territory, it was realized that this coexistence could not go on for ever, and forced conversions of the Moors, and especially of the Jews took place repeatedly. At the beginning the neophytes, those converted to the faith, known as *conversos* and *confesos*, were considered as new sons for the Church, saved by their baptism and included in the *community of the faithful*. But when it was demonstrated on numerous occasions that among these people there were many apostates who returned to their old beliefs, they began to be looked on in a different light: rather, there were those who defended them en masse, and those who attacked them likewise,[12] so that a clearly defined social class was created – that of the 'new Christians', which, placed thus in opposition to that of the 'old Christians', constituted a seedbed of troubles. These were linked with those produced by the lineages and factions of the type described in the last chapter, since in cities like Toledo, Córdoba and Seville, the 'new Christians', and earlier the Jews, flocked to the standard of one of the great houses, which would protect them, or showed their sympathies for one party rather than another – even in disputes for the crown, as seems to have happened in the time of Pedro the Cruel and Henry of Trasta-mara (when the Jews were more inclined to the former than to the latter), or when Henry IV was fighting against the Infante Don Alfonso, when the *conversos* were more in favour of the former.[13] By the establishment of the Inquisition it was intended to put a stop to the riots and rivalries. On the one hand to prevent persecutions by the populace of the 'new Christians' accused of apostasy, and on the other to punish severely those apostates who were in fact guilty. Among the penalties imposed on these not the least terrible were those which extended the guilt to their descendants, branding them as 'infamous', ineligible for a great number of honours, dignities and offices; far-reaching penalties which shocked some people from the very beginning.[14]

Now, it is a known fact that during the fourteenth and fifteenth centuries the Jews possessed great wealth, and that the rich 'new Christians' attempted to safeguard their children's futures immediately by buying some benefices in churches and cathedrals, generously endowing others, giving them an education superior to the majority, etc. So, in a few generations, it was notable that on all sides there were outstanding bishops, canons, abbots, priors, friars and clergy in general of Jewish origin; that in the courts and chancelleries scholars of the same race exercised the most delicate legal, diplomatic and economic functions, and that houses of 'old Christians' of the highest social pretensions came to intermarry with these people whose sincerity as Christians was in some doubt, and upon whom the Holy Office vented its wrath at the beginning of its existence.[15]

As a counteragent to this penetration sodalities, schools, convents, etc. began to be founded, from which the descendants of condemned apostates, or even 'new Christians' without further qualification, were excluded, and these statutes provoked bitter struggles even within the fifteenth century.[16] But from the moment the Inquisition was founded we may say that the statutes had a clear field throughout the whole of Spain, and came to root themselves among the tenantry and in the townships, the religious and military orders, cathedrals and the numerous professional guilds and brotherhoods, so that in the course of the next century the whole of Spain was dominated by a preoccupation with the concepts of 'purity' and 'cleanliness of blood' and of 'impurity', 'stain' or 'blot'; this 'purity of blood' being equated with 'honour', and impurity with 'dishonour', and at the very least, ineligibility for the competition for honours.[17] The results of this criterion, based upon a strange valuation of *blood*, that is, of *Gothic* blood as the better and *Jewish* blood as the worse, were much more complex than would be imagined from a simple glance. According to old Castilian law every man belonged, in principle, to the same social class as his father; that is, the son of a noble was noble, even if his mother were a villein, while the son of a villein was a villein.[18] There was in force, then, a patrilineal system which upheld the lineage system which has already been examined.

But on the establishment of the statutes of purity of blood, those who furnished evidence for their entry to a renowned or honourable institution which demanded such evidence, were asked for proof of purity on all four sides – that is, of both grandfathers and both grandmothers, and if there was impurity in one of the four lines the candidate was immediately declared ineligible. Now, the case might arise in which a man of noble and powerful lineage was 'stained' because one of his forbears, masculine or feminine, had married a 'new Christian', and so neither the honour inherited by direct line of male to male, nor the estates, titles, etc, which he possessed could (in theory) wipe out the result of the conflict between his *nobility*, expressed by this diagram, in which only one line is taken into account:

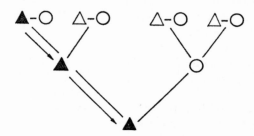

and his *impurity*, which can be shown by this diagram, in which all the lines are taken into account:

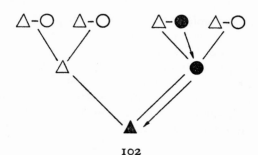

In this way there arose with appalling frequency problems in which the 'honour' of a family was placed in suspense because they sought 'honours' which might be denied them. Any system of honours has in any case as its counterweight a system of affronts, insults, outrages and disgraces. It is incredible how many anonymous or signed denunciations were sent during the sixteenth and seventeenth centuries concerning the ineligibility of numerous families to receive such honours as the habits of the military orders, and the disgraces which followed from them. In *Rinconete y Cortadillo* the leader of the Sevillian underworld at a certain point reckons up a veritable audit of the common affronts which were to be carried out 'on commission', among which, apart from beating up with bottles, smearing with pitch, mocking, frightening, organizing, uproars and mock stabbings, were the *publicación de nibelos*, by which he means libels, and the 'hanging of *sambenitos*' and 'horns'[19]; the latter to insult some husband, and the former to make public the fact that a family was not very *pure*, that one of its forbears had gone to the pillory in the penitential habit given by the Inquisition to those it reclaimed, an absolute sign of disgrace and dishonour for heretics in general, and above all for the so-called 'Judaisers'.[20]

We should here note the fact that the penalty of 'public shame' has its material expression as long as the old regime lasts, both in certain monuments, such as the penitential pillars and pillories[21] and in certain habits, such as the *sambenitos* themselves or the conical hats on which different offences were shown by different devices. Thus there were symbols for witches, panders, complaisant husbands, etc. It was expressed in the sentences themselves too; that of flogging for example, was highly injurious. For this reason the attempt to inflict it upon a noble on some occasions provoked great upheavals and troubles.[22]

But it was the 'stains' or shames derived from inquisitional sentences which were pitilessly recorded from generation to generation. The so-called 'church registers', the 'green book of Aragon', and the 'Tizón' attributed to Cardinal Mendoza y Bovadilla, were copied over and over again, although their possession was an offence because they were defamatory to many great families.[23] The moralist theologians of the seventeenth century considered collective memory a salutary means of maintaining the faith. Those of the eighteenth began to think, however, that this insistent recalling of blots in the lineage, and family shames and dishonours in general, was neither prudent nor commendable, and the politicians initiated a revision of the legal concepts admitted by the Holy Office, from a new philosophical point of view, which in the next century was part of the liberal programme.[24] It can safely be asserted that much of what the liberals carried out between 1812 and 1869 is to be found in the form of projects in writings of the eighteenth century, by politicians whose views were typical of the enlightenment. But what is more surprising is that many of these measures are found to be proposed by Spanish writers of the seventeenth century, of perfect Catholic orthodoxy and convinced monarchic ideas.[25] And apart from this, the very mechanism which governed the proofs of purity of blood, etc, was the object of much criticism, as we shall see, and the cause of the discrediting of these investigations.

4

Until the time of the Napoleonic invasion and the war of Independence the concept of the 'old Christian' held sway. It constituted an honour to be thought one, and by way of complement it was offensive or shameful to say of anyone that he had some Jewish, Moorish, or, in general, 'new Christian' blood, or that his family name was recorded in the church. Indeed, in the churches were hung the *sambenitos* and the lists of those punished by the Holy Office in each township or district, and these 'records of infamy' were periodically restored or replaced. In the south of Navarre these lists were known as *mantas*, and although by the second half of the eighteenth century they began to be removed, they did not finally cease to exist until the abolition of the Inquisition.[26] Now, as systems of concepts work in one way and the social realities which are said to be adjusted to them very often work quite differently, it was soon obvious, to the most rigorous in religious matters as well as to the mass of the outraged, dishonoured, ineligible, or whatever we care to call them, themselves, in different generations, that many and repeated cases of false purity occurred in certain sectors of society, even in the highest nobility, and that in the last instance 'wealth' wiped out 'shames' and bought 'honours'. The satiric poets who flourished in the time of Philip III and Philip IV constantly allude to this *concrete power* of money.

Don Luis de Góngora, in a series of plays upon words, says this in the fourth rondelet of his *burlescas*:

> '*Cruzados hacen cruzados,*
> *Escudos pintan escudos,*
> *Y tahures muy desnudos*
> *Con dados hacen condados;*
> *Ducados dejan ducados*
> *Y coronas majestad*
> *Verdad.*'[27]

(Cruzados make crusaders, escudos paint armorial bearings, and very shabby gamblers make earldoms with their dice; ducats produce dukedoms and crowns real majesty.)

This is to say that the coins known as *cruzados*, *escudos*, *ducados* and *coronas* were able to buy a noble the *cross* of an order, to procure him a pedigree with a *coat of arms*, to make *dukes*, and even to obtain royal *crowns*. Finally, the gambler who plays with dice (*con dados*) may come to possess an earldom (*condado*).

Quevedo says more directly on one occasion:

> '*Alguno ví que subía,*
> *Que no alcanzaba anteayer*
> *Ramo de quien descender*
> *Sino el de su picardía.*
> *Y he visto sangre judía*
> *Hacerla el mucho caudal*
> *Como papagayo, real,*
> *Clara ya su vena oscura.*'[28]

(I saw one who was climbing up, who the day before yesterday could not reach any branch from which to trace his descent, except that of his own roguery. And I have seen great wealth make Jewish blood royal, its dark taint becoming bright as a macaw.)

There is no need to amass examples. In my book on the Jews in modern Spain there are many which show clearly how, especially in the time of Philip IV, the most honourable offices, habits, etc, were given to persons who from the point of view of 'pure blood' were unable to conceal some antecedents which, if taken into account would have disqualified them from the contest for honours, according to the laws then in force.[29] So I have come to feel that the conflicts arising between the force of that concept and the power of wealth made no slight contribution to the cracking of the foundations of a social structure modelled, in the time of Ferdinand and Isabella and the early Hapsburgs, on bases as contradictory as that of the supremacy of conferred or inherited honours on the one hand and the real power of money on the other – in fact, upon a self-contradiction which could not help but be the target of countless criticisms and mockeries, synthesized in the proverb glossed by Quevedo himself:

> '*Poderoso caballero*
> *Es Don Dinero.*'[30]

(Sir Money is a powerful Knight.)

We find, then, essentially, the paradoxical situation that if on one hand the tradesmen, merchants, etc, among whom there were many 'new Christians', were despised, on the other they were growing ever more important not only in the economic but also in the political life of an age of great commercial enterprises.

In brief, once again there was a clash between two sorts of 'prestige': that based on military achievement in the service of the monarch or on noble, warrior and victorious ancestry, and that based on the money which flowed in ever larger quantities into Seville, Madrid, Lisbon, etc, to the horror of certain old-fashioned moralists[31] and the open amusement of some disinterested observers such as, for example, Huarte de San Juan, the penetrating psychologist, who, defining what makes a man truly honoured in society, says (and this in the very middle of the sixteenth century) that the following things contribute, and in the order indicated:

(a) The man's personal quality in (i) prudence, (ii) justice, (iii) spirit and (iv) courage. This was the most important.

(b) Property.

(c) Nobility and antiquity of his family.

(d) Dignity or honourable office.

(e) A good surname and a pleasing Christian name.

(f) Elegance and personal pomp.[32]

This idea, in opposition to that of many of his contemporaries, may be related to that of some 'new Christians', reflected in some verses by Antonio Enrique Gomez, a Jewish-Spanish writer of the seventeenth century:

> *'El mundo tiene dos linajes solos*
> *En entrambos polos:*
> *Tener está en Oriente*
> *Y no tener asistá en Occidente.'*[33]

(There are only two families in the world, at its two extremes: the Haves in the East and the Have-nots in the West.)

And in what he himself says in the 'Life of Don Gregorio Guadaña' (chapter I): 'The most well-born has always been he who lives best.'[34]

5

It may be said, however, that as much according to the medieval system of lineages as to the criteria of 'cleanness' and 'purity' imposed by the absolutist regime, the concept of 'good' or 'low' birth is intimately connected with personal honour. But given the possible contradiction already indicated between the 'pluri-lineal' lack of 'purity' on one side and the general patrilineal nobility, it came about that the idea began to spread that it was precisely in that social class which had always had least social pretensions – which had lived cut off from honours on one hand and from the business which produces wealth on the other – that it was possible to find the purest, most essential honour of the 'old Christian'. I refer to the villein class, the country labourers, subject to the king or to private overlords.

There are many texts emphasizing the scorn which this class had always provoked in the nobles and city people: it is sufficient to recall the pejorative senses of the words 'villain' and 'villainy' (Spanish, *villano, villanía*) to demonstrate it. But churchmen of villein origin who had attained lofty positions, soldiers, scholars, etc, of humble birth, campaigned more or less deliberately to rehabilitate them; and as a final resort the monarchy more than once sought the support of the common people against the nobility.[35] Thus it comes about that in the end the honourable villein is a classic literary figure in the Golden Age. A great deal of the drama is dedicated to the consideration of his virtues. Lope de Vega was especially interested in this theme. To bring it out he did not hesitate to dramatize to his liking events related in the medieval chronicles. Thus in *El mejor alcalde el rey* he changes the prosaic story of a Galician noble plundering some lands into the rape of a woman, the beautiful Elvira, betrothed to Sancho, an honourable villein. In *Peribañez y el comendador de Ocaña* (1605?), a work later remodelled by Rojas Zorrilla in his famous play which had the significant title of *Del Rey abajo ninguno* ('All equal beneath the King'), he insists on the idea that the only justice sufficient to avenge the wrongs inflicted upon a villein is that of the monarch.[36] Calderón advanced the theme further, and his play *El alcalde de Zalamea* is the quintessence of the drama based upon conflicts of honour: its action is founded on the pride of the different social classes and the ordinary man's consciousness of his own honour, 'the patrimony of the soul', of divine origin. The countryman enjoys this patrimony with the best, because he is as pure an 'old Christian' as the best too. Therefore the noble cannot dishonour him with impunity, nor repair his dishonour with material offers, but only in the way that would satisfy a member of his own class. So, also, when the countryman executes a just sentence upon him, he is supported by the king, as occurs in this play and in others – which, however, still rather reflect a wish or a theory than a palpable everyday reality.[37] But in the drama we should always see more of an ideal and a proposed model for the future than a copy of reality. And this ideal of the countryman's honour, or of the honourable rustic,

ust also have had its corrosive virtue, as a criticism of society. It may even have had more force when instead of presenting the cases of individuals it took a collective form, taking as a fact the existence of what we might call a 'people's honour' – that is to say, of a section of the population within which affronts, wrongs and insults were not submitted to from anyone, whatever his rank. In *Fuenteovejuna*, perhaps Lope de Vega's most famous play, this idea of popular solidarity in the face of the excesses committed by a noble against several commoner families is very clearly expressed. When the officers of justice, in the inquiry, ask the members of these families one at a time who killed the commendador, the source of the trouble, they all reply that it was the

village, Fuenteovejuna, 'as one man'.[38] And this popular honour
of divine origin is set in contrast with bought public dignities,
and with the vanity of the poor nobles who, to preserve their
dignity and keep their lives free of any action they thought
shameful, suffered hunger and poverty and even lied and dis-
sembled, provoking their neighbours to mockery or pity. The
most perfect picture of this sort of personage, pathetic and
absurd, is that of the poor squire in *Lazarillo de Tormes*.[39]

6

We can see then how by a process of dialectic and by a series of
contradictions which would delight a Hegelian, the Spaniards
of the sixteenth and seventeenth centuries carried through a
severe criticism of the principles by which their ancestors had
lived, and according to which they themselves still lived. But
the situations of conflict which we have already examined were
not the only ones which gave rise to more or less radical and
violent criticism. There were others which may have contributed more than these to the undermining of the bases of the
established codes of honour and shame. Let us look at them.
Well into the eighteenth century, and in England, David Hume
said (in his essay on 'The Rise of Arts and Sciences') that the
point of honour and what the English call 'gallantry' were
modern inventions, that the resolution of certain differences by
means of the duel was so too, and that the 'small indecencies'
which in practice are often most offensive to punctilious persons
can never be prevented by this type of action.

He considered, too, that all the ideas which had formed
around affairs of honour were not only useless but pernicious,
since, in fine, they separated the 'man of honour' from the
'virtuous man'.[40] What would this brilliant philosopher have
said had he lived in seventeenth-century Spain? There the man of
honour often became a violent, baroque figure, as he appears in
the memoirs and autobiographies, of which perhaps the most
illustrative is that of the Toledan gentleman Diego Duque de
Estrada.[41] What we know of the lives of naval and military
officers, too, such as Don Antonio de Oquendo and Don Tiburcio
de Redin, may be given as an example of the meaning of this sort
of honour, founded almost exclusively on the idea of individual

prestige, regardless of other considerations and carried to the limits of 'personalism'.[42] Thus, this sort of man might try to kill or let himself be killed for the sake of what was known as a point of honour, or for what Hume would have described as a 'small indecency' – that is, a smile, a glance, a greeting which he considered insufficiently respectful, a few ironic words. The man who refused a challenge was 'disgraced'. I feel that a clear relationship exists between this type of hypersensitive, punctilious man and a famous literary figure; that of Don Juan. Many theories have been built up around this personage.

However, with all respect to those who make his behaviour depend upon a problem of hormones or sexual insufficiency, and those who have occupied themselves in seeking out the secondary sources of his story, I feel that a case can be made out for Don Juan as the literary result of a society in which personal 'prestige' or 'disgrace' has come to exercise an obsessive influence. The figure of Don Juan, in its more elaborate forms, is the quintessence of the punctilious, fiery man, always ready to challenge another; who, to demonstrate his superiority in all aspects of a young man's disorderly life has to be not only the one who risks his life most, kills most, gambles most, spends most, wears the most elegant clothes, but also the one who conquers the greatest number of women, and who brings the greatest ingenuity to their seduction. For since the honour or shame of the female sex was a matter of such concern to their families, the demonstration of personal supremacy in this constituted one of the most remarkable triumphs.[43] In other words, I think that the figure of Don Juan needs to be explained in sociological terms, and not in terms of psychology or psycho-pathology. And this figure in itself, like that of the honourable rustic and that of the man of dubious descent loaded with honours, constitutes a criticism of the state of society, even though the myth has fired generation after generation and has found living examples in the figures of Don Miguel de Mañara and other gentlemen whose lives are less well known, and served to inspire the fear of eternal punishment or to demonstrate that, in the last resort, if a man is a believer in his heart and capable of repentance, there is always a chance of salvation, however many crimes he may have committed.[44] In fact, this morality of 'prestige' through individual force is always the morality of the soldier, which is acceptable and even desirable so long as there are danger and good luck, but becomes un-tenable in civilian life. So in Spain, as in other countries, excellent soldiers have been recruited among wild lads (*crúos* as they were already called in seventeenth-century Andalusia),[45] capable of outraging and insulting solely for the pleasure of being esteemed in brothels and gaming-houses; lads who formed groups known by such names as the *banda del cuervo* ('The Raven Gang') and *los de la cáscara amarga* ('The Trouble-makers').[46] But it is clear that care was taken not to let them run too wild, and that on occasion some of them were handled with excessive severity.[47]

If this were not enough, we should note that many witnesses of the seventeenth century give the impression that while an extreme sensitivity reigned in the social relations of those who lived under the sway of this concept of honour, there was an immense lack of real decisiveness, expertise or fighting quality in precisely those who were most punctilious. The papers of the reigns of Philip IV and Charles II allude quite consistently to the lack of courage in generals and military officers, which is roundly stated by a historian of the time of the last of the Hapsburgs: the Spanish soldiers had no heroes to command them.[48] Now, when such a feeling dominates a community the supremacy of the idea of prestige based on individual fighting qualities must also reach a crisis. And this in fact occurred, as the conclusion derived from a series of negative impressions concerning the strength of the ideals and basic concepts of social life. We should not be surprised that not very long after the time we have been discussing, new concepts imposed themselves.

Chapter Three

I

We have seen, then, that the basic institutions of Spanish life in the sixteenth and seventeenth centuries carried within themselves the germ of their destruction. And for one reason and another it may also be said that there was an awareness of the fact that much of society lived, up to a point, in a state of anomia. From 1599 when Mateo Aleman published the first part of the *Life of Guzmán de Alfarache*, until the appearance of the last picaresque novels, far into the seventeenth century, the idea was spreading in Spain that many of its population lived a miserable life remote from any norm of honour or shame; for, in brief, the *picaro* or *picara* of literature is the archetype of what today is popularly known as the *sinvergüenza* (shameless person), and the picaresque is the product of *sinvergonzonería*, a term much in use in modern times.

Whether the subject is Guzmán de Alfarache, Pablo de Segovia, Don Gregorio Guadaña, the Bachiller Trapaza, Estebanillo Gonzalez, or any other *picaro* of the male sex, or whether it is the Justina of Andrés de León, 'la Garduña' de Sevilla, or Teresa de Manzanares of Madrid, their counterparts of the female sex, we meet persons of low birth who live by adventure; but not noble adventure, only the sordid type of adventure, based upon deceit and very often on the pretence of rank or dignity. It is clear that there were many real people of this sort, as may be appreciated from reading some of the letters written by various Jesuits and other persons in Seville to Father Pereyra; letters which together form a magnificent record of events in Spain between 1634 and 1648,[1] and it is clear, too, that the picaresque was extremely popular. But if the real or imaginary cases of picaresque and shameless lives aroused great curiosity in

Spain, and many reflections were made upon them and the commonplaces of Christian moralizing poured out over them, other examples show us that there were also many men and women who, without being *picaros* or anything of the sort, suddenly broke with all social conventions and barriers and faced the greatest dangers to satisfy a passion which went against all the canons of the age. Here is a case which occurred in 1635, recounted by the same Jesuit who collected some facts on picaresque lives: 'What happened was that this gentleman,' he says, referring to one whom he does not name, 'came from Piedrahita, where he had become very much attached to a nun in the convent there, both of them being elderly, and she so desperate for him that one night she left the convent without his knowledge and went to his house. The old man was very much upset to see her; she said to him: "Take heart, for I'm not going back to my cell; let us go out into the world." "Let us go," said the good old man; he collected together that night what money he could, and with only one mare, on which the good lady was riding, and her lover on foot, they were able to get as far along the road for Portugal as Ciudad Rodrigo. There the police of Avila (under whose jurisdiction Piedrahita is) came up with them and took them; she returned to her convent where she will die imprisoned or immured; he was taken to Avila, where today he was executed . . .'[2]

The single fact has more tragic quality than hundreds of dramas. But what it shows us, above all, is how life presented situations which are scarcely reflected in the literature of the period. For given that the drama and the novel had to adjust themselves to certain norms and serve as an example, any course of action which was outside the system of accepted values was bound to be excluded from both forms of art, even if it ended in punishment. The old nun's passion for the poor Castilian gentleman already stricken in years was outside the scope of any order of morals or aesthetics then in force, outside any 'plan'.

So Spanish literature reflects no more than the existence of certain scenarios and certain authors: it is always more abundant in references to aristocratic or knightly life and to popular ways of life than in allusions to certain sectors of society which only in much more recent times have earned the attention of novelists and playwrights. There are, then, few old plays or novels in a truly bourgeois setting. Yet the bourgeoisie was already in existence and beginning to create rules of honour which clashed not only with the medieval ones, but also with those imposed by the absolute and theocratic monarchy.

2

The researches of economic historians show us, above all, that from the sixteenth to the seventeenth century there was a middle class growing up in the cities, and even in the towns, made up of lawyers, scholars, doctors, functionaries and merchants. It arouses no great interest as 'literary material' but in fact is much more important than is admitted in histories of a romantic and impassioned kind.

Our information on the way of life of this middle class is drawn from very varied sources, including some merchants' memoirs such as those of Raymond de Lantery, who worked in Cádiz from 1673 to 1700[3]; and these show us a world much nearer to our own, or to that of our fathers and grandfathers, than that of the cloak and dagger plays or those with plots drawn from the middle ages which at that very period and even later were being written by the successors of Calderón and Moreto.[4] Theories have been worked out, hypotheses have been constructed about the historic fate of Spain based on the idea that for the Spaniard of the classic period manual tasks, skilled trades, industry and commerce were so much base and dishonourable drudgery.[5] On many occasions the decadence of the country has been attributed to this lack of respect for work, to this incompatibility between honour and 'prestige' and professional life.[6] But the truth is that this is not valid for the whole of Spain, nor is it absolutely true even considering as typically Spanish those regions such as Castile and Andalusia where it is said that the idea that the possession of an immaculate 'honour' is incompatible with participation in arts, crafts or trade exerted most influence.

Between the sixteenth century and the seventeenth the people of the Basque provinces evidently made the change from a social structure in which the factions and lineages and the honour of the blood were dominant to one in which the families best known as heads of factions lost almost all their influence to other, newer ones whose pretensions were rooted only in a sort of collective nobility common to all natives of the provinces and compatible with the exercise of the humblest professions of artisans and labourers, and above all with that of industry and commerce on a large or small scale.[7]

In the eighteenth century the Jesuit Larramendi made a fervent eulogy of this sort of popular, collective nobility which he contrasted with the aristocratic scruples against work of some Castilian gentlemen, and with the very descendants of the old lineages and faction chiefs.[8] But we should emphasize that long before his time in Castile and Andalusia there were many families of businessmen and merchants, who had a claim to honour and influence and did acquire great honours by wealth or services, and that in the seventeenth century it was a fact that many titled gentlemen, knights of military orders and so forth were involved in land transactions, trade, etc. Thus Ruiz de Alarcón in *El semejante a si mismo* could put into a character's mouth this reflection, at the beginning:

> '*Es segunda maravilla*
> *Un caballero en Sevilla*
> *Sin rama de mercader.*'[9]

(It is another marvel when a gentleman of Seville has no connection with trade.)

In Burgos the majority of the local nobility of the seventeenth century were descended from merchants of the fifteenth and sixteenth centuries and in Madrid even in the seventeenth century Portuguese 'new Christians' were very powerful and obtained honours in competition with the Genoese, Flemings, etc, who were everywhere abundant.[10] The middle class, upper or lower, was thus growing in importance until we may say that by the end of the eighteenth century it was very satisfied with itself, and even felt itself superior to the aristocratic and the plebeian. All the previous criticisms of ideas about honour and shame took new forms with the triumph of the philosophical ideas of the eighteenth century and their glorification of virtue and efficiency in work, utility and the general good. The idea of 'prestige', the challenges and duels, the battles between rival clans and even the concept of 'pure blood' were considered antiquated. ('Gothic' – it had become an adjective of disdain

then, equalling in intensity the admiration of 'Gothic' descent
at the end of the middle ages.) And not only antiquated but
wrong.[11] The thinkers and politicians born between 1720 and
1760 made severe attacks in their writings on the behaviour of
their ancestors, whom they considered irrational. And as the
Gothic and Baroque styles were discredited by neo-classicism,
so the chivalrous and monarchic ideals were banished by a
philosophical moral code which is also neo-classical up to a
point; for the thought of men like Jovellanos, for example, is
nearer, in the consideration of honours, to that of Cicero in his
treatise *De Officiis* than to that of a Spanish classic writer of the
seventeenth century.

3

As often happens, the concepts which in the seventeenth century
had still served to govern the lives of nobles and gentlemen of
rank later served only, adapted and perhaps simplified, to rule
the lives of persons of low birth. In the first place, it is significant
in itself that the novels of chivalry of the Carolingian cycle,
equally with those of the Arthurian and others of diverse origin,
were reprinted in the form of chap-books until very near our
own times and that, especially in the south of Spain, they were
the favourite reading of drovers, farm-hands and other working
people, who were able to build up from their reading the picture
of an alien world.[12] In this plebeian sector of society the equivalent of the gentleman of easily affected honour is the professional
bravo, the bullying braggart, the dandified tough. Don Francisco
de Quevedo has a series of poems on men of this type. Cervantes
lists the places where they preferred to congregate and in the
novels of Gonzalo de Céspedes y Meneses they also figure
frequently.[13] These types drag out their existence, half criminal,
half archaic, during the eighteenth and nineteenth centuries.
And the chap-books themselves have popularized, in printings
up to the beginning of this century, the exploits of *majos* and
guapos (such as 'the *guapo* Francisco Esteban') and others of their
sort, who based their whole existence on a 'personal prestige'
within a popular society of loose women, panders and *mozos
crúos*.[14]

At the beginning of the twentieth century the last representatives of popular 'swaggering' of this sort were eradicated by the Civil Guard in areas as widely separated as southern Navarre and parts of Castile and Andalusia. The Civil Guard also had the responsibility of combatting a personage sometimes related to them: the bandit, about whom we should make some comment.

The Romantic Movement, being a reaction against the ideals of the eighteenth century, tended to be interested in whatever that century had despised or fought against, from medieval events and the seventeenth century drama to the plastic arts of those periods. In this revaluation the knights had their turn, together with Don Juan and even other colourful persons, such as the bandits. Local and archaeological colour served as a standard for the writers. Tales of bandits became fashionable, and they even came to be portrayed as men often involved in an archaic problem of honour.[15] But this revaluation did not succeed in destroying the foundations of eighteenth century morality, nor in acquiring expressions which could bring it down from a literary or artistic level. During the nineteenth century the process clearly begun in the previous one was brought to a conclusion. Thus, during it the 'statutes of purity of blood' which had weighed so heavily on Spaniards' honour were abolished; while the penalties of inherited shame and the very tribunals which had most often enforced them, such as that of the Inquisition, were also suppressed.[16] There is no need to add, too, that the laws ceased to recognize certain previously accepted principles, such as that of *mas valer*, and that they contested the existence of so-called 'affairs of honour' and laid down how wrongs were to be redressed. The Romantics had been somewhat given to challenges and duels, but once the first romantic fever was over violent campaigns were carried on against the duel and duellers, who were attacked with a subtle weapon, that of ridicule. When towards the end of the nineteenth century the Marqués de Cabriñana published a work entitled 'Affairs of honour between gentlemen', there were not a few critics who took both the author and his book as a joking matter.[17] In other words, just as at the end of the fifteenth century one cycle closes and another opens, so in the nineteenth century this second cycle clearly came to an end, and to some extent the problems of 'honour' were reduced in their proportions, so that certain of the concepts analysed in the two previous chapters of this essay were limited in their scope. But it must not be thought for this reason that there are now no situations of conflict like those which arose in other ages.

In these last few pages I shall try to give a brief description of some of them, as far as possible from personal observation.

4

It may be said that today the word *honra* is in quite common use in Spanish, and of course with a broader, more general meaning than the word *honor*. *Honra* is applied to many types of action, and it is considered that in principle any person who has not publicly come into conflict with certain legal dispositions possesses it; and that it is greater according to the degree of virtue and capability in his profession of the individual. The concept of *honor* seems more archaic and always poetic, applicable on a few occasions to problems of 'prestige' and 'disgrace' and to certain sexual questions. It is a sort of superstructure built up on the concept of *honra*, the latter tending to be associated with the possession of the virtues as defined in the philosophical systems of antiquity, in religion and in the doctrines of the eighteenth century. Thus, in the ordinary life of the towns and villages reasons for dishonour, or *enfamamiento* as the Partidas say, are adultery, premature remarriage of widows, procuring, usury, homosexuality, open cowardice, theft . . . The idea of 'shame' in relation to these dishonourable acts has a deep significance in the individual and collectively, although it might be possible to establish a nuance of distinction between ill-fame and sheer shamelessness.

In villages of small or moderate size there is a sort of collective consciousness in matters of honour and shame. They do not welcome cases of illegitimacy, or the presence of loose women or of men who are complaisant husbands or possess unpleasant habits in money matters. All these persons are 'shameless', or those who have lost their honour, according to the standard applied – for the term *sinvergüenza* has sometimes an overtone of banter which other words used in the same context have not. It may even happen that, as in the time of Calderón, a woman loses her honour as the result of a rape – and in fact until the beginning of this century such events provoked memorable collective reactions.

As an example of these we may adduce that of the Extremeñan village of Don Benito, in connection with a notorious crime. A young noble of the family of the famous Renaissance military leader García de Paredes, in complicity with his servant and a night-watchman, broke into the house of a poor girl who had no male relatives and who had repelled his advances, raped her, and then fearing discovery killed her. It was soon discovered who had committed the double crime, and in what circumstances it had been committed. García de Paredes and his accomplices were arrested. But since he was believed to be influential in the province, the whole village, intending to avenge the dead girl at all costs, took up a threatening attitude when it was suggested to transfer him from the local prison to the provincial one; and the state of vigilance and alert did not end until the trial, sentence, and even the garrotting of the criminals had taken place in the village itself. Only by this means did the population feel itself satisfied.[18]

We should remark, however, that in the noted popular reaction new elements may have intervened; for at that time, especially in the south of Spain, the idea was spreading, as it still is, propagated by political writings, that the *pueblo*, the mass of artisans and labourers, possess certain virtues lacking in the more powerful classes; thus, basing themselves upon the figures of the honourable poor man and the rich man lacking in honour and generosity, numerous socialist or anarchist, or generally proletarian campaigns have been carried on. So, too, not only an awareness of the *pueblo* as a physical, geographical entity has been created, but also an awareness of its collective honour as a group of the poorer class. In the absence of commendadors and *ricos-hombres* who, shielded by the power of arms, inflict wrongs, rape maidens, and so forth, the archetype of evil is found in the rich man who is shielded by the power of his wealth.[19]

5

Leaving aside for the present the question of the claims of the poor as a political problem, and concentrating on the study of social and ethical values, we may say that in connection with the possession of wealth as related to 'honour' and 'shame', there has grown up a set of accepted ideas according to which the wealthy man *must be*, almost inevitably, a wicked exploiter of the working classes.[20] But the latter, in turn, are obsessed by the idea of the omnipotence of money, and accept as valid the old affirmation of the 'new Christians' that there are only two families in the world: the Haves and the Have-nots. The Have-nots are exposed to all dangers, even including dishonour. Thus it is thought that the poor man's daughter is more likely to prostitute herself, or his wife to deceive him on account of his poverty – as says the old epigram, attributed to the Conde de Villamediana:

> *'Tienen los que pobres son*
> *La ventura del cabrito,*
> *O morir cuando chiquito,*
> *O llegar a ser cabrón.'*[21]

(The poor have the same fortune as the kid; to die in infancy, or to grow up to be he-goats. *Cabrón* has the double meaning of he-goat and cuckold.)

The poor man who, on the one hand, proclaims the honour of his class and the lack of honour in the wealthy, fears the personal and individual wrong, the insult, the injury done to him by the rich man so obsessively that he pictures all the forms of this injury. He lives in a state of tension on account of a series of stories in which this wrong is made obvious. On his side, the rich man takes little care to prevent repetition of the cases of popular irritation, and even hysteria; and the man who having been poor becomes rich believes more firmly than anyone that anything can be done with money. The idea of 'prestige' based upon the strength of the lineage, personal courage, and manliness, has been succeeded by that of economic 'prestige', or what Don Francisco de Quevedo would have called *Dinerismo*:[22] a 'prestige', as tormenting and aggressive as the older one, which affects honour, if this is taken to be equivalent to virtue, and even has some connection with *honor* and *honras*.

For the idea that honour may be menaced by money problems weighs upon the greater part of the consciousness of Spaniards, not only of the lower classes, and the problems arising from the confrontation of the two forces are very varied. It would be premature to discuss them now, since we should require a series of studies which would bring out clearly the part played by money in different communities, the significance given to it by the people, the ways of getting and spending it, and other points which to the shame of economists and sociologists are not at all clear, and which in poor countries are perhaps more important than in rich ones. By way of illustration I shall give here a few brief notes on one particular point in the relationships to which I have referred; that of money-lending.

Contrary to what is publicly proclaimed, the scourge of usury is still the cancer of many of the villages of the South. The usurer as an archetype is an infamous personage, and of ill-repute. But in ordinary everyday life usurers, women as well as men, exist in great numbers: from the woman who lends money in the markets to the local women according to the classic formula of 'one peseta on every five' (per week!) to the man who makes loans, mortgages and loan covenants on large properties.

Now, in matters of actual loans at interest, the man who in difficulty has recourse to borrowing, has the same interest in keeping it secret as the man who lends in contravention of morality. The utmost discretion is little enough, for two honours are in question: that of the man who lacking money feels that he is 'disgraced', and that of the one who has money gained by dis-honourable means. And this necessary secrecy gives rise to strange cases. Just as in the time of the classic bandits, in the recent period of insecurity in rural life due to the *maquis* (out-laws for political and other reasons) there have been villages, notably in the Málaga area, where money obtained as ransoms for kidnappings, loot from armed robberies, etc, was entrusted without any real security by the authors of the crime to usurers, for them to lend out at high interest. And even after the men of action were dead and their gangs broken up, the money remained in the hands of the prudent and crafty money-lenders. Money matters among the lower classes, and even others, are generally treated with a discretion bordering on secrecy, the concealment of truth on principle. It is felt that no business may be begun except after infinite probings and strategems, and in this sort of conduct rather than honour what matters is the idea of personal 'prestige' reduced to shrewdness, astuteness, a capacity for argument, a prestige of which some well chosen words and elementary rhetoric are the greatest expression, and one in which too much trust is sometimes placed.

By contrast, among these people to whom discretion is so important, popular forms of the same 'prestige' which still had some significance until a few decades ago are not acceptable. Only in low eating-houses, bars and places of ill-repute are insults, brawling and physical aggression still acceptable. These things come into the class of actions known as *chulerías*. The *chulo*, who originally was the man who lived on what women would give him, applied the idea of individual 'prestige' to things of trifling importance. His reign, as such, has ended. At the beginning of this century his figure had some popularity in Madrid and other large cities. Closely related to him was the *matón* or professional thug, occasionally made use of in political struggles. Both of them were the object of severe satire in the most purely popular theatre; for example in the plays of Don Carlos Arniches, in whose farces and operettas the *chulo* and the thug always come off badly.[23]

6

In conclusion we may say that in Spain the concepts of 'honour' and 'shame' have exerted great pressure on society at different periods, but that in every age they have been charged with a rather different significance. Leaving aside the relationship which exists between honour and the Christian virtues as set out in the catechism (that is the three theological virtues which have God for their object and are Faith, Hope and Charity; and the four cardinal virtues of Prudence, Justice, Fortitude and Temperance), or the moral code of philosophers such as Aristotle or Cicero, also based in essence upon the four cardinal virtues, we may clearly see that honour is also related to the question of birth, of status, not to say of social class. The honour connected with lineages and a system of honours and shames, offences and revenges as conceived by the late middle ages gives the best illustration of this assertion.

But we may consider as another example that of the honour linked with a division within the community of the faithful, such as that which held sway as long as the statutes of pure blood and their consequences were in force. Finally, when we speak of the 'people's honour' or that of the bourgeoisie, we establish a social division which invalidates any ethical principles. The tendency is always then to consider the problems of honour and shame as social problems; problems with a great number of fortuitous and variable elements. It is interesting to note, however, that in the middle ages and the Golden Age as today, there has been severe criticism of the means of honouring and dishonouring – criticisms which have ended by bringing entire legal systems into discredit. And it is no less interesting and significant that it has consistently been economic arguments which have made most impression on the public consciousness (or at least, the most lasting impression), in the criticism of a system. Another factor which has effectively contributed to changes in the concept of honour is the idea of *mas valer*. From the period at which it was conditioned by chivalric ideals until the present it has been changing its objectives. Even today we find it influencing Spanish life, but referred by the middle classes especially to a sort of professional competition, such as examinations, academic contests, etc, where the new Amadises and Palmerins are measured against one another in the light of memory tests, mechanical and sterile criteria which I believe to be a real scourge of civil life. But this is not the time to make out the case against such a system of 'prestige' nor against the bureaucratic mechanism for the concession of honours which is linked with it, in spite of their exceptional importance within the structure of contemporary Spanish society.

Among ordinary people there survives, to my knowledge, no trace of the idea that honour is connected with long genealogies, although it is thought to be related to the quality of the parents, and of the 'breed' or 'nation' in general. Nor are ideas relating to purity of blood very widespread now, although it may be said that in the north of Spain an idea existed, semi-popular only in origin, according to which the people of the south are in general the product of mixtures and bastardies, which affect their morals. But in defiance of the indications of historic investigation, it is with reference to the dubious Moorish ancestry, not to the Jewish, that the Andalusians, and southerners in general, are considered a 'bad breed'.

The honour of the middle class is still highly thought of by the members of that class, and the same may be said of the working classes: but there is no doubt that on the one hand leftist political propaganda has diminished the idea of middle class honour among the people, and that revolutions, on the other hand, have contributed to the calling in question of the honour of the poorer classes on the part of many conservatives. In short, there is evidence of a new crisis. What we cannot know yet are its consequences, either short or long term. For it is unimaginable that social structures could again be created on a basis of the supremacy of certain families and the dominance of the chivalric ideals, nor yet on the ideals of a theocratic monarchy; nor does it seem likely that present political systems are capable of setting up a standard in this or other matters which would survive for any length of time. Today wealth, and nothing else, seems an almost physical force, against which there is no means of fighting. In the long run this very force will take us somewhere. But I do not believe that in the future it can weigh more heavily than other values which have gradually lost their dominance, as has happened with the lineage, physical strength, the scorn of death, etc, all of which began to diminish in vitality precisely at the moment when society had come to be obsessed by them.

NOTES

CHAPTER ONE

1 Quevedo *Obras* XXX p. 110, no. 345 in *Biblioteca de autores espanoles* ed. Rivadeneira, B.A.E. 69.
2 Much has been written about the sense of honour in the light of literature, especially the drama. R. Menéndez Pidal in 'Del honor en el teatro español' in *España y su historia* 2 (Madrid 1957) pp. 355–95, collected together a series of facts which may be considered as an example of the generally accepted point of view, which is very different from that given here.
3 For a clear understanding of the Roman world, from this viewpoint, the best thing is to read Cicero's treatise *De officiis*, which had considerable influence later, as will be shown. For the use of such words as *honor* and *honestas* see any Latin dictionary.
4 J. Corominas *Diccionario crítico etimológico de la lengua castellana* 2 (Madrid 1954) p. 938.

5 Juan de Valdes *Diálogo de la lengua,* edition with an introduction by J. Moreno Villa (Madrid 1919) p. 166.

6 Vicente Garcia de Diego *Diccionario etimológico español ę hispánico* (Madrid 1954) pp. 326 and 797 (note 3282).

7 Sebastián de Covarrubias *Tesoro de la lengua castellana o española* edited by Martin de Riquer (Barcelona 1943) p. 696.

8 *Segunda partida* titulo 13, ley 17 (edition in *Los códigos españoles concordados y anotados* 2 (Madrid 1848), vol. I of the *Código de las siete partidas* p. 398).

9 *Segunda partida* titulo 13, ley 18 (ed. *cit.* 1, p. 399).

10 *Segunda partida* titulo 13, ley 4 (ed. *cit.* 1, p. 390).

11 *Segunda partida* titulo 13, ley 4 (ed. *cit.* 1, p. 390).

12 *Segunda partida* titulo 19, ley 2 (ed. *cit.* 1, p. 455) refers in detail to the affronts which enemies may offer to the king.

13 *Séptima partida* titulo 6, ley 2 (to be found in vol. 4 of the *Códigos españoles* . . . (Madrid 1848), 3 of the edition of the *Siete partidas,* p. 306).

14 *Séptima partida* titulo 6, ley 3 (ed. *cit.* 3, pp. 306–7).

15 *Séptima partida* titulo 6, ley 4 (ed. *cit.* 3, p. 307).

16 *Séptima partida* titulo 6, ley 5 (ed. *cit.* 3, pp. 308–9).

17 *Séptima partida* titulo 6, ley 7 (ed. *cit.* 3, p. 311).

18 The relationship between 'honour' and 'shame' is laid down by Cicero (*De off.* 1, 35, 127), but he makes 'verecundia' almost a physiological condition: 'hanc naturae tam diligentem fabricam,' he says, referring to the constitution of the body, 'imitata est hominum verecundia'. Aristotle *Ethic. ad. Nicom.* 4, 9 (1228 b) considers shame as a sentiment or state of character, not as a virtue.

19 Ed. *cit.* 3, p. 397.

20 Ed. *cit.* 3, p. 92.

21 *Séptima partida* titulo 5, leyes 1, 2 and 3 (ed. *cit.* 3, pp. 304–5).

22 Lope García de Salazar *Las bienandanzas e fortunas* ed. Angel Rodriguez Herrero (Bilbao 1955) p. 167.

23 I have had occasion to make three studies of the lineage system: one on the desert nomads; another on villages of the north of Morocco; and another on the medieval Basques. Julio Caro Baroja *Estudios saharianos* (Madrid 1955), *Estudios mogrebíes* (Madrid 1957) and *Linajes y bandos* in *Vasconiana* (Madrid 1957) pp. 15–61. Since then I have continued to study the theme within other frames of reference. The bibliography is immense.

24 The two best known works of Salazar y Castro are *Historia genealógica de la casa de Lara, justificada con instrumentos y escritores de inviolable fe* 4 vols. (Madrid 1696) and the *Historia genealógica de la casa de Silva* 2 vols. (Madrid 1685), leaving aside other works.

25 Covarrubias *Tesoro* . . . ed. *cit.* p. 47.

26 Covarrubias *Tesoro* . . . ed. *cit.* p. 51.
27 *Séptima partida* titulo 9, leyes 1–23 (ed. *cit.* 3, pp. 330–44).
28 *Séptima partida* titulo 9, ley 1 (ed. *cit.* 3, p. 330).
29 *Séptima partida* titulo 9, ley 3 (ed. *cit.* 3, p. 332), M. Menéndez y Pelayo *Historia de la poesia castellana en la Edad Media* 1 (Madrid 1911–13) pp. 248–51.
30 The 'Coplas del Provincial' are also studied by Menéndez y Pelayo *Historia de la poesía castellana* ed. *cit.* 2 (Madrid 1914) pp. 292–7.
31 *Séptima partida* titulo 9, ley 4 (ed. *cit.* 3, p. 333).
32 *Séptima partida* titulo 9, ley 5 (ed. *cit.* 3, p. 333).
33 *Séptima partida* titulo 9, ley 6 (ed. *cit.* 3, pp. 333–4).
34 I quote as an example of the law of insult a portion of law 2 of section 3 of book 4 of the 'Fuero Real de España' (*Los códigos españoles concordados y anotados* 1 (Madrid 1847) p. 403): 'Qualquier home que à otro denostare, é le dixere gafo, ó sodomético, ó cornudo, ó traydor, ó herege, ó a muger de su marido puta, desdígalo ante el Alcalde, y ante homes buenos al plazo que él pusiere ante el Alcalde: a peche trecientos sueldos, la meitad al Rey, y la meitad al querelloso; é si negáre que lo no dixo, é no gelo pudiere probar, sálvese asi como manda la Ley: é si salvar no se quisiere, faga la emienda, é peche la calumnia.' See also, in the Romance version of the 'Fuero Juzgo', book 12, section 3, 1.7 (*Los códigos . . . cit.* 1, pp. 190–1).
35 'Apellidar' says Covarrubias (*Tesoro* . . . ed. *cit.* p. 130), 'es aclamar tomando la voz del rey, como: Aquí del rey o Viva el rey; y *entre parcialidados, declarándose a voces por una dellas.*' In my study on 'Linajes y bandos' (quoted above) in *Vasconiana* p. 52 (note 48) I analyse the progressive insults offered to each other at one time by the chiefs of Oñaz and Gamboa, according to Lope García de Salazar *Las bienandanzas e fortunas* pp. 249–52.
36 For example, the general observations to be found in the *Crónica del halconero de Juan II, Pedro Carrillo de Huete* ed. J. de Mata Carriazo (Madrid 1946), pp. 160–1, on the general laws for the restriction of the plague, enacted in 1434, I give further general indications in 'Linajes y bandos' in *Vasconiana* p. 60 (notes 97 and 98), but they could be multiplied to an extraordinary degree. The factional feuds and the conflicts arising from the love of two persons belonging to enemy families are elements made use of by Shakespeare in *Romeo and Juliet* (1595–6), which might have been inspired by several texts. Lope de Vega in *Castelvines y Montescos* and Rojas in *Los bandos de Verona* made use of the same theme. The factional feuds in Castile and Leon have furnished plenty of literary material too. Even so late an author as Don Antonio de Zamora (1660 or 1664–1728) wrote the play entitled *Mazariegos y Monsalves*, in which the quarrels of two Zamora lineages are dramatized. The

Spanish novel abounds in allusions to the same matter. It is sufficient to recall here those Cervantes makes in *Don Quijote*, part 2, chapter 60, to the feud between the Niarros and Cadells of Catalonia, which was still continuing in his time. Don Diego Clemencia in a note on Cervantes' text (*El ingenioso hidalgo Don Quijote de la Mancha*, edition with commentary by Don Diego Clemencia, notes by Miguel de Toro IV (Paris 1914) pp. 296-7, eruditely illustrates this point and shows that in the *Diálogos de contención entre la milicia y la ciencia* by Francisco Nuñez de Velasco (Valladolid 1914) folio 47 we read as follows: 'En Algunas ciudades destos reinos de España aun no se acaba de extinguir el fuego destos negros bandos, especialmente en Trujillo, Cáceres y Plasencia, adonde no sola-mente la gente principal es banderiza, pero aun la común y plebeya está dividida entre Carvajales y Ovandos.'

37 On revenge see the study by R. Menéndez Pidal, quoted above, 'Del honor en el teatro español' in *España y su historia* 2, pp. 360-4 especially. A strictly sociological study remains to be made.

38 *Séptima partida* titulo 12, ley 2 (ed. *cit.* 3, p. 358).

39 *Séptima partida* titulo 12, ley 1 (ed. *cit.* 3, p. 357).

40 'Ordenanzas reales de Castilla', book 4, section 9, law 9 (*Loscódigos españoles* . . . 4 (Madrid 1849) p. 394).

41 Alonso de Maldonado 'Hechos de Don Alonso de Monroy, Clavero y maestro de Alcántara' in *Memorial histórico español* 6 (Madrid 1851) pp. 1-110.

42 A fact which I emphasized in 'Linajes y bandos' in *Vasconiana* pp. 26 and 49 (notes 30 and 31).

43 M. Menéndez y Pelayo *Origenes de la novela* 1, (Buenos Aires 1945) pp. 471-2.

44 This text, which Menéndez y Pelayo copies in entirety, *Orígenes de la novela* I, p. 327, is found in the 'Obras' of Fray Luis, I, p. 327, published in the *Biblioteca de Autores Españoles* (VI).

45 Menéndez y Pelayo *Orígenes de la novela* 1, pp. 452-8, gives the opinion of various authorities.

46 'Jornada de Omagua y Dorado' in *Historiadores de Indias* 2, *Nueva biblioteca de autores españoles* 15 (Madrid 1909) p. 458.

47 'Jornada de Omagua y Dorado' ed. *cit.* p. 469.

48 'Libro de la vida y costumbres de Don Alonso Enriquez de Guzmán', in *Biblioteca de autores españoles* (continuation) 126 (Madrid 1960) p. 105. The formula is worth copying here: 'Esta se haze en memoria de lo syguiente porque, aunque en las voluntades esté escrito, pues dellas salió efetuarse, es bien que cada qual de nos, de los dos, lo tenga firmado, para afirmarlo en nuestros juizios, por no herrarnos, pues tanto nos va en ello, y prendar nuestras palabras y fee de caballeros, pues tenemos prendadas las ánimas y obligadas

las conciencias. Y es verdad que martes antes de mediodía a doze de noviembre, año de Nuestro Salvador de mill e quinientos e treynta e dos, don Alonso Enriquez e yo, Pero Ortiz de Cuñiga, entramos en la yglesia de Sant Miguel, perrochia en la çiudad de Sevilla, y pusimos nuestras manos derechas encima de un ara consagrada que el sacristán de la dicha yglesya nos entregó y juramos por Dios en ella consagrado y por su consagración de ser hermanos en amor y muy firmes amigos y buenos desde el dicho diá hasta el postrero de nuestras vidas, del uno o del otro, y de ayudarnos y defendernos, en dicho y en hecho, en presencia y en ausencia, con nuestras personas y haciendas contra todos los que a el y a mi y a mi y a el quisieren ofender, aunque tengan deudo o otra douda alguna ni sea hermano natural y amigo, que para esto dezimos que esto prezeda a todo, y que antes ni después con otro alguno abemos hecho no haremos el tal juramento, hasta que el uno de los dos fuese muerto. Y que demás desto que lo prometemos como cavalleros hijosdalgo una y dos y tres vezes y tantas quantas vezes el derecho y ley de cavallería permite. Fecha en el mismo dia y firmada de mi el dicho Pero Ortiz que rescivo otro traslado désta, y del mismo don Alonso.' Furthermore, this book gives a very clear idea of how, in the sixteenth century, Seville and other cities of the south were enmeshed in feuds, rooted in the lineage wars and it also shows the troubles which the author incurred on account of his hypersensitivity in matters of honour and 'prestige' (*valer mas*).

CHAPTER TWO

1 The examples given and many others may be found in the *Refranero general ideólogico español* compiled by Luis Martinez Kleiser (Madrid 1953) pp. 354–6 (nos. 31-241-31. 474).

2 'If wealth is unaccompanied by civil power or nobility, it rather makes a man wretched than fortunate' said Sancho IV of Castile, *Castigos e documentos* chapter 75 (B.A.E. 51, p. 205).

3 On this point see my book on the Jews of Spain in the modern period, chapter 4, part 4.

4 *El libro de buen amor* lines 490–2 (ed. Michaud, Paris, pp. 81–2). Furthermore, the power of money is a commonplace in love poetry, already subscribed to by Propertius and Ovid.

5 We have already seen, in note 36 to the previous chapter, that the factions continued in some regions into the seventeenth century. This explains how an anonymous writer of the first half of the sixteenth century could say that the term *apellido* is used 'quando hay vandos entre Señores, como Niebla y León, en Sevilla; Oñes y

Gamboa, en Vizcaya; Giles y Negretes, en la Montaña; Avilas y Villaviçençios, en Xerez de la Frontera y otros muchos semejantes', 'Floreto de anécdotas y noticias diversas' (*Memorial histórico español* 48, Madrid 1948, p. 353). But at this time too, such feuds were being severely punished or were losing force.

6 'De la guerra de Granda, comentarios de Don Diego Hurtado de Mendoza,' a work of which there is now an edition by Don Manuel Gómez Moreno, in the *Memorial histórico español* 49 (Madrid 1948).

7 This may be appreciated by reading local histories of various towns and different regions. See as an example that of Baltasar Peña Hinojosa, *Pequeña historia de la villa de Campillos* (Málaga 1960) pp. 42-75.

8 The proverb which runs 'Iglesia, o mar, o Casa Real,' which Cervantes recalls in chapter 39 of *Don Quijote* part 1, to situate the beginning of the story of the captive, and which is repeated in many other texts of the period, reflects the situation very clearly: 'quien quisiera *valer* y ser rico', comments Cervantes himself (ed. *cit.* 2, p. 219) 'siga a la Iglesia, navegue ejercitando el arte de la mercancía, ó entre a servir a los Reyes en sus casas'.

9 The House of Austria was very strict in this matter. See the monograph by Don Antonio Rodriguez Villa *Etiquetas de la casa de Austria* (Madrid 1913).

10 In any case, the expression 'grandes' is already found in the *Segunda partida* titulo 9, ley 2 (ed. *cit.* 1, p. 360).

11 Both the general histories of Llorente and Lea and the histories of particular cities where tribunals of the Holy Office were set up allude to these quarrels and disputes. But not to amass references, I will recall here only the events in Córdoba in 1643, recounted in the 'Cartas de algunos pp. de la Campañia de Jesús' 5, pp. 73-5 in the *Memorial histórico español* 17.

12 Don Alonso de Cartagena, bishop of Burgos, and himself a *converso*, collected together in his defence a great quantity of doctrine, considered by theologians to be excellent. His work *Defensorium unitatis christianae* has been edited in our time by Father Manuel Alonso (Madrid 1943).

13 I study this point in my book on the Jews, part 1, chapters 6 and 7.

14 The chronicler of Ferdinand and Isabella himself, Fernando del Pulgar, discusses the beginnings of the Inquisition with some surprise *Crónica de los Reyes Catolicos* 1 (Madrid 1943), pp. 438-40, etc.

15 Don Manuel Serrano y Sanz in his 'Origenes de la dominación española en América' (vol. 25 of the *Nueva biblioteca de autores españoles* Madrid 1918), collected a great number of documents on this point, more Aragonese than Castilian. Since then Marcel Bataillon, Américo Castro and others have gathered more facts and

observations. In my book, quoted above, they are examined at length, in part 4.

16 Leaving aside now my own investigations, see the thesis by Albert A. Sicroff *Les controverses des statuts de 'pureté de sang' en Espagne du XVᵉ au XVIIIᵉ siècle* (Paris 1960).

17 This is the definition of both given by a jurist of the seventeenth century, Juan Escobar de Corro, in his *Tractatus Bipartitus de puritate et nobilitate probanda* (published in Lyon 1773, the first edition bears an imprimatur of 1632) p. 46: '*Puritas* igitur dicitur qualitas e majoribus in descendentes proveniens ex eoquod illorum nemo, cujus sit memoria ex Judaeis, nec Mauris, nec Haereticis, conversisve originem trahit, nec horum eos minima inficiat macula. Est que quasi quidam mitor ex co proveniens, quod majores, et parentes omnes fidem intrepide et constanter observarunt: catholicam in eorum descendentes derivatus.' '*Impuritas* vero e contra dicitur macula orta e majorum prava legis Mosaicae, sectaeve Mahometanae, et haereticorum observatione, et ad universos omnes descendentes transmissa et derivata, quae ab honoribus et oficiis puritatem requirentibus omnino arcentur et repelluntur, velut infames, et detestabiles personae, quorum progenies in infinitum impura dicitur.'

18 *Segunda partida* titulo 21, ley 3 (ed. *cit.* 1, p. 468). The problem of hidalguía has occupied many students, but a definitive study on this institution is still to be made.

19 Miguel de Cervantes *Novelas ejemplares* ed. Ricardo Benavides (Santiago de Chile 1956) p. 199.

20 Covarrubias in his *Tesoro* p. 925 discussing *sambenitos* says: 'De manera que aunque para el mundo sea ignominia y afrenta, si los que los traen reciben en paciencia lo que dirá el vulgo, pueden pava con Dios merecer mucho'. At first sight the way in which the Christian penance of the *saco bendito* and public shame combine seems strange. But there are other cases in which the same thing happens.

21 The monograph by C. Bernaldo de Quirós *La picota. Crímenes y castigos en el país castellano en los tiempos medios* (Madrid 1907) needs to be rewritten.

22 See, for example, the account given by Fray José de Sigüenza in his 'Historia de la Orden de San Jerónimo' 2 (*Nueva biblioteca de autores españoles* 12, Madrid 1909, p. 444, part 3, book 3, discourse 10) of events at the Escorial when the famous monastery was being built, in 1577 concerning a riot among Biscayan and Montañes masons, because the chief *alcalde* intended or gave out that he intended to have one of them flogged riding on an ass, a punishment which could not be inflicted on *hidalgos*. 'Vestido en pompa y a

caballo' says one of the convicts jokingly of the bawd who appears in chapter 22 of the first part of *Don Quijote*, alluding to this punishment. But Sancho Panza comments: 'Eso es, a lo que a mí me parece, *haber salido a la vergüenza.*'

23 Although in the reign of Philip IV, by a decree dated 10th February 1623, it was forbidden to have the *libros verdes* or the *libros del becerro* which were those in question (see the 'Novisima recopilacion' book 11, section 27, law 22, 5 *Los códigos españoles* 9 [3 of the code indicated, Madrid 1850] p. 514), manuscript copies of them have survived until modern times, sometimes copied for scholastic purposes, and sometimes with scandalous intent.

24 In this, the short period of office of Don Gaspar Melchor de Jovellanos (1744–1811), as Minister of Justice is noteworthy. It was he who protected Canon Llorente in his project for preparing a work on the Inquisition which should expose all the legal excesses which it had committed. In 1813 the *Cortes* of Cádiz, following the decree of abolition promulgated by their enemy Napoleon put an end to it, and to these *Cortes* is also due the suppression of the statutes of 'purity of blood' and other measures which open a new age.

25 The controversy however was heated, but the anticlerical intent given to many measures in the nineteenth century was not apparent in the seventeenth, because it would have been impossible.

26 In the Archivo Histórico Nacional de Madrid, Inquisición de Toledo, may be seen a considerable number of documents concerning the 'ineligible' persons in various towns and various actions against individuals who had flouted their ineligibility; see *Católogo de las causas contra la fe seguidas ante el Tribunal del Santo Oficio de la Inquisición de Toledo* (Madrid 1903) pp. 131–40. In my book on the Jews, part 2, chapters 2 and 4.

27 B.A.E. 32 p. 491.

28 B.A.E. 69 p. 88 (no. 313).

29 The most extraordinary case is that of Manuel Cortizos and his family, all Jewish. This did not prevent him and his brothers, sons and brothers-in-law from being titled and knights of Calatrava, while Manuel's wife and aunt were being prosecuted by the Inquisition. In the eighteenth century a member of this family ended his days in London as an openly practising Jew. See my book on the Jews, part 3, chapter 5 and part 4, chapter 5.

30 B.A.E. 69 p. 93 (no. 325) in the 'Musa quinta'.

31 In Portugal the bitterest enemy of the new way of life was perhaps Sá de Miranda (1481–1558) who praises the ancient virtues of the gentleman and the countryman as against the vices of seamen, merchants and courtiers.

32 Juan Huarte de San Juan *Exámen de Ingenios para las ciencias*,

digression in chapter 16 (Madrid 1846) pp. 225–6. I must point out here that in the notes collected in the 'Floreto' quoted above (see note 5 to this chapter) pp. 360–2, on nobility and honour, the order laid down by Huarte is followed almost word for word.

33 B.A.E. 43, p. 374.

34 B.A.E. 34, p. 259.

35 The Archbishop of Toledo Martinez Siliceo was one of those who were most influential in carrying out their intentions of implanting the statutes of purity in the primatial Church, to rehabilitate the class to which he belonged. And a letter attributed to him has been preserved in which he speaks openly of his origin: 'Yo os quería casar con mi sobrina,' he wrote on one occasion to Dr Santiago, 'y pues también araron vuestros parientes como los mios, no tendréis què dezir a vuestra mujer, ni ella a vos,' 'Floreto', *cit.* p. 187.

36 By recalling other examples we may appreciate the importance which the villeins placed upon saying that they were 'old Christians': 'Ellos, en fin,' says Dorotea, referring to her parents at the beginning of her story, in chapter 28 in the first part of *Don Quijote*, 'son labradores, gente *sin mezcla de alguna raza mal sonante, y como suele decirse cristianos viejos rancios* (o ranciosos) pero tan rancios, que su riqueza y magnifico trato les va poco a poco adquiriendo nombre de hidalgos y aun de caballeros . . .' Sancho Panza, who had not such pretentions continually boasts of his being an 'old Christian' (part 1, chapter 21; part 2, chapters 3 and 4, etc.).

37 It should be pointed out that the plot of *El alcalde de Zalamea* was taken by Lope de Vega, the author of the first dramatic version later superseded by Calderón from a story by Masuccio. But in this the protagonist is a Valladolid gentleman who avenges his dishonour, not an *alcalde* of villein stock. R. Menéndez Pidal, 'Del honor en el teatro español' in *España y su historia* 2, pp. 370–1. The intention, then, is clear.

38 It seems that in this case Lope de Vega did not have to alter anything in the sources of his work. The rebellion of Fuenteovejuna must have happened in 1476 and the comendador was the Comendador de Calatrava Hernán Gómez de Guzmán, J. Diaz del Moral, *Historia de las agitaciones campesinas andaluzas*. Córdoba (Madrid 1929) pp. 36–40. In the middle of the seventeenth century there were cases in which the vassals of a harsh overlord killed him, as the overlord of Lozoya was killed by shots from an arquebus in 1647. But I do not think that this episode ended in a Calderonian manner, or as in *Fuenteovejuna*, but with great slaughter among the guilty. 'Cartas de algunos pp. de la Compañia de Jesus' 7, *Memorial histórico español* 19 (Madrid 1865) p. 27 (letter from P. Sebastián González to P. Rafael Pereyra, dated Madrid July 16th of that year).

39 Sancho Panza (part II, chapter II) also alludes to 'aquellos hidalgos escuderiles, que dan humo a los zapatos y toman los puntos de las medias negras con seda verde', as people at odds with fortune.

40 David Hume *Essays and treatises on several subjects* I (London 1764) p. 150.

41 'Comentarios del desengañado, ó sea vida de D. Diego Duque de Estrada, escrita por él mismo' in *Memorial histórico español* 12 (Madrid 1860).

42 The deeds of these and other gentlemen of the period are to be found recounted in the letters and communication of contemporaries, like those of the jesuits, Pellicer, Barrionuevo, etc.

43 It must also be pointed out that from the starting-point of the idea according to which outraging, affronting or dishonouring another, especially an enemy, are positive deeds which demonstrate one's own superiority, the simple figure of the *burlador*, as drawn by Tirso de Molina, and even that of the *infamador* of Juan de la Cueva (1543-1610), who possibly took the character of Leucinio from reality, fit into a well-defined social structure independently of what may be argued from a psychological point of view for or against the realism of these characters and of the moral view which we may hold of those who take pleasure in deceiving and dishonouring others. For even in the plays of Tirso de Molina we find another figure, that of *El vergonzoso en palacio* which shows how in a young man an excessive sense of shame was not highly esteemed by many women, who made a mock of him. Today too the so-called *machismo* (virility) imposes itself over certain virtues in certain matters.

44 The type of the 'repentant sinner' is seen in Don Miguel de Mañara, Don Tiburcio de Redin, Duque de Estrada, etc. without having recourse to fiction. In others piety and lust, if not other passions, always run parallel – in Philip IV himself, whose correspondence with Sor María de Agueda, studied by students of politics, should have received the attention of psychologists.

45 True today too.

46 In a letter from Don Diego de Garay or Don Diego Gómez, Inquisitor of the Supreme Court, to Father Diego del Marmol, dated Madrid, 14th September 1638, we read this: 'De esta corte fueron dos compañias de hijos-dalgo de más de 400 hombras; de la una su capitán D. Rodrigo de Tapia, y de la otra D. Francisco Luzón. Los más de estos son gente moza y alentada, de los que comunmente llaman "crudos" y a lo, moderno en Granada, los de "la banda del cuervo" y de la "cáscara amarga"; todos se precian de la hoja, y están tan ejercitados en la espada y broquel que los mas de ellos los llevan consigo,' 'Cartas de algunos pp. de la Compañia de

Jesus' 3 *Memorial histórico español* 15 (Madrid 1862) pp. 28–9. The expression 'de la cáscara amarga' has undergone several semantic changes.

47 As is shown by the case recounted by Gaspar de Velasco to Father Diego de La Fuente Hurtado, in a letter dated Madrid, 14th September 1639, which I give here: 'De Málaga escriben un caso atroz, y es que pretendiendo entrar un D. Fulano de Torres, sobrino del cardenal Torres en el refectorio de las comediantas, quiso impedirlo el alcaide, y despues de algunos remoquetes dijo al dicho Torres que era un picaro, y él respondió que mentia como un infame, y echó mano a la espada para defender el mentis. Mandó el alcaide que le prendiesen, y aquel mismo dia le sentenció a degollar; apeló el caballero de la sentencia, mas el alcaide fué por la noche á la cárcel con un esclavo, y alli hizo que le degollasen, y pidiendo el caballero confesión, dijo: que a picaros como él no se les habia de administrar los Sacramentos, y después de todo eso le hizo colgar de piés de una reja de la ciudad. Ahora aguardamos á saber lo que se ha de hacer de este mal cristiano; parece que nada basta.' 'Cartas de algunos pp. de la Compañia de Jesús' 3 *Memorial histórico español* 15 (Madrid 1862) pp. 334–5.

48 This was already felt at the time of the wars of Catalonia and the separation from Portugal, from 1640 onwards, as we see in many of the letters in Father Pereyra's collection. The text of the historian to whom I refer runs thus: 'Ni puedo dexar en este lugar de hazer memoria de las grandes proezas que han executado los Españoles en todos los siglos, aunque aora parece que se ayan amortiguado sus hazañas, que mas que falta de valor, y denuedo, es porque no tienen Heroes que los dirijan.' Juan Alfonso de Lancina *Historia de las reboluciones (sic) del senado de Messina* (Madrid 1692) p. 497.

CHAPTER THREE

1 For example, the letter from Father Juan Chacón, dated Valladolid, 17th September 1634. 'Cartas de algunos pp. de la Compañia de Jesús' 1 *Memorial histórico español* 13 (Madrid 1861) pp. 95–8.

2 Letter from the same Father Chacón, dated Valladolid, 2nd December 1635, *Cartas . . . cit.* 1 (*op. cit.*) p. 341.

3 *Memorias de Raimundo de Lantery, mercador de Indias en Cádiz,* 1673–1700, ed. Don Alvaro Picardo (Cádiz 1949).

4 However in some plays, such as *El dómine Lucas* by Don José de Cañzares (1676–1750) there is already an interesting satire on the vanities of the nobility.

5 Recently Don Américo Castro has revived this idea, already old in

Spain, and even more in Europe. *La realidad histórica de España* (Medico 1954) pp. 558–61, 582–7, 600–6, etc. Américo Castro even considers the existence of a caste, not a class, system.

6 Literary evidence has also been abused to support this point, in disregard of other documents which contradict the theory. Even Sancho Panza in the dialogue with his wife (*Don Quijote* part 2, chapter 5) shows by his jokes that the stability of the supposed castes was not a thing which was considered at all real.

7 In a report from Don Antonio de Mendoza to the Conde Duque de Olivares at the time of the troubles in Vizcaya the change which had occurred is made clear. The old families of the time of the factions had been superseded in importance in the life of Bilbao and the ports by people engaged in trade and connected with foreign merchants. *Discursos de Don Antonio de Mendoza, secretario de Camara de Felipe IV* (Madrid 1911) pp. 139–48.

8 Manuel de Larramendi *Corografía o descripción general de la muy noble y muy leal provincia de Guipuzcoa* (Barcelona 1882) pp. 121–54.

9 See the introduction to *Rinconete y Cortadillo* by Don Francisco Rodriguez Marín (Seville, 1905).

10 Larramendi *Corografía . . . cit.* p. 133 says: 'Ya para pruebas de colegios, catedrales, de hábitos, no se tiene por embarazo el tener padres, abuelos y parientes comerciantes en grueso y de lonja, como dicen.' But his '*ya*' could have been written a century before. For Seville see Santiago Montoto *Sevilla en el Imperio (siglo XVI)* (Seville 1937) pp. 181–4 where several comments are copied from Fray Tomás Mercado in the *Suma de tratos y contratos* (Salamanca 1569). In Burgos the families of the great merchants of the fifteenth century and the early sixteenth (such as the Malvendas) succeeded in obtaining knightly honours, and the Genoese bankers, etc. even became titled Castilian nobles.

11 Here the following points should be emphasized: In the *Nueva Recopilación*, a legal code compiled in the time of Philip II (1567), there are as many as eleven laws (book 8, section 13) on challenges and accusations. But in the *Novisima*, made in the eighteenth century, they have already been suppressed (*Los códigos españoles . . .* 11, Madrid 1850, pp. 244–7). In the *Novisima*, on the other hand, book 12, section 20, are collected the following laws on challenge and duels: (a) A law of Ferdinand and Isabella, dated 1480, against those who make placards and challenges; a thing which is considered frequent 'at this time' (*agora*). (b) A decree of Philip V forbidding them absolutely (16th and 27th January 1716) ratified by Ferdinand VI (9th May 1757) and in which they are described as 'detestables y malditos'. (c) Another decree dated 21st October 1723, laying down that no one 'pueda tomar por si satisfacción de agravios o

injurias' (ed. *cit.* 4, pp. 68–71). In the seventeenth century decrees were enacted to restrict the frequency of challenges, such as one of the 29th August 1678, and a number of duellers were punished. From another angle, we should take into account the restrictions and penalties set out from the point of view of moral theology in treatises like that of Fray Antonio Montes de Porres, *Suma, Diana recopilado en romance* . . . (Madrid 1657) pp. 264–5 (*Duelo*).

12 Menéndez y Pelayo does not take this fact into account when, in the *Origenes de la novela* 1, p. 208, he speaks of the ephemeral and un-Spanish nature of the genre, nor yet of the previous text of *Don Quijote* part 1, chapter 32, which shows us the reapers of La Mancha gathered together outside the inn listening to one of their number reading in their hours of rest one of these books, which were also so much enjoyed by the innkeeper and his wife.

13 See the above quoted introduction to *Rinconete y Cortadillo* by Rodriguez Marín (note 9).

14 The cultivators of the so-called 'criminal anthropology' of the end of the nineteenth and beginning of the twentieth centuries, strongly influenced by the Italian school, took an interest in these personages. See as an example the book by Rafael Salillas *El delincuente español. Hampa* (*Antropologia picaresca*) (Madrid 1898) pp. 502–16. But without wishing to offend their memory, I think that we may say that they contented themselves with utter formalities.

15 When the famous historian of the Muslims in Spain, R. Dozy, begins his account of the personage of Omar ben Hafsun [*Historia de los musulmanes españoles* trs. Don F. de Castro 2 (Madrid 1877) pp. 213–19] he dedicates several pages full of what we might call 'enthusiasm' to the bandits who in his time or a little earlier had occupied the mountains in the South, and whom he compares with that forceful character. Rochfort Scott, Custine, Mérimée and others had given him the material for these pages.

16 On the last days of the Inquisition and the changes of criteria referred to, see my book on the Jews, part 5, chapter 6, where I make use of the earlier bibliography and of some documents little used in it.

17 During the first two decades of the twentieth century there were, however, more or less sporadic cases of challenges between politicians, journalists, men of letters, etc.

18 Much was written at the time about this crime.

19 Glorifications of the poor classes in Spain may be found in some Protestant writers of the second half of the nineteenth century. For example the Rev. Hugh James Rose *Among the Spanish people* 2 vols. (London 1877).

20 Now that we can see the facts from a distance we realize that we

have no good studies of the influence of popular novels in the preparation of revolutionary politics. *María o la hija de un jornalero* by W. Ayguals de Izco is the first work of this type of a socialist nature by a Spanish author.

21 'Cartas de algunos pp. de la Compañia de Jesús' *Memorial histórico español* 16, Madrid 1862) p. 352.

22 B.A.E. 23, pp. 415–16 in *La isla de los Monopantos*, a short antisemitic work.

23 Recall *El santo de la Isidra* (1898) and *Es mi hombre*, very much later.

J. K. Campbell

HONOUR AND THE DEVIL

Honour and the Devil

1 Aspects of Honour

Honour[1] as the recognized integrity and value of the individual
personality is profoundly important to Greeks whether they are
peasants or cabinet ministers. The self-regarding values of
honour, however, recommend behaviour that is very different
from the prescriptions of Christian charity and fellowship. Yet
if the minority of sophisticates and agnostics among the urban
middle class is excepted, the majority of Greeks remain committed practising members of the Orthodox Catholic Church.
It is a problem of some interest to consider how they succeed in
reconciling these conflicting social and religious ideals. I examine
it, however, only for a particular community of Sarakatsani,
Greek shepherds with a transhumant pastoral economy. This
canvas is admittedly small but the definition of the contrast is
precise. The Sarakatsani continue to live by an austere code of
traditional honour while they are also conscious of their complete
dependence on the protection and beneficence of God.

The population of the community is about 4,000. In summer
they graze their sheep and goats in the mountains of the Zagori
district in Epirus, where the families of the community are dis-
persed over an area of some 390 square miles of difficult country
among certain villages of the district which own wide grasslands.
Since 1938 local gatherings of 100 to 300 Sarakatsani have had
citizenship and grazing rights in the particular village of their
summer pastures. But in the winter, when climatic conditions
force the Sarakatsani to move their flocks to the narrow valleys of
the Epirote seaboard, many families do not have village citizenship which automatically assures them of grazing rights. Then
pasture must be rented at high cost from village communities or
private individuals, if indeed it can be found at all.

The local groups of families which happen to graze the lands of the same village community have no corporate functions. Nor does the community as a whole possess any formal political institutions. The critical unit of social organization in the community is the family, whether in its elementary or extended form, and a number of families related by kinship or marriage generally co-operate in the management of their sheep. Such a 'company' (*parea*) normally numbers between fifteen and fifty individuals of all ages and in a majority of cases it is dominated by a group of married brothers. Unrelated men seldom belong to these associations unless they are paid shepherds. Indeed between men who are unrelated by kinship or marriage there is deep distrust which in practice prevents any effective form of co-operation. For the Sarakatsani, therefore, there are three categories of persons in the community: kinsmen by blood, recognized to the collateral degree of second cousin through the mother or the father, affinal relations by marriage, and strangers. Persons in the first category are loved, cherished, and trusted; one must never cheat or lie to a kinsman. One should also deal honourably with persons in the second category, the affinal relations; yet one does not trust them. With these people there is co-operation but only a qualified confidence. Unrelated Sarakatsani, on the other hand, the strangers (*xenoi*), are almost enemies. A man would be foolish and weak to trust them, unmanly not to exploit them within the limits conventionally allowed.

Kinsmen and affines must offer one another moral and practical support in a hostile world. But some forms of assistance are not permissible; and others, although possible, are not categorically enjoined. For instance, a father must always put the interests of his own family of marriage[2] before the needs even of a brother. However large his flocks he cannot give away any of his stock to assist a poorer kinsman, nor is he under any obligation to avenge the death of a kinsman or the dishonour of a kinswoman unless that person is a member of his family of marriage. Thus the family is a kind of social isolate facing the majority of the community on terms of hostility and distrust, and receiving important but, nevertheless, qualified support from kinsmen and affines.

This hostility is chiefly expressed in aggressive denigration of the reputation of others, in secrecy, theft, and incidents of physical violence. Conversation between two unrelated men or women is a verbal engagement where both sides probe for the least hint of the other's intentions or activities. It is not concerned with sociability but is rather an expression of social opposition and distance. The reciprocal theft of sheep used to be an endemic occupation until severer penalties restricted its incidence. Men now prefer to steal each other's inadequate grazing by organized trespass at night across the boundaries of their neighbours. Fights occur between shepherds after insults or imagined slights. Sometimes these are the consequence of the kind of trespassing which I have just mentioned. A sheep strays across a boundary, a stone is thrown, a fight begins. But generally the Sarakatsani are careful that these brawls do not lead to killings, for the cogent reason that since it is only within the family of origin of an unmarried man, or the family of marriage of a married man, that there is a categorical obligation to revenge a killing, this small group is peculiarly ill-equipped to carry on any form of protracted vendetta.

More generally the shepherd's way of life is too vulnerable to tolerate more than a certain measure of violence in the community. Sentiments of opposition and exclusiveness between families find a more extended expression in competition for name and prestige, which hold the concern of Sarakatsani in every context of public action and give purpose and meaning to their lives. The sociological importance of competition is precisely that it represents a kind of opposition which is often indirect. In this case families compete for social recognition which depends entirely on their acceptance of, and adherence to, a shared system of values; and on the grudging approval of their performance by the other members of the community, the majority of whom are unrelated and hostile. Thus although the values of prestige encourage the intense consideration of a man's own interests, they also have a most important associative function in a community remarkable for its degree of fragmentation. They are, as it were, the rules of the game.

The basis of social reputation for a family is the recognition that it has honour (*tīmē*), a word which is also used in Greek to describe the monetary price, or value, of an object or service. *Tīmē* expresses the notion of worth whether this is an economic value in a market, or social worth evaluated in a complex of competing groups and individuals. Yet there is this difference. With the exception of those persons in certain families at the lowest level of the prestige hierarchy, all Sarakatsani are born with honour into families of honour. It is difficult, then, to talk of competition for honour. But it is a quality in a family which may easily be lost in certain situations where it is typically violated or betrayed, as in homicide, the drawing of blood in a fight, verbal insult, seduction, rape, or a broken betrothal. Honour, then, is a condition of integrity, of being 'untouched' by this kind of attack, insult or betrayal. The integrity of a family and its equality (at least) of status is recognized when others take care not to give offence in these particular ways. If they do gratuitously commit an outrage against a family, they make it clear that they consider its social existence of no account. In that case, whether the violation is accidental or not, the outraged family must answer at once, and with violence, if its reputation is to survive.

The honour of the family, and its solidarity, are symbolized in the idea of blood. In marriage a man and woman mix their different blood to produce 'one blood' which is the blood of their children. Relationships in the family are a participation in this common blood. It provides the reason and the sanction within the individual's conscience for the fulfilment of the exigent and uncompromising duties of family membership. The relevance of blood to intelligence and moral character, and their inheritance, is an idea with a long history.[3] But for the Sarakatsani, the blood which children inherit not only represents, but it 'is' the physical and moral attributes that form their social personalities. If a man is not of honourable lineage his blood does not 'take fire' at an insult; and when he is faced with sudden danger 'his blood is cut' (*kopēke to aima tou*). These are not metaphorical usages. The blood centred in the heart is both the medium and the agent of emotional thought and feeling. Thus blood is intimately related to courage. And it is a matter of common observation that as a man loses blood, he loses strength. Since courage and physical strength are particularly the qualities that men require in order to defend the reputation of their families, it is entirely consistent that for the Sarakatsani the honour of the family is literally the honour of its blood.

Without honour there is no possibility of social prestige. Yet social prestige is compounded also of certain material attributes, particularly wealth in stock and the number of sons in a family. Indeed honour itself, as well as other important attributes of prestige such as the quality of marriages contracted or the effective display of pride, are dependent on numbers[4] and wealth. Families of extreme poverty are denied the recognition of honour even though no positive accusation of dishonour can be pointed against them. Quite small incidents, which are not in themselves exactly questions of honour, are seized upon by the community to show prospectively that such a family, if it were faced with the duty of defending its honour, would be found wanting. These are 'lost' families (*chamenes oikogeneies*), both morally and practically.

Honour invariably has some reference to the corporate family, for in this community the individual can only be taken account of, and evaluated, in relation to his family membership. Yet the honour of the family is drawn from the qualities of its individual members and from public commentary on their behaviour; and these members are few in number and can never, in anonymity, escape the burden of their representative responsibility. The intrinsic principles of personal honour refer to two sex-linked qualities that distinguish the ideal moral characters of men and women: these are the manliness (*andrismos*) of men, and the sexual shame (*dropē*) of women which the majority of Sarakatsani are assumed to possess 'by nature', although in the fallen condition of this world a reputation for manliness or shame is easily lost. In this sense it is not difficult for a man to move in a direction opposite to the true inclinations of his nature. One aspect of honour, then, is a struggle of self-discipline over cowardice and sensuality, flaws of animal nature that continually threaten to limit the natural nobility of man.

In general, the qualities of manliness are obvious and familiar. A man must be strong in body and spirit. But there is also a nuance of meaning peculiar to a community where values are agonistic and social reputation is frequently at risk. In these circumstances a man must have boundless self-confidence in his own powers. Where few men owe him more than conditional support, and the great majority none at all, he must rely on himself. Manliness implies not only the condition of being courageous but the ability of a man to do something efficient and effective about the problems and dangers which surround him. For in this complex of values results count for almost everything and intentions[5] for very little.

The physical characteristics of manliness are important. A man must be *varvatos*, that is well endowed with testicles and the strength that is drawn from them. The word also describes a certain ruthless ability in any form of endeavour. Here again we see the 'efficient' aspect of manliness. But *varvatos* is in no sense a moral term, and in other contexts it may describe the dishonourable conduct of a man who rapes a woman or bullies weaker men. The manliness that is related to honour requires this physical basis, yet it must discipline animal strength and passions to its own ideal ends. Virginity before marriage is the ideal.

The quality required of women in relation to honour is shame, particularly sexual shame. Subjectively the woman's sexual shame is not simply a fear of external sanctions; it is an instinctive revulsion from sexual activity, an attempt in dress, movement, and attitude, to disguise the fact that she possesses the physical attributes of her sex. Maidens must be virgins, and even married women must remain virginal in thought and expression. But honour is always something imputed by others. In these matters the individual woman can never retreat within her own conscience. Her honour depends upon the reputation which the community is willing to concede, not upon the evidence of facts in any case difficult to determine. Therefore she protects her honour most effectively by conforming in every outward aspect of her deportment to a code of sexual shame.

This kind of shame is a quality that is thought to descend in the female line from mother to daughter, but its loss always implicates the honour of the men of the family, reflecting on the manliness of the husband, and, more generally, on the whole social personality of brothers and, particularly, sons. The woman is soiled (*leromenē*), and blackened (*mountzouromenē*): and she marks with her dishonour all those who are close to her through kinship or marriage. Clearly manliness and shame are complementary qualities in relation to honour. The manliness of the men in any family protects the sexual honour of its women from external insult or outrage. The women must have shame if the manliness of their men is not to be dishonoured.

Honour considered as the possession by men and women of

these qualities is the attempt to relate existence to certain archetypal patterns of behaviour. Female values are referred to the ideal conduct of the Mother of God: modesty, virginal attitudes, and selfless love. Male values appear in different exemplars. Christ is the ideal of continence and selfless sacrifice even of life for those to whom one is committed: the horsed and warlike saints George and Demetrius present the pattern of assertive courage, physical, spiritual, and invulnerable. Nearer to the realities of a shepherd's life, these two aspects of ideal manliness meet in the legendary image of the Klephtic hero, a man who so refined his powers of courage and continence that he partly transcended the limitations of the material world. Bullets could not find their mark on Katsandonis. Shepherds in Zagori know the place where he leaped his horse a hundred paces across a chasm. Such heroes are both prepotent and efficient. Whatever the odds these men always defeat their enemy, except in the final contest when only the pre-ordained moment of fate and the presence of Charon succeed in taking away life. Men and women, then, struggle to attain these ideal modes of being and conduct. Where they fall too far short in the effort of identification, honour is lost.

In addition to the general qualities of manliness and shame which are the prerequisites of honour, other specific qualities and behaviours are required of men and women in the different roles they play as they pass through their life cycle. A man (or woman) who succeeds in approaching the ideal type personality that is appropriate to his sex and time of life is described as honourable (*tīmios*). The adjective is clearly a word with a considerably wider reference than *tīmē*, honour, the values of which are always specific and unchanging. What is honourable (*tīmio*) may even in certain circumstances be a risk to honour (*tīmē*). For instance, if a head of family fails to avenge the breaking of his daughter's betrothal because there is no adult son, it may be argued that as an 'honourable' man his inaction is due to his concern that, if he acts, he must at best serve a prison sentence and his family will be without a leader. But if circumstances of age and family commitments excuse to a degree the loss of honour, nevertheless honour is lost.

An account of the general expectations of different roles in the Sarakatsan community is unnecessary in the context of this essay.

Here I need only mention those characteristics of male roles which are relevant to the development of my argument. Between the age of twenty-three after he has returned from military service and the time of his marriage (when he is generally about thirty years old), a young man belongs to the *pallikari* age group of adult but unmarried men. The *pallikari* is the hero warrior with physical strength and assertive courage who is prepared to die, if necessary, for the honour of his family. For him physical perfection is an important ideal attribute and any kind of physical deformity is fatal to his reputation. These, indeed, are the years of perfected manliness when a young shepherd is still free from the responsibilities of family leadership and the need for caution, compromise, and lies, which it inevitably imposes.

The critical moment in the development of the young shepherd's reputation is his first quarrel. Quarrels are necessarily public. They may occur in the coffee-shop, the village square, or most frequently on a grazing boundary where a curse or stone aimed at one of his straying sheep by another shepherd is an insult which inevitably requires a violent response. In any case some account of the event becomes public property. If the quarrel occurs before unrelated bystanders, the community may obtain a reasonably factual account of the fight. If it is not witnessed by an impartial audience, the contestant with the fewer marks of injury and the greater number of persuasive kinsmen wins the day. It is the critical nature of these first important tests of his manliness that makes the self-regard (*egoismos*) of the young shepherd so extremely sensitive. It is not only the reality of an obvious insult which provokes him to action, but even the finest of allusions on which it is possible to place some unflattering construction.

When a man has assumed the status of head of family he becomes more cautious. He resorts to violence only when he must. For he now has to consider what will happen to his family if he loses his life or is thrown into prison. The family, it will be remembered, receives only conditional assistance from the kinsmen and affines of its members. Cleverness is the quality he must cultivate. It implies a quickness of mind and a degree of foresight; also the skill to plot with guile, and to lie with effect. In some respects this period of leadership is perhaps more testing for a man than his years in the *pallikari* age group. Expediency must be balanced against honour in ways that do not endanger reputation; this is not always easy. Only after his retirement when his reputation is definitely established does a man at last enter a period of life which is free from competitive strain.

Both honour and the notion of the honourable man are, in a certain sense, sanctioned by the sentiments of self-regard (*egoismos*)[6] and shame (*dropē*). Self-regard is the inner necessity and obligation to achieve identity with the image of the ideal self. This image, of course, is a stereotype presented by society, there is little room for individual speculation, nor would it occur to most Sarakatsani to question its traditional content. Self-regard is concerned with what must be positively achieved, that is the ideal of a social personality with particular moral qualities but also certain material attributes. It is not concerned with a code of moral or ritual interdictions governing behaviour towards God and one's fellow men which, simply, must not be transgressed.

Self-regard is molested where a man is insulted or defamed, or believes himself to have been so treated. If a man behaves towards another in such a way as to suggest that he is not worthy of consideration and recognition, his self-regard is molested; for he only acts in this way towards another when he considers him to be of lesser reputation and, by inference, less honourable. In such circumstances the core of a man's social personality is touched, his manliness and prepotence are questioned. He must respond with violence if he is to avoid self-disesteem. The need is even more pressing if his humiliation has been observed by others and his reputation for honour is at stake.

If self-regard is the need to achieve an identity with the image of an ideal self, shame is the emotion experienced by an individual when he clearly fails to do so. As in the case of self-regard, although a man may feel shame for shortcomings or sufferings that remain secret, it involves at all times some idea of comparison with the achievements of others, and it is all the more acute when a man's inadequacy is publicly exposed. A man may feel shame not only for his own shortcomings, but also for those of other persons with whom he is closely identified in any situation. And it may also be a sentiment imputed by others when they make critical comments on a man's behaviour or condition. They may say that his conduct in a particular situation is a matter for shame, that is, if he were an honourable man, his sense of shame would have prevented him from acting in the way that he did. The notion of failure underlies the different contextual uses of the term. In the critical instance of the sexual shame of a girl it may be said that she has shame in two respects. She is aware of the power of her sexuality which threatens the honour of men; in a sense she has already failed by being a woman at all, and for this she 'feels shame'. She is also a girl 'with shame' in the sense that she carefully conforms to a strict code of modest behaviour and movement. This expresses the fear of failure in disciplining sexuality according to the ideal pattern of maidenly conduct. It is clear that to some extent the sentiments of self-regard and shame are sex-linked. Self-regard encourages a positive competitive attitude especially between men of similar age and standing, and it is not generally a quality for self-congratulation in a woman. On the other hand, the restrictive regime, which an extreme sense of shame imposes on an individual, is incompatible with the social role of the head of family who must generally assert himself and on occasion, for the sake of his family, may even be forced into questionable or sinful actions. This is not to say that a man does not equally feel shame when he is judged to have failed. It means, rather, that unlike a woman he cannot remain always in a state of shame, in the sense of guarding against imminent failure by a careful restriction of behaviour and bearing.

In the present context three things are important about the system of social values that informs this fragmented community of opposed and competing family commonwealths. Firstly relationship radically affects the forms of approved behaviour. Since everything depends on the conservation of honour, it is believed that the misfortunes of a family which falls from grace through poverty or dishonour in some way validate the status and integrity of the others. Thus it is almost a virtue, within conventionally defined limits, to denigrate and deceive non-kinsmen, while the same conduct to kinsmen would be sinful and shameful. The values of honour and prestige are exclusive and particularist.

Secondly they are plainly self-regarding. The concept of *timē*, honour, expresses essentially the idea of worth, the worth of the individual or his family, as this is measured explicitly against ideal patterns of behaviour, and implicitly against the conduct of others. It is, as we have seen, a condition of integrity, of being untouched by attack, insult, or betrayal. The sentiments of self-regard and shame internal to the individual social personality support the notions of honour and 'the honourable man', and present the obligation to achieve identity with the image of the ideal self.

These concepts and values, then, are concerned with self-regard, not regard for others. In each case it is a question of a man attempting to realize a particular ideal pattern of conduct. What interests him is the success of this quest, not the effect of his actions on the affairs of others. When a man appears to insult you, you do not pause to consider whether he may have mis-understood what you previously said, you do not in charity accept his apology (which in any event no Sarakatsanos would offer). You consider only your honour and the consequences his remarks are likely to have if you do not act. Self-regard forbids any action which may be interpreted as weakness. Normally this would include any altruistic behaviour to an unrelated man. Co-operation, tolerance, love, must give way to autarky, arrogance, hostility. Even where a man of nobility moderates his conduct because it would disastrously affect the fortunes of another family this is the result of an acute concern about the purity of his own motives which spills over into an only incidental concern for others.

In self-regard there is a sense of tension between what a man is and what he ought to be. But what a man is depends on the evaluation by the community of what a man is alleged to be, or to have done. The need to equate the community's evaluation of himself with his own ideal image often leads a man into a form of unconscious cheating, or self-deception. In the appearance of being a *pallikari*, he becomes a *pallikari*. A man boasts and asserts himself the more when there is little fear that he may be called on to prove himself. And knives are pulled with greater bravado when it is certain that others are present to prevent their use.

The third important consideration about the values of honour is the emphasis they place on strength and skill. As we have seen, physical strength is an important element in the critical quality of manliness. Chronic sickness in a wife is inexcusable. Strength in numbers, it may be remembered, is also significant. A family without sons will find it more difficult to protect the honour of its daughters. It is more prudent to offend a man without a brother than a man with brothers. Weakness is despised. In itself it tends to diminish prestige even before it has led to dishonour. It follows that generally there is no shame in delivering insults, only in receiving them.

Cleverness, cunning, and skill, are prized because without these capacities stock is managed inexpertly, indifferent grazing is chosen, and bad bargains are made. If he lacks these qualities a man is likely to be, or to become, poor. If he is poor he has no prestige. And without prestige honour, too, is in doubt. For honour is always a question of ascription, not a matter of fact or individual right. Reputation, then, is impossible without strength, skill, cleverness. Man is good only when he is also by implication strong. Although aimless violence is dishonourable there is no missing the pleasure it gives when a man tells of a killing he was obliged to make; nor the prestige which it brings him. There is no more conclusive way of showing that you are stronger than by taking away the other man's life. Conversely all forms of weakness are shameful. So the weak, the humble, the modest, even the merely good-hearted and co-operative, are not virtuous.

It becomes abundantly clear that the values of honour, particularistic, egocentric, and related to an ideal of disciplined strength rather than ethical goodness, contradict in most respects the principles of Christian fellowship.

2 *The Sins of Adam*

The formal relationship of the Sarakatsani to the Orthodox Church, as an institution, is somewhat tenuous. In the face of the almost open contempt and hostility of villagers they attend church only at some of the more important festivals, generally with the purpose of taking Holy Communion which a man or woman ought to do at least once and preferably twice a year, the most significant of these occasions being, of course, at Easter. The Eucharist in the simple way that they understand it as the sacrifice of Christ's blood, which overcomes the barrier of sin separating man from God, is the central belief of Sarakatsan religious life. But they do not understand the structure of the liturgy. Indeed, since it is written in a form of Greek they do not use, they understand only the shorter and more frequently repeated phrases and petitions. Yet they have a clear if sometimes unorthodox conception of God the Father, Christ the Son, the All Holy Mother of God, and the Saints; the divine archetype family, and those transfigured human beings who through self-discipline and the sanctity of their lives are the appropriate models for the guidance of weaker men, and the natural inter-cessors between them and God.

The Sarakatsani are very conscious of their dependence on God. The margin of security possessed by each family in its relative isolation is narrow. There are many anxieties; the sickness of children, the diseases of sheep, the scarcity of pasture, social prestige and personal health. These are matters which concern each family separately and each family in seeking to enlist God's aid and mercy attempts to establish a particular relation with Him which ignores, in this context, their fellowship with other men. They find a ready justification for these attitudes in the sacred form of family institutions referable to divine arche-types. In their simple and frankly pragmatic prayers it does not occur to them to pray for other men or suffering humanity. Yet they are aware that this is not the Christian ideal. They them-selves continually lament the degree of disunion, envy, and distrust, which separates unrelated men, and they derive from this source all the troubles of the community. They know that Christ sacrificed Himself not for one but for all. Not the least miracle of a Sarakatsan Easter is the measure of enjoined good-will. Unrelated men smile at one another, give away their milk on the Saturday of Easter to the poorer shepherds of their own com-munity, or to villagers, visit each other's homes on Easter Monday; simple gestures, but they represent an impressive reversal of the normal attitudes of distrust and tense aggressive-ness. But if, as these considerations suggest, the world of the Sarakatsani is at other times far from ideal, how are they yet able to represent themselves as men of nobility and honour. The answer to this lies in their conception of sin.

Man is separated from God by sin. Sarakatsani express this in the idea of 'a weight' (*varos*) which depresses the spirit and in a literal sense draws man downwards away from God. The Sarakatsani, however, make a distinction between two kinds of sin, personal sin (*oi amartīes mas*) and ancestral sin, or the sins of Adam. Both divide man from God but while the individual is wholly responsible for personal sins, he feels little sense of guilt for the other kind of sin which he sees as a condition of the world into which he was born.

The sins for which a man is individually responsible, and for which he merits the punishment of God, fall into three categories. The first includes those acts which are wanton and personal insults to God Himself, acts in which a man shows himself to be impious through denial or mockery of God. Perjury is the greatest of these; for in this act a man calls on God to witness the truth of his words, that is, he attempts the impossible task of implicating God as a collaborator in his own sin. Although the Sarakatsanos lies as a matter of habit and policy at other times, it is only in situations of extreme difficulty that he will perjure himself.

The second category of personal sin relates to family life and especially to certain fundamental and axiomatic attitudes and duties on which the moral solidarity of the family institution is based. The family for the Sarakatsanos is not merely a human and social group, it is a complex of relations divinely instituted and sanctioned by God. The Holy Family of God the Father, the Mother of Christ, and Christ the Son is on a transcendent and spiritual plane, the archetype for all earthly families. As love, respect, compassion relate the three Holy Persons, so these qualities ought to regulate the relations of the members of earthly families. Where this is not so there is a condition of sin and God's punishment may be confidently awaited. Thus this category of sin includes the unnecessary brutality of fathers towards small children; provoking a premature separation of sons' households; laziness or dereliction of duty which leads a family into serious want; in that sense gambling or chronic drunkenness; public insult to a parent by a son or daughter; maltreatment of aged parents; striking a parent; physical violence between brothers; wanton cruelty towards, or neglect of, the family's horses, sheep or goats.

The third category includes those sins which exist in the field of general morality in the behaviour of one man towards another. A man feels little obligation to discipline himself in his conduct towards an unrelated person, but there are limits which ought not to be transgressed, and generally speaking these limits are related to the consequences that immoderate behaviour would have for the victim's family. To exploit a very poor man, or refuse charity to a beggar, is sinful. To slander the name of an unmarried girl is a sin. In these instances there enters a hint of the idea of *hubris*, an arrogance of act, or thought, overstepping bounds set by God and involving wrong-doing to others which threatens the moral or physical existence of another family and is not excusable on grounds of essential self-interest.

Sin is wilful rebellion against God and His institutions. And for acts of personal sin a man may expect to be punished by God through sickness, death, or some catastrophe that leads his family into want and distress. Sarakatsani visualize the punishment of God as being realized essentially in this world either against themselves, or their children. Hell is a place of vaporous darkness where sinful men suffer in cauldrons of pitch; Paradise is a plain of well-watered grass covered with spring flowers. These conceptions exist, yet seem to make little impression. If an evil man dies unpunished, men are not content with thoughts of the torments he may suffer in Hell; they concentrate their attention on the misfortunes that will certainly overtake his children in this world. The wages of sin is death. But it is not the spiritual death which follows physical death which holds any real terror for the Sarakatsanos, but rather the spiritual death which precedes physical death. For sin interrupts the communion between man and God on whose provision and protection a man and his family are, in the final analysis, entirely dependent. The consistency between this view of divine punishment and the system of prestige values is clear enough. In both cases it is the events of this life, and this world, which are significant.

On the other hand, the Sarakatsani do not expect to be punished individually in the same way for ancestral sin. For this kind of sin refers to the general human condition not to individual transgression of particular interdictions. The two sins they particularly include under this rubric are sensuality and envy. Both are conditions which imply an attachment to material things which leads man away from a concern for his spiritual relationship with God. It is equally inevitable that every man must succumb, in some degree, to both these sins. However, the attitude to sensuality and envy is not precisely the same. The consequences of sensuality destroy the integrity and honour of the family. Sensuality is a condition which constantly threatens to undermine this institution from within. It must, therefore, be disciplined by all the strength and will of each man and woman. Even in marriage sexual activity is something 'out of alignment' (*anapodo*). In some way it pollutes. After sleeping with his wife a shepherd ought to wash his hands before milking a ewe, a sacred animal. Intercourse must occur in darkness, without speech, and the woman must remain motionless and passive. Conversely virginity is a quality that provokes the deepest respect and a sense almost of awe. It is obligatory for maidens and preferred in youths. The noble *pallikari*, the self-disciplined warrior youth, as yet innocent of sexual experience with women, presents the Sarakatsan ideal.

Unlike the protestant puritan who attempts to win his battle by destroying sensuality itself, and feels individually responsible and guilty when he fails, the Sarakatsanos accepts that sensuality is part of the human condition, but that he must struggle to contain and discipline it. The important restraints are essentially external. Unmarried men and women, who are not kinsmen or affines, have few legitimate opportunities to meet, and none where they may speak to one another. The unmarried daughter seldom goes to the well alone, and when she passes a man on the path she lowers her eyes. It is a tight prudential control, collectively exercised. As the Sarakatsani say, 'If you put your hand in the fire, it gets burnt.' A man of God may win an individual and inward control over the condition of sensuality, but ordinary men need the help of kinsmen and the support of institutions in the unequal fight. Sensuality is part of ancestral sin and as such a man or woman does not feel individually guilty for its existence. But it remains a threat to honour. And in this respect the struggle to control it is so fundamental to the belief in their own nobility that in a community where masculine values are paramount it has led the Sarakatsani to a form of sexual dualism in which women must bear the main responsibility for this collective sin. In this context woman has a natural predisposition to evil. Her powers of sexual attraction are of a supernatural order. Even unconsciously she may lure a man to disaster without a glance or gesture. But through self-discipline and shame she may redeem her condition in bearing noble sons who will protect the honour of family and race. Although the grim consequences[7] of a breach of sexual propriety obviously cannot be reconciled with Christian teaching this general Sarakatsan view of sexuality is not entirely inconsistent with the moral prescriptions of the Church. But an important difference remains. In terms of honour the problem is a question of self-discipline and the conservation of a reputation for maidenly or faithful conduct; in terms of religious values sensuality is part of the fallen condition of the world and must therefore be referred to ancestral sin.

Envy, however, does not threaten the family in the same way from within, nor does it conflict with the values of honour and pride. Indeed, the emphasis on competitive values, the need to achieve identity with ideal types of social personality, the competitive opposition of family groups, are social values and relationships which inevitably breed envy. Like the fingers on a hand, all men are not the same, Sarakatsani explain. Those who are less fortunate, or less evidently honourable, must envy those others who surpass them. Envy, they admit, leads directly to deceit and cunning. In the form of the evil eye it is a force of psychic hostility and wickedness which pervades the world, spiritually separating man from man, and man from God. Focussed through the eyes of an envious man, it may create physical effects of sickness and destruction. These things, it is agreed, are evil, but they arise from the external conditions of a world of limited resources and contrary human wills, not from the conscious sinfulness of individual men. The force of envy is felt to be so pervasive that it would be futile to struggle to control it, as one must struggle to control sensuality; particularly since a man may put the evil eye on another without conscious knowledge or intention. All that an honourable man can do in these circumstances is to avoid in his conscious actions the consequences of excessive envy. Since the family is, after all, a copy, admittedly imperfect, of a divine form, and since each man has a sacred duty to respect the institution as such, but also to struggle to support his own group, it is inevitable that he must fall between these two obligations and sin in this way. The Sarakatsani are fully aware of the dilemma. There is grudging admiration for the expertise of the shrewd, scheming, leader but regret that the means to success must be these. The word *kakos*,[8] bad or evil, is sometimes used to indicate a skilful man, especially in operations where cleverness or cunning is required. And *kalos*, good, in some contexts of character description may refer to a man who is merely weak and irresolute.

In this manner the Sarakatsani, through their view of ancestral sin, reconcile the nobility of man which is a premise of the values of honour, with his sinfulness which his sense of complete dependence on God imposes on him. Nobility depends on the struggle of the individual to achieve ideal patterns of being and behaviour. The sins which produce feelings of individual guilt and, therefore, directly qualify the nobility of his nature, do not constitute an impressive list, and they are transgressions which the Sarakatsani do not easily commit. On the other hand, the ancestral sins recognised by the Sarakatsani are general forms of sin which the Orthodox Church holds to be peculiarly grave and, moreover, sins which the Sarakatsani are continually committing; in the instance of sensuality because they are human, and in the case of envy because the social institutions and values encourage it. Yet the Sarakatsanos avoids any personal responsibility for these sins by insisting that they are exterior to his individual will. They corrupt the condition in which he must live, but not the potentialities of his nature. Sensuality was the consequence of Adam's sin, not his. Envy was the sin of the Devil in his act of rebellion against God.

Nevertheless these are sins which separate man from God. If they provoke no sense of personal guilt, a man feels a heaviness, a depression of his spirit, when he thinks of his need to be near God, and of this inherited condition of sinfulness. In this situation it requires the grace of God, conferred through the sacraments of Baptism and the Eucharist, to make communion possible. Inevitably if a child dies unbaptized, innocent of the world but still implicated in the appalling consequences of original sin, its soul is lost. The baptized Sarakatsanos is free of the original guilt, yet participation in the world of sin again separates him from God and he requires, therefore, the periodical renewal of his state of grace which the Eucharist effects.

In this resolution of their difficulties the critical importance of the Passion of Christ is clear to the Sarakatsani. In becoming a man like themselves He asserted the essential nobility of men. And in His death His blood effected a union between man and God which overcame the separating barrier of ancestral sin.

Each Easter at the climactic moment when the cry, 'Christ is risen', is heard, they know that His liberating blood will always be at hand to save them from abandonment to the Devil.

The fitness of Christ for this role lies in His origin from God the Father on the one hand and His human mother on the other. 'He was a man, then, like us' it is said both in folk tales and in comment on the events of His life. From His mother the divine Son of God took on a condition, in all respects, like that of man, except that through His virgin birth He remained outside sin. Born of a virgin, a virgin in His life, it needed the sacrifice of a Being, divine, human, exposed to sin yet untouched by it, to bring man and God together. In their own experience the Sarakatsani see the reflection of the sufferings of Christ. From the moment of His birth He was persecuted and humiliated, yet He did not lose dignity or nobility. Nor in similar circumstances, the Sarakatsani believe, do they. 'Christ is our brother', they sometimes say. He made the first shepherd's flute. He rounded up the wild goats, beasts of the Devil, and tamed them by placing His seal on the joints of their forelegs. He stands always by their side. They have only to think of Him and make the sign that recalls His sacrifice.

The wine of Holy Communion is at one and the same time a symbol of the first sacrifice and a material substance in which divine energy exists. It represents and it is the blood of Christ. If he is properly prepared to receive the sacrament a man's sins are forgiven. But the receipt of the sacrament is not a passive act. Men must give some pledge of their will to turn to God during the preceding days, by sincere repentance, fasting, continence, and goodwill. For a period, at least, the hold of material things and the senses is loosened.

The related elements in Sarakatsan religious life, then, are simply these: the nobility of the Sarakatsani; ancestral sin in the forms of sensuality and envy for which they are not individually responsible; the consequences of this condition of sin which tends always to separate them from God; and the sacraments which from time to time reunite them to Him.

3 *The Devil*

Over against God stands the Devil, the agent and first cause of evil. Evil, the Sarakatsani believe, entered the universe through his contrary and rebellious will, particularly in the form of envy. His object is simply to turn men away from God or, where this is not possible, to destroy them physically.

'The Devil has many feet,' the Sarakatsani say, that is he works out his evil in many ways, assuming whatever physical appearance is suitable for his purpose. His power is immense and particularly in the wilderness of the mountains and forests outside the circle of men's homes protected by the grace of God; but even these he sometimes enters. In keeping with his degenerate nature, he appears frequently in the form of an animal, particularly as a black dog, donkey or hare. Sometimes he is half man, half animal, with horned head of a goat or wild pig. When he assumes human form it is generally as an old man with a face black 'like an Arab's' and lame. In one instance he appeared as an Orthodox priest in red robes. Often he pretends to be a Sarakatsanos.

Some manifestations of the Devil are plural and of either sex. Bands of male demons (*satanaraioi*) with their leader the black-faced limping Devil sometimes surround and torment a lonely shepherd. The female demons are referred to as the 'ladies of good fortune' (*oi kalotyches*), a propitiatory euphemism which indicates their power. Like their masculine counterparts, these ladies prefer the mountain tops and forests or a lonely meadow in the plain. Very often they join the male demons in an orgiastic feast, the ladies of good luck wearing long white dresses, the men in kilts of the same colour. On a night when there is wind one often hears the Devil's music in the high crags. Otherwise when they are not feasting or provoking humans they pass their time eternally spinning, and very occasionally one comes across a spindle-weight[9] which one of them has dropped.

Devils come from and disappear into the air which is thickly populated with spirits both good and evil, although in the imagination of the Sarakatsani the evil forms predominate. One of the tasks of Christ on earth was to cleanse the air of evil spirits so that the souls of men could find a way upwards to God. High winds, storms, whirlwinds, are manifestations of demonic power. Evil spirits of the air (*ta aerika*) may attack men and animals invisibly or without taking a more definitive form than a passing shadow. Two considerable classes of these spirits are 'the shadows' (*ta iskiomata*) and 'the things that terrify' (*ta skiasmata*).[10] After dark the former beat men and women about the head and are the cause of pains in the head and teeth. They take hold of your arm or foot and twist it sharply. The latter often attack the sheep which in panic rush in different directions, injuring one another and losing milk.

In general, the frustrated enmity of the Devil and his attendant spirits is directed physically against the bodies of the Sarakatsani and their animals. If the Devil falls on the sheep and mounts them, they swell, bleed and die. If he comes on a shepherd asleep, particularly under a fig or mulberry tree, he presses down with great weight on his chest and attempts to strangle him. The 'ladies of good fortune' may attack a woman who goes out alone to cut wood, with the possible consequences of paralysis or loss of speech. But the greatest peril is that one may step, unknowingly, on the table (*patas tavla*) which a group of male and female demons have laid for a feast. One woman who had this misfortune was found unconscious on the mountainside. She remained in a deep coma, shrinking physically, until she died after forty days the size of a small child.

But the persons in greatest danger from direct assault by the Devil are 'the innocent' (*athooi*), particularly children and young unmarried shepherds. For the innocent person 'does not work in his heart', he does not require to plot or scheme against others, his being is not seized by envy and jealousy, he is quiet, detached and free. The Devil unable yet to corrupt him morally, turns in a fury of frustration to destroy him physically. Recently a small boy was found dead with his hands over his face and no mark of injury on his body. He was not wearing a phylactery and nobody doubts that this was an assault of the Devil. A young shepherd sleeping on a hillside awoke to see a Sarakatsanos with a mule approaching him from a precipice where no man or animal could pass. There was a moon and he saw that the man's face was black. He said he was Michael Raftis but the shepherd knew he was the Devil. Fortunately he was using as a pillow a bag of salt, an apotropaic substance of the greatest value. By keeping his head on this pillow and refusing to speak he passed the night in safety. In any appearance of the Devil the essential precaution is to remain absolutely silent whatever the provocation or enticement. Once a man has entered into communion with him through speech he cannot resist his will. The least consequence, then, is the loss of speech; but more probably the shepherd is led to his death over the edge of a precipice. These apparitions of the Devil are relatively common and most shepherds claim to have had at least one experience of this terrifying kind.

Fortunately God has provided the Sarakatsani with a variety of prophylactic means to resist most forms of demonic assault. Some of these are magic substances with apotropaic power, others are symbolic objects, words or rituals through which the grace of God confronts and defeats the power of evil. The Devil cannot approach salt or pass fire. The exorcisms of St Basil the Great and St John Chrysostom are read by the priest over possessed persons or animals. Thornbush, a cross of boxwood, incense, are powerful repellants. The red egg that is dyed on the Thursday of Holy Week, or the head of a viper that has been sanctified at forty liturgies in church, is buried in the sheepfold to protect the animals. A powerful protection for a woman who is approached by the 'ladies of good fortune' is a black-handled knife, particularly when formed as a cross with its scabbard. A shot from a pistol or rifle when fired with the left hand dismisses any apparition. In one instance a child's phylactery contained the dried blood of a priest shot by Communists. But perhaps the most efficient protection in an armoury which this miscellany does not exhaust, is simply the sign of the cross and the silent repetition of the thought, 'I see Christ, I see Christ, I see Christ.'

God and the Devil fight a pitiless and continuing battle for the souls of men in which the three elements are the grace of God, the cunning and subtlety of the Devil, and the will of man. The Sarakatsani consider man's nature to be a trichotomy of spirit (*pnevma*), soul (*psychē*), and body (*kormi, soma*). Although the views of different informants are not always clear about these conceptions (for instance some people see no difference between spirit and soul) nevertheless certain simple assumptions appear to be generally accepted. Spirit and soul together form a union with the body, yet between the first two elements and the last there is a degree of tension. The body is a product of material and sexual generation and is only redeemed when it is informed by a nobility of spirit and soul. Conversely, when the spirit and soul are dependent on the values and passions of the body, honour is lost and communion with God is interrupted. Spirit refers to the intellect plus the conscience. Its natural inclination is to prompt a man's will (*thelēsē*) to lead his soul upwards to God. It is associated in a man's mind with the Holy Spirit whose nature is imperfectly understood as some divine energy. Evil befalls where for one reason or another the power of a man's spirit is not guiding his actions. Of a Sarakatsanos who shot his brother accidentally while cleaning a pistol it was said that 'his spirit was not concentrated'. And it was added, 'the Devil pulled the trigger'. The soul is the divine element in the individual human personality. Perhaps spirit and soul are the active and substantive aspects of the same thing. Both strive in an upward direction, but if the individual as a total personality does not incline his will towards God they become corrupted by their union with merely material things; and this is the end sought by the Devil.

It may be added that where a high value is given to the related notions of honour, strength, and manliness, the body cannot be considered as evil in itself, but only under the aspect of its subjection to sensual passion. Man, then, who is by nature noble normally moves towards a closer communion with God but is held back partly by the sinful condition of the world in which he lives, and sometimes more seriously by the turning of his free will away from God. God will come to a man's aid when he asks for it with a 'good heart', but he cannot join the fight unless man wills it. It is on this contingency that the Devil's opportunity and power depend.

In a fallen world the temptation to have, at least, occasional dealings with the Evil One is very great. The Sarakatsani believe that if a man is willing to deny Christ, almost any material favour is possible. Not unnaturally unusual prosperity tends to be explained in this way by less fortunate individuals. Similarly, sexual temptation by the Devil is expressed in the belief that the Devil is able to have sexual intercourse with women in their sleep and that 'ladies of good fortune', who are peculiarly beautiful even if their hair is sometimes in the form of snakes, try to entice lonely shepherds into 'marriage'. These generally are the explanations accepted for erotic dreams in either sex.

One of the Devil's chief concerns is to corrupt those relationships of kinship and marriage which are instituted by God. His success is, of course, more likely where there are inherent strains, particularly between the wives of brothers still living in an extended family, and sometimes between the brothers themselves. When one man attacked and nearly strangled his brother, people said, 'The Devil has entered into him', and they meant this in a quite literal sense. When the shepherds hear of a case of father daughter incest among the villagers of Thesprotia, they can only understand such an enormity as a plot of the Devil.

It must be emphasized, however, that the sins into which a man is led by the Devil's temptation always possess a certain reference to external agency. If a man has sinned in a way not easily understandable it is said, 'The Devil pushed him.' A man by not placing his whole trust in God, inclines his desires towards material and sensual attachments. He is, then, as it were, physically unable to resist the Devil who chooses the sin, and sets the scene of temptation in the knowledge that his victory is assured. But the sin by which the man is tempted is the work of the Devil. Through these modes of thought the Sarakatsani are able to appreciate themselves as an essentially noble and God-fearing community struggling under the limitations of the human condition which, so far as the physical and political environment is concerned, they are able to represent as being, in their case, peculiarly severe.

The definitive loss of the soul to the Devil is the basis of the appearance of *vrykolakes*, the bodies of dead men and women which return from the grave in a hideous distended form often to terrify members of their own family. They are persons whose lives were corrupted in sin, committed suicide, drowned or were unbaptized; or persons whose bodies were not guarded by their kinsmen in the period between death and burial, or whose bodies although guarded were leaped over by a cat. In these various ways, and particularly in the first, the soul is lost to the Devil. Instead of departing through the mouth (as some imagine it in the form of a small bird) and rising to God, it passes through the anus to the Devil. And since the body and soul, whatever the internal tension between them, form a unity, the body also falls into the power of the Devil, remains undissolved in the earth, and possessed by the spirit of the Devil emerges from its grave to mock at the sacred institutions of family life by attacking or terrifying those to whom it owed, in life, the greatest obligations.

A person known to have the evil eye (*to kako mati*), 'has an eye infected by the Devil'. In a sense, the envy of men expressed in the belief in the evil eye is the great triumph of the Devil;

firstly, because it implies a whole complex of vices including enmity, greed and deceit; and secondly, because without the Devil requiring to set any particular temptations almost all Sarakatsani, in their pursuit of the elusive and competitive ends of prestige with their mixture of spiritual and material values, are necessarily involved in this form of sin. They succeed in avoiding individual guilt for it, but they cannot deny their collective responsibility, nor can they ignore the existence of the barrier which it represents between themselves and God.

A family attributes the majority of its misfortunes to this evil force. The range of effects attributed to its activity is wide. The diseases of sheep and other animals, almost all children's illness, and the sickness of adults, especially when it is accompanied by the onset of sudden pains in the body, may all be referred to the evil eye. A woman is anxious if another sees her kneading the dough for her bread; for, then, it may not rise. The impotence of a bridegroom may be the result of the evil eye of a woman with an unmarried daughter. The force behind this action of the eye is the attraction of things which are envied (*zēlevta pramata*). And it is significant that the two things most important for social prestige, children and sheep, are the two things most prone to attack. It is men who are prosperous, or more especially men, in a sense, too prosperous, or lucky, who stand in particular danger. It does not please a man to be told by another that his sheep are in excellent condition. Praise and admiration, it is thought, indicate the desire of the admirer (which may be quite unconscious) to possess what is pleasing to his eyes. And since that is not possible, frustration is inevitably followed by envy.

Many substances are used as protective charms in the phylacteries of children, or tied to the tongues of sheep bells. Some of these operate sympathetically such as garlic, thistle, and pubic hairs. Others like a small wooden cross of boxwood, incense, a cross woven from flowers or a candle taken from the representation of the Tomb during Easter week, are objects with sacred connections that mediate protective power. If, despite these precautions, a person (or sheep) is bewitched, relief is generally found in a procedure which first identifies the possessor of the evil eye and then counteracts its influence. A bowl of water is taken and a hair of the bewitched person (or a strand of the sheep's fleece) is placed under the bowl. Small pieces of wood carbon are taken from the fire and after the surface of the water has been crossed three times the first fragment about the size of a small finger-nail is dropped into the water. The operator, who is almost always a woman, puts to the piece of carbon the name of a person she may suspect. If the carbon floats the person in question is not guilty, if it sinks one evil eye at least is known. If more than one eye is suspected the process is continued. When the operator is satisfied that the worst has been uncovered, the sick or otherwise afflicted person is crossed with the water in the bowl forty times on the brow, the hands, the feet, and the afflicted part, if pain or other symptoms are localized. Finally the patient drinks a little of the water from the bowl.

In putting names to the pieces of carbon the operator is guided by various considerations. Who, to her knowledge, has recently seen the afflicted person or animal? And, of these, who is generally noted for an envious nature, or has a reputation for unconscious bewitching, or is simply disliked by herself and her family? If none of these proves to be guilty, other names chosen at random are put to the carbon. But this rarely happens. In practice about one fragment of carbon in every five sinks. Therefore the guilty person almost invariably is among those whom the operator considers to be likely possessors of the evil eye. And this confirms the validity of the procedure.

It is not, of course, strange that the envy of the evil eye is associated with the Devil. Envy is inherent in the material world of limited resources and numerous contrary wills. Lacking what another possesses and thinking of that rather than of his relation to God, a man is easily led by the Devil to destroy what he himself has not. This tendency is so inherent in the nature of the situation that even kinsmen and affines bewitch one another, although such is the strength of the moral element in these relationships that the effects are not believed to be produced with conscious intention. And it is interesting to note that honour and the quality of being honourable, which suggest the ideal equality of members of the community and the conception of the Sarakatsani as men united in the desire to live in accordance with honour, do not of themselves necessarily lead to envy between men, for they are spiritual values of a kind; on the other hand, those elements of prestige which inevitably differentiate men and possess a pronounced material aspect, wealth, numbers, marriages, dowries and so on, are precisely the values competition for which must breed envy in those who are not successful.

4 *An opposition of values*

The problem of the opposition of two systems of values, one social, the other religious, has yet to be explicitly considered. On the one hand, we have social values of honour, prestige, strength, and pride with their exclusive and particularist reference to the individual and his family; on the other, is the community's wider membership of an Orthodox Christian culture. Contradictions and inconsistencies, of course, exist in the values and beliefs of many societies. The difficulty for the Sarakatsani is that they affirm so unambiguously that existence has only two aspects of transcendent value, honour and dependence on God. Inconsistency at the centre of such a simple philosophy of life is not so easy to tolerate. And although it is true that the relationship of the Sarakatsani to the Orthodox Church, as an institution, has been sufficiently tenuous to result in a popular religious life that is a gross refraction of Orthodox dogma and practice, yet the value of the Christian ideal of the fellowship of all men in Christ, with the universalist ethical values that follow from it, is not to be avoided. How is this opposition of values resolved or accommodated?

There is no great problem of fellowship between Sarakatsani who are related by kinship or marriage. By associating The Father, The Son, and The Mother of God in a holy archetype family, the institutions and relationships of the Sarakatsan family, even the concept of honour and the duty to defend it, are given a categorical quality and a divine sanction; and by extension kindred and affinal bonds receive a similar validation. It is true that even within this restricted circle certain Christian values cannot enjoy a general application. Modesty, meekness, humility are values only admirable for women. Some Christian prescriptions have to be entirely set aside. One ought not to forgive a kinsman who has betrayed his trust, at least until he is dead. And to protect the prestige of his family a man must avoid the company of a kinsman who is despised for his poverty. The poor are not blessed. Yet love, mutual trust, truth, and altruism are important Christian virtues which are the ideal values of Sarakatsan family and kinship life. Men would extend the circle of their application if they could, but the conditions of life in a fallen world prevent this, particularly limited resources, the divinely sanctioned honour and interests of a man's own family, the condition of envy.

But in their commitment to the concept of honour as the guiding principle of behaviour, the Sarakatsani cannot admit themselves to be anything but noble; and this must be said not only of the soul but the body also, for honour is related to physical strength and manliness when this is disciplined and spiritualized. The original guilt for sin must be placed elsewhere. This is the role of the Devil. Sensuality was the sin of Adam, but only after this had been thought of and presented to him by the Devil with the assistance of woman. Envy, the more fundamental sin, was originally the cause of the Devil's rebellion against God. 'The Devil envied God,' the Sarakatsani say. Indeed the Devil is the symbol and the efficient cause of all those many tensions and hostilities which prevent the Sarakatsani from living in the values of Christian fellowship. Not only is he the original cause of the miasma of ancestral sin, the provoker of the evil eye and the tempter to sexual lusts, but in his desire to injure physically where he cannot corrupt morally his action on the spiritual plane parallels the mutual hostilities and social isolation which each family experiences in social life. In this way the Sarakatsani avoid personal guilt for their own implication in these sins. Even in the case of personal sins for which individual guilt is admitted, Sarakatsani would say that the fault of the man was in the act of turning away from God, not in the sin itself. For without the grace of God he cannot resist the Devil who then leads his victim to the sin he has chosen for him.

However, just as children inherit responsibility for the sins of their parents, the responsibility for the sins of Adam cannot be avoided. The condition of sin in which a man lives, although it is exterior to his individual will, interrupts his communion with God on which life and honour depend. It is in this situation that Christ comes to save men pouring out the sacrifice of His blood to reunite man with God, a salvation, however, which is contingent on man freely turning from the Devil towards God. In a certain sense, then, these forms of sin are a kind of pollution, for which the Devil is originally guilty and responsible, and from which Christ is the saviour. But this analogy must not be pressed too far. This salvation requires moral action on the side of man. In his daily life he must struggle to discipline sensuality and he must avoid the ultimate consequences of envy. For, the fact that all earthly families are imperfect copies of a divine archetype places a limit on the amoral ruthlessness that unrelated men may show towards one another in circumstances where such conduct seriously and unnecessarily endangers the existence of another family. And at certain periods of religious celebration, such as Christmas, Easter, and the feast of Assumption, the sins of Adam must be altogether suppressed through universal continence, goodwill, and the symbolic sharing of food.

Thus, in one way, Christian beliefs are accommodated with the particularist values of honour and prestige through the idea of the holy archetype family. The institutions of family life and honour are thereby sanctified. At the same time the sanctity of the family marks a limit to the ways in which one man may exploit another. A poor man may not be cheated of his bread, nor the name of an unmarried maiden be slandered. Each family in relative isolation faces the majority of the community with sentiments of hostility and envy. These are not, in the Sarakatsan view, inherent in the nature of the values of prestige and honour but are a consequence of life in a fallen world and a concoction of the Devil, their original author. It is the Devil who schemes to separate family from family, who prevents men from achieving their natural union in relation to God, and consequently interrupts communion between God and man. It is Christ who from time to time through the sacrifice of His blood saves the Sarakatsani, not only in His love and pity for them as sinners but also in free recognition of their innate nobility of soul.

NOTES

1 A more extended discussion of the concept of honour is included in my book, *Honour, Family, and Patronage* (Oxford 1964) chapter 10 *passim*. I am grateful to the Delegates of the Clarendon Press for permission to use material from this source. I also wish to thank

Professor E. E. Evans-Pritchard and Dr Rodney Needham who read this essay in manuscript.

2 In his family of origin the individual is a child and a sibling; in the family of marriage a spouse and a parent.

3 See R. B. Onians *Origins of European Thought* (Cambridge 1951) pp. 48, 121.

4 *Cf.* below, pp. 166–7.

5 I refer here to the relation between a man's true intention (*ie* his purpose known certainly only in his own conscience) and his public reputation for honour. On the other hand, intentions imputed to a man by public judgement are of critical importance particularly in situations where his behaviour may bear more than one interpretation.

6 Although the Sarakatsani use the adjective *philotimos* to describe a person who 'loves honour', they do not use the substantive *to philotimo*, a 'sense' of this honour, which is a concept of popular thought extremely common in many parts of Greece. It is clear, however, that *egoismos* is a close analogue.

7 An unmarried girl discovered in a premarital affair ought to be killed by her father or brother; similarly an adulterous wife by her husband.

8 *Cf.* Carsten Höeg *Les Saracatsans, Étude Linguistique* (Paris and Copenhagen 1926) vol. 2, p. 168.

9 On the sites of prehistoric settlements.

10 See Angelicke Chatzimichalis, *Sarakatsanoi* (Athens 1957) vol. 1, Part A, p. ρλθ″. [In Greek.]

J. G. Peristiany

HONOUR AND SHAME IN A CYPRIOT HIGHLAND VILLAGE

Honour and Shame in a Cypriot Highland Village*

Honour and shame are two aspects of an evaluation. An evaluation implies the possibility of choice within an accepted hierarchy of values controlled by taxonomic ideals. An ideal held in common by two actors provides a basis for evaluation, communication and prediction. It provides a common value language. What is the scale of values in which honour and shame are reflected, in what contexts they are invoked, what groups are affected by these evaluations will, then, be the main concern of this paper.

The three social categories with which a Greek identifies himself most readily are the family, the community of origin and the nation. They provide, in most contexts, the duality necessary for differentiation, for the cleavage – and opposition – between the Us and the They. I hope to show that most identifications and oppositions assume either of these forms.

Although I believe that some of my statements may be applicable to communities other than the one with which I was personally concerned they did arise from observations made in Cyprus in one particular village where I spent six months in 1954 with the most generous help of the Nuffield Foundation. It will, therefore, not seem out of place if I sketch in the background of my frame of reference.

There are twenty-two villages on the western slopes of Mount Tröodos which are known by the collective name of Pitsilia, their inhabitants being known as Pitsilloi. Pitsilia is not an administrative division; the common name is a recognition of the distinctive characteristics which are said to single out the inhabitants of this area. The Pitsilloi take pride in the belief that they are the purest

* This paper refers, in the present tense, to the economic, political and social situations as they were in 1954.

Greek Cypriots – racially and linguistically. The other Cypriots point to them as a repository and the living embodiment of the traditional values of manliness, perseverence, hardihood and generosity. At the same time the name of the area was associated with squalor and backwardness, an accusation which the Pitsilloi impute to the inaccessibility of their villages (the first car arrived in the central village in the nineteen-twenties). In the characteristic manner of turning blame into praise, the Pitsilloi claim that the inaccessibility and unworldliness of their villages made them places of refuge under Turkish domination. Some of these villages were included in the royal domains of the French Lusignan dynasty and in this area are to be found some of the most impressive Cypriot Renaissance chapels and frescoes.

The village I know best is the village of Alona. It has only 650 inhabitants and the small size of its population made it possible to establish contacts with most of its inhabitants and to follow their social activities with some knowledge of the nature of their kinship and other bonds. This village acted for many centuries as the religious and cultural centre of eastern Pitsilia, providing priests and schooling for a large section of this area. At the same time its economic and social problems are representative of those encountered in this part of Cyprus.

The elevation of Alona (3,500 ft), the rocky nature of its soil, the extremes of temperature, the poverty of its water supply and the erosion of its soil which followed the merciless deforestation by both peasants and some of their ex-rulers limit not only the number of crops which may be grown here but also necessitate that a balance be preserved between the remunerative but time and capital consuming crops and those which need less water and a more modest outlay of capital and labour.

The main source of cash income is the hazelnut. The hazelnut bushes grow at the foot of a deep ravine at the foot of the village. Bacon curing, wine, almonds and grapes come next in importance. The average net income of each family from these sources was under £77 per year. From this income the villager has to pay his taxes, buy wheat as well as, in order of importance, beans, oil, shoes and clothing. He also has to provide a dowry for his daughter and fees for the secondary education of his son. Two of the results of the attractiveness of education have a direct effect both on the social morphology of this area, and on the problems with which this paper is concerned. This unanimous desire for education not only forces the parents to part with their holdings or to engage in forms of work which are considered as undignified but may make marriage more difficult and in many cases improbable – for a large number of maidens. Indeed, the young men who have spent long periods in towns, where the secondary schools are located, are attracted by city life and wish to live there permanently. After the completion of their studies, their first requirement is a cash dowry which will permit them to acquire in the city a plot of land on which to build their home. In order to provide for these dowries the peasants have to sell their land, but parcelling, the constant rise of wages and the relative cheapness of their products in relation to the rising value of other goods renders their land almost valueless. Many of the girls over eighteen years of age are still unmarried and the marriage market has now become so competitive that punctiliousness concerning questions of female honour is as fierce as ever. At the same time not to provide for a daughter's marriage marks the failure of a man to live up to the expectations of his family and opens the way to a type of 'shame' which reflects on the close kinsmen of the unmarried female.

The salient feature of Cypriot administration under foreign government, that is for the past four centuries, has been direct rule. In most Cypriot villages (and in most of Pitsilia) authority is only represented by the Government headman and his assistants, all representing and all being directly appointed by the central authority. The government headman (*mukhtar*) is mainly responsible for acting as a link between the central authority and the villagers and he perceives – or, rather, he is entitled to perceive – some registration dues on the transfer of animals, while his assistants receive fees for attending boundary disputes.

Apart from the headman, who is often more feared than considered, the most respected office holders are the priest and the teacher. They are often known not by their personal name but by their calling. The priest represents in the eyes of the Greek community, not only the autocephalous church of Cyprus, but the only legitimate authority. Since the end of the twelfth century, that is after the end of Byzantine rule and the instauration of a Frankish kingdom, political authority has been linked in the mind of Greek Cypriots with rule by foreigners who – until British occupation – were considered not only as enemies of the local inhabitants but also as enemies of the Church. In 1260 Pope Alexander IV issued the *Bulla Cypria* which raised the Latin Archbishop to the position of supreme head of Latins and Orthodox. As a result the Cypriot Church was dispossessed of its properties and firmly subordinated to the Latin clergy. The Turks – phenomenon common to the Eastern Orthodox world – revived some of the privileges of the Orthodox Church but, as Moslems, they remained within the category of enemies of the faith. Under Turkish domination the Church in both Greece and Cyprus was responsible for teaching the Greek language and the Orthodox faith and for keeping alive the spirit of Greek identity. Indeed the Greek language and the Orthodox faith are so intimately interconnected that the Greek Cypriots find it difficult to differentiate between them. All westerners to this day are called *Frangoi* – they are persons who, however openly their other qualities might be admired, are not to be trusted in questions affecting one's spiritual salvation or even in matters of earthly honour. A Greek is a Greek insofar as he is an Orthodox; when he is a member of another Christian church he is said to be not a Greek but a Frank. The priest is, therefore, always a firm believer in the Enosis movement, as Enosis, to him, means the reunion of the temporal and the spiritual which have been artificially disjointed. He is also a firm propagandist for the conservative party which is identified with the Enosis movement. In Alona the task of the priest was simplified by the unanimity of political opinion – all the inhabitants being pro-Enosis conservatives. The priest is not only in the main stream of the struggle for liberation but, in contradistinction to the government headman, he is freely chosen by the village community in the same way as the Archbishop of Cyprus is chosen by the laity. Thus the priestly office and the values it represents are both enduring and actual.

The authority and power to shape opinion of headman, priest and teacher is unassailable, each in his own sphere, when they co-operate or, at least, as long as their disagreements are not openly vented. When this happens the cleavage of opinion and of interest show clearly the spheres of competence proper to each office. The ideal headman, as understood by the villagers, is the one who uses least his government derived authority and prerogatives as only this restraint enables the villagers to forget the stigma of the foreign derivation of his authority. To act as a government agent is to act as the representative of a foreign authority – foreign not only in its more literal sense but also in that of a city – not of a village – controlled executive. It is only when the headman has quarrelled with his fellow villagers and turned a deaf ear to the advice of School and Church that he accepts this role of 'foreigner'. When this happens those amongst the peasants whose interests make them more dependent on town and government goodwill compromise with the headman and find a *modus vivendi* which, while protecting their interests, makes them, through their silence during governmental visits of inspection, accomplices of the *krimata*, the 'iniquities', of the headman. In a context of local strife the teacher may also be reduced to a passive role as, being a government servant, he may be disinclined to quarrel with the local government authority. In this situation only the priest is relatively free to represent – and to act in the interest of – his parishioners.

Apart from these three office holders the most respected members of the community are those who are said to come from families which on both the paternal and maternal side are noted for their respectability (*entimotēta*). In addition it is required of them that they behave like *archontes*. *Archontas* has the connotation of leadership, largess, nobility of manner and punctiliousness in all matters related to honour (*timē*). An *archontanthropos* is a man conscious of local tradition and prepared to identify himself completely and unwaveringly with its code of behaviour. In all matters in which the local values are antithetical to the values of the city or of the Franks the archontas must try and secure the greatest material advantage to his community without laying himself open to suspicion, the suspicion that he has identified himself with an alien status or an alien value. In this, as we shall see, he differs profoundly from the returned expatriate who shows skill as a mediator between city and village values but whose skill is not equated with honour.

The first lead in our understanding of 'honour' in this Greek Cypriot community is the fact that two value systems, here the rural and urban ones, cannot be bridged by translating the utility of the returned expatriate's knowledge (or wealth) into steps of the village scale of dignity. In Alona the returned expatriate who had achieved success in a city environment wished to trade on this success as a means of achieving immediate recognition in his village. The expatriate, that is, especially the one who had absented himself for long, considered that the single fact of having lived and worked in a town exalted him above his fellow villagers, and further that his financial success raised him above the confines of the village hierarchy. When attempting to translate his city status into degrees of village status the expatriate automatically assumes the superiority of the city scale, that is of achievement untempered by dignity, so that the lowest steps of the city ladder are made to correspond to the uppermost steps of the village scale of values. The patronizing attitude of the returned expatriate is seen by the villagers to rest not on an assertion of superiority within, and resting on, the village status system but as the assumption of the inapplicability of the village scale of values to the expatriate who transcends it through his association with the city. In anger at his behaviour the villagers sometimes ask an illuminating rhetorical question: what does he mean by strutting about in this manner? Does he take himself for a Frank? This is a reference to one of the main grudges of the Cypriots and perhaps of all foreign-administered people. It points to the deep-seated Cypriot belief that members of the ruling power, whatever their class provenance, assume automatically the attitude of superiors in their relations with the autochtones, their sole claim to superiority resting on the non-recognition of the local system of values due to the 'natural' transcendence of their own. Thus an expatriate is said 'to ape the ways of the Franks' in that, in his attempt to ascend rapidly the prestige hierarchy, he disregards the local moral system. The very opposite is true of the archon-like leaders who identify themselves in speech and action with the local conception of what is proper.

I shall now turn to the evaluation of honour and shame within the village and in so doing I shall first examine the village as a unit of moral evaluation and the segments of which the village is composed. As these basic segments are the constituent families, I shall relate honour and its antonym to age, sex and position within the family.

The basic word in this discussion is *timē*, meaning esteem, honour, dignity; also, as in classical times, social worth, ranking and value. *Philotimos* is said of the person inspired by self-respect, of a 'high-souled and generous person', a person animated by *megalophrosynē*, who places considerations concerning his good name, of his social image and of its social ranking above other – and more immediately profitable – considerations. *Atimos* is the condition of the person who lacks *timē*. If he does nothing to remedy this situation he is also *adiantropos*, that is he lacks shame, he is shameless. Having reached that stage, the stage in which he has lost his self-respect and disregards his social evaluation by others, he puts himself outside the moral order. He is a menace to the community as his actions are unpredictable.

The longer I remained in the field, the clearer it became to me that, in the context of the evaluation of conduct, the individual actor was conceived as the protagonist of a family and that the village was commenting upon and evaluating every action.

The Greek family is, and as far as we know has always been, bilateral with, I believe, a stress on patrilineality expressed, in Alona, with the greater formalism related to agnation, with the moral ascendancy of the male and with the surname, a recent innovation, which follows the paternal line. All evaluations affect the standing of a family in the village, that is of all those in the first instance who bear the same surname – and of the daughters, even after their marriage, when the evaluation refers to sexual modesty. At the same time there is a realignment of loyalties with each marriage as at that moment both bride and groom are endowed by their respective parents with a substantial share of their inheritance. In future their interests and loyalties will be in each other and in their children rather than in the families of their own parents or in those of their brothers or sisters. Thus two meanings are given here to the category 'family'. It is first used for agnates bearing the same surname. They are the *soï*. Anything reflecting on the surname they bear also affects them, but the distance from the actor is taken into consideration. Also, disregarding the affines, the family, *oikogeneia*, in the strict sense is composed of parents and children. This social group is most effective when the children are not yet married. It is to the smaller unit that I shall usually refer.

I consider the Alona family as a social isolate moving in a field of common values so that as one moves from family to village, from one's own village to that of one's neighbours and from there to the city and to the Franks, the moral vacuum increases. Economically the Alona family is self-sufficient to a degree. The herding, irrigation, vine- and tree-tending and ham curing, which are its main economic pursuits, do not necessitate the employment of external help. The home, except on rare festive occasions, is closed to non-kinsmen. Even outside the home relations with kinsmen, when no para-kinship relationship has been entered into, are fraught with suspicion as, if they are of an economic nature, the protection of the interests of self and family is expected as a matter of course and in most other face-to-face relations one has to guard against slights which, if disregarded, undermine a man's good name by holding it up to ridicule. The villagers share no common immovable property. The upkeep of the irrigation system necessitates little, if any, communal effort and the apportionment of water creates more ill-feeling than solidarity. The school is maintained by common contributions but these are assessed by a government appointee and the teachers are not chosen by the villagers. Of all local institutions the Church is nearest the heart of the people and the priest is chosen by the villagers but Church property is controlled by a see distant in both social and spatial terms. Finally, in a village solidly united under the national flag there are no political factions which might unite together a number of families and so provide a grouping intermediary between family and village in terms of collective self versus collective other. It is, then, possible to say that, within the village community, the family is the basic unit which acts for the preservation of its economic interests and of its moral integrity and that the assessment of these actions by village public opinion lays the foundation for the standing of the family in terms of the honour hierarchy.

Family relations follow a pattern of superordination-subordination between proximate generations, between elder brother and younger brother and, within the same generation, beween male and female. Mutuality between brothers decreases with age and reaches a low point at marriage and the death of the father, that is with increasing differentiation of personality and with growing obligations to mutually exclusive families. Since most economic matters have been settled before marriage and grandchildren form the growing point of their relationship, parents-in-law may gradually draw closer together. The opposite prediction may frequently be made concerning relations between brothers as these are marked by a series of oppositions and by gradual alienation.

The closest relations are those between the parental couple and their children and between these unmarried siblings. The first qualification for a man of honour is to be honoured in his own family.

The unmarried son in the presence of his father is expected to behave with the kind of decorum which singles out, through their prohibition, certain actions denoting equality of rank. Thus the son should rise when the father enters the room, leave the coffee-shop when his father enters it and discontinue a gambling game on noticing his father's presence. Even in the early years after marriage it is reprehensible for a son to smoke in his father's presence, to mention even platonic relations between the sexes or to venture an opinion indicative of a judgement in which his father had no share. To show disrespect towards one's father by publicly provoking or flouting his authority is said to be 'shame-ful'. The son himself is said to be 'shameless', to be lacking in 'the knowledge of what is good without which there is no shame' and his behaviour is said to 'shame' his father. The rigidity of this behaviour decreases with age and tends to become more egalitarian with the setting up of an independent home, and it may alter radically when the father is old and incapacitated. The economically and jurally independent son who continues through life to behave towards his father as though he were still under his authority is said to be inspired by *philotimo* and the son himself is said to be *philotimos*. This simple example points to the fact that the neglect of one's duty is sanctioned by a negative evaluation expressed by *ntropē*, shame, or by reference to *lack* of *philotimo*, the shame reflecting both on the actor and on the person humiliated by lack of consideration for his rank. On the other hand the simple fulfilment of the duties of filial piety does not entitle a man to be called *philotimos*. This term is reserved for those who act as ideal rather than as average persons.

We have seen that the non-recognition by the son of the respect owed to his father shames both the father and the son. A person may also be shamed, *ntropiazetai* or be deprived of honour, *xetimazetai*, by the unethical behaviour of the actor even when this is not directed against him. This is the case when the personality of the actor is not clearly differentiated from that of the person or group which he shames. It applies to subordinates or dependents whose actions are said to mirror those of their superior and to characteristics which are the collective property of the family and as such are to be defended against all comers. The main reference, here, is to feminine honour.

Woman's foremost duty to self and family is to safeguard herself against all critical allusions to her sexual modesty. In dress, looks, attitudes, speech, a woman, when men are present, should be virginal as a maiden and matronly as a wife. If it were possible to combine the concepts of virginity and motherhood the ideal married woman would be a married mother virginal in sensations and mind. It is as though we were moving in the field of ritual prohibitions for a maiden is defiled not only through contact or awareness through one of the senses but also through the unwitting arousal of desire. She may even be sullied if her name is constantly on the lips of men. The anachoretic, anti-sensate, anti-intellectual armoury with which the early fathers of the Church tried to undermine the Greek representation of mind and body and of their inter-relations is partly responsible for these attitudes. A woman who behaves according to the code of honour regulating the behaviour of her sex is said to be a *timia gynaika*, an honest woman and the expression *timēmenē* which refers not only to her honourability but to her being honoured, is frequently used. A woman of light virtue is said to be *atheophovē*, not God-fearing, *anomē*, lawless, *skylla*, a bitch, *adiantropē*, shameless, *xetsipotē*, skinless (this is connected with the popular saying that a woman has two 'skins', or shows her 'skin' to two persons only, the midwife and her husband, so that her honour would be sullied should anyone beside them see her body), thus a 'skinless' woman is a woman lost to all feeling of shame.

For an unmarried woman shame reflects directly on parents and brothers, especially unmarried ones, who did not protect or avenge her honour. The moment a woman is married these responsibilities pass to her husband. This transfer of responsibility is, perhaps, clearly seen from the fact that when, after the usual two- to three-year period of engagement the bride goes to her wedding an expectant mother, those who are mainly shamed are the wedding-sponsors who are said to *phoresan to stratouri*, that is to have been made to wear a saddle. Here again the metaphor of lawlessness, of animal-like behaviour is used.

The military imagery, full of castles, conquests and destructions, used for extra-marital relations is indicative of the lack of a scale of values common to both sexes. It is true that this does not apply to Greek Cypriots only. It is also true that in a country where feminine honour is almost exclusively associated with sexual modesty this attitude assumes a particularly violent and socially significant form. Feminine honour involves not only a woman's total personality but also that of the group she represents. This is apparent when the female is seen not only as the representative of her family and sex but as that of a hostile community or class.

Philotimo, it seems to me, is neither an inspiration nor a sanction of action in situations where the type of relations is so clearly structured as to allow but little freedom of choice. At the opposite pole this would apply to situations where a claim on personal relations being non-existent no standard of common evaluation may be used. If one could use as an example an imaginary village priest one might find that his advice was closely patterned on a rather narrow interpretation of the New Testament and of the rules of conduct laid down by the Fathers of the Church. Once or twice a week he would hold meetings whose main topic would be Body versus Soul. In this new manicheism all sensate, all body-inspired actions would be condemned as of doubtful inspiration unless they were ultimately validated by procreation within wedlock. But even this would leave smoking, drinking, dancing, games-playing and spectacle attendance within the satanic orb. This very same *papas*, in discussing local boys who made good abroad, would carefully examine their behaviour in relation to their family, their nation and their church, but he might not consider it necessary to examine publicly and in detail their business ethics.

If one mentioned in the same context a procurer practising in the same area he would be condemned outright by both priests and peasants. A man can sell firearms and remain a man. He may even be admired as a brave *tolmēros*, an adventurous man. But however far from his homeland and amongst whatsoever people he practises, a procurer is a *man* who has *abdicated* his manhood. He is *adiantropos*, he has no shame, no self-respect, he is *atimos*, he lacks honour, he is *tou klotsou kai tou mpatsou* – he is, that is, a man who may both metaphorically and actually be kicked and slapped with impunity. A person of this kind is said to lack *philotimo* and to be *aphilotimos*. The same may be said about a woman. Immodesty marks woman's abdication of her femininity, the betrayal of her nature and therefore of her divinely prescribed role, of her family of origin or marriage which, of necessity, entrusted her with its honour, that is with its most precious possession. It is also a betrayal of her community which will become the butt of ridicule for its neighbours. It matters not when or where she acted immodestly; the stigma, when known, will mark and diminish her in all social relations through time and space.

In the last two examples we have seen that honour ordains man and woman to behave in a certain way – mostly positive in the case of man, mostly negative and passive in the case of woman – whatever the context of the situation. Thus certain aspects of honour are sex-linked. In the first example we saw that it was not the action itself but its results, not the means but the ends, which were being evaluated. This occurred when the two actors were considered as two social isolates interacting in a neutral field of values. In such a context *homo homini lupus* and the more *lupus*, that is the more successfully self-seeking, the more *homo*. In order to have true isolates interacting in a neutral field of values, in order that conduct might be solely determined by self-interest undeterred by reference to values, actors must not be endowed in each other's eyes with a social personality. The moment they are seen as parents, children, as hosts or guests, as rich or poor – or even as protagonists of their culture – an evaluational element enters the relationship, and with it questions of honour and *philotimo*. Thus even an honourable man might believe that peddling narcotics in distant foreign lands was, as he put it, 'carried out by walnuts from all walnut trees', that is that it was a trade open to and practised by nationals of all nations. This man's attitude might have been radically different had he been made to see that this is everywhere a disreputable occupation and that the man carrying it out is not simply an anonymous 'trader' but a wrong-doer whose actions reflect on the nation he represents.

Moving in the direction of increasing social distance, we come to a field of values which is common to both parties but which remains non-operative as long as the relations of the actors are not clearly defined. Some examples may illustrate my meaning. An Alona peasant visits a town shop for the first time. The shop-keeper and the peasant have stereotypes concerning each other which inspire them with mutual distrust. As long as the be-haviour of the two actors conveys the impression that the rela-tionship is to be a transient interaction between two stereotypes, each of them, within limits not coterminous with those of the law, will seek the maximum immediate profit. It is, therefore, in the interest of the weaker actor to convert the impersonal relation-ship into a personal one, so that the actual transaction will seem to be the latest link in a chain. The means of doing this is for the weaker actor to lay claim to a relationship with the more potent one. Examples: 'I am X, the best man of your son's godfather', or even 'I was sent by Y, one of your old customers'. Even an acknowledgement of the other person's relative superiority limited to the particular context of interaction is a way of trans-lating an anonymous interaction into a personal relationship. Thus, 'I am a father of many children. I have to buy cheap and good.' To acknowledge the claim is to recognize the existence of an obligation other than to self. Even better, it is the awareness that an act of generosity including fair dealing will be appreciated as such, and not ascribed, as it might be by outsiders, to unmanly softness, foolishness and inexperience. Again it is *only* within the context of *shared* and *active* values and in relations between *persons* – not between anonymous individuals – that *philotimo* becomes operative.

These examples may be pursued endlessly. I shall only refer to the relationship between a citizen and a civil servant, and to that between two rankholders within the same institution. When a citizen, and more specially a peasant, approaches a civil servant the two actors conceive their relations in the following way: the citizen thinks of the civil servant as of a person in whom power is vested by a group from which the citizen is excluded. The civil servant has rank and personal affiliations. In one sense he is a member of a family other than, and opposed to, the family of the citizen. This administrative family has power and this power must be tapped in a way beneficial to self and kindred. The civil servant himself considers all others as outsiders who try to use his position in the administrative hierarchy for the furtherance of their own private ends. The administrative 'family' has been given power over all the other families. This power is a distinctive attribute of the civil service's status in its relations with citizens. It is, therefore, the civil servants' duty (to self and through self to his administration) to stress the distance separating him from the common citizen. The civil servant does not disclose to the citizen the internal organization of his own administrative family in terms of either administered regulations or hierarchy. In his relations to the citizen he is the embodiment of the administration. With reference to his sphere of competence, he considers himself to be a plenipotentiary. In the impersonal interaction between citizen and civil servant the only claim upon the latter's *philotimo* is that of his own sectional interests, and these call for the assertion of his administrative dignity, for arrogance and the marking of social distance. In his relation with him the citizen is isolated, mutual relations are not conditioned by concepts of a common citizenship and of public service, but by the effect that the service will have, once rendered, on the two hostile persons and groups, those of the citizen and the administrator. Obvious conclusions may be drawn from this. All citizens are not equal. Their importance varies with their relationship to the senior grade of the administration and to persons who may exercise pressure. In my chosen example, that of the insignificant peasant dealing with the representative of an all-powerful organization, the peasant must claim some relationship either with the civil servant he is dealing with or with powerful patrons respected or feared by the administration. The most successful approach is the one which aims at segregating the officer concerned from the service to which he belongs and even further, the creation of a personal link of such a nature that a claim on *philotimo* will transcend those of affiliation to a service. All forms of kinships (consanguineous, affinal and spiritual), friendship, host-guest, patron-client, relationships either with the civil servant concerned or his colleagues are used to good effect. In these situations there will be a conflict of duties. The claim on *philotimo*, in this context, is the incitement to act in a manner prescribed by a particular relationship. It is a claim to be treated as a person and not as an anonymous citizen, it is a claim to disregard the general for the particular with the risks that this entails.

Within an organization, be it a public service or a large private enterprise, the primary obligation is to self and rank. In relations of rank undiluted by personal relations the superior asserts his authority in terms of naked power and the inferior resents his anonymous subordination. The two *philotima* are competing for recognition and it is with good reason that *philotimo* and *philonikia*, quarrelsomeness (literally love of victory) were closely associated in classical times. It is only when a personal relationship has been established that the inferior's *philotimo* permits him to subordinate himself without self-abasement and tempers the necessity for the superior to constantly flaunt his superiority.

What is specific to this social situation – or, rather, to the morality reflecting social relations in societies of this type – is the non-recognition of impersonal moral obligations in terms of citizenship or common humanity. The only obligations which are here immediately meaningful are those to family, village and nation, and those to self in situations in which one's honour is at stake. The significance of common humanity, common citizenship are not apparent in most contexts, and this lack of clarity affects the evaluation of actions judged by absolute standards – that is by standards which do not take into consideration pre-existing relationships between two parties. Duties are well defined and one knows one's place in relations of kinship and to a much smaller extent in relations of a similar type, friendship, hospitality, host-guest, community and nation. Outside these situations the Pitsillos is hard put to as to how to act unless he can convert the unusual relationship into a known one, the general to the particular. Should he find this impossible or if he attempts it and is brushed aside, his *philotimo* is apt to become so sensitive that he senses slights which were never intended. More simply, in unknown relations, the Pitsillos stands on his dignity. The Pitsillos in general is prepared to some extent to play (act) a role which might show him in a non-dominating position as long as this is not misunderstood as a lack of masculinity. In a field of kinship or semi-kinship there is no fear of his actions being misinterpreted as self-abasement or servility, and self-protection is not the overweaning motivation.

Some conclusions
  (a) In societies of this type, that is in societies without clearly

delimited spheres of competence, each male individual finds it constantly necessary to assert either his superiority or his *isotimia*, that is his right to be treated as a person entitled to equal esteem. Hierarchical relations are resented and resisted as, whenever the superior stresses his rank, the inferior stresses his manliness. *Ki' esy moustaki ki' ego moustaki*: we both have a moustache, we are equals in our manliness. When spheres of influence are not clearly delimited each actor fears an encroachment on his area of insecure prerogatives and he asserts them against all comers. This insecurity is one of the reasons for self-assertion. The Greek-Cypriot highlander discussed here in all novel situations is not antagonistic but agonistic, parading round the assertion of honour, the social rank, or the knowledge to which he is laying claim like a bird round his mating ground. Prompted by this constant need for a situation in which to prove himself from ancient times to now the Greek who does not find opponents of honour commensurate with his own pits himself against Fate or the Gods. This is the sin of *hubris*. A true man is one who is prepared to stake everything on one throw of the dice. This Greek is a keen gambler attracted more powerfully by the risk than by the gain, more, that is, by the opportunity of proving himself than by the prize.

(b) The conceptual framework of the field of obligations of honour is that of the family and of families linked together by common obligations to honour – in reality by a common honour to defend. The Greek loves his family and his nation, and the true head of the nation is the father-like figure of the King. A nation is a family of men sharing the same national name and prompted by the same motivation to defend its honour. The social machinery of the state demanding of its citizens not proof of their masculinity in its defence, but passive subservience to its local representatives is looked upon as something alien and expendable. The Pitsillos does not readily recognize impersonal, anonymous, moral obligations. A common humanity, a common citizenship may have to be redefined in terms of recognized relations. Duties and one's own relative position are well defined in kinship relations and in those which may be assimilated to them, friendship, host-guest, and, in some contexts, community and nation. Outside these situations the Pitsillos is hard put to know how to act unless he can convert the unknown relation into a known one, the anonymous into the personal, the general to the particular. Thus, in relations in which the actors and/or the situation are new, in order to assert at least his equality with all present, the Pitsillos stands on his dignity.

(c) *Philotimo* is involved in two basic contexts. In the first the nature of the relationship and the social context of the situation, are of little significance. In the second it is the situation itself which determines whether honour is involved.

The first category refers to sex-linked characteristics – in a man: manliness/assertion of masculinity; in a woman: feminin-ity/passive modesty. An unmanly man, an immodest woman, betray their nature. They dishonour, that is, not an achieved status or any particular type of relationship but their sex-ascribed characteristics. They betray their *physis*, their 'nature'. I use the term 'nature' literally. The Greek-Cypriots, to describe a characteristically masculine or feminine action say: it is in the *physis* of man (woman), it is *physiko* to man (woman) that they should act in this way. Here the evaluation of an action, or of its effect, uses as a standard not the character of the person or of the relationship in which he or she is involved, but the ideals of masculinity and femininity. In situations where a woman is involuntarily shamed or a man's honour is attained through his mother, the only way the dishonoured patient may be trans-lated into that of honour-seeking actor is to die.

(d) Excessive centralization goes against the grain of this Greek-Cypriot conception of moral values. This centralization, viewed against the Pitsillos' excessive emphasis on the family, is a constant cause of political inefficiency. The State is of little significance as a catalyser of values and loyalties. The family, on the other hand, is all-important. In this social context nepotism is not considered as an anti-social action, but as a moral duty.

(e) What is stressed in *philotimo*, apart from the basic ingre-dients of masculinity and the honourability of the family name, is what is *achieved* rather than what is *ascribed* – thus skill, prowess, courage in preference to brute strength, generosity in preference to egoistical use of wealth.

Finally, I shall ask one question: 'What is the relation of honour to honesty?' I do this only in order to provide myself with an opportunity for a lapidary answer which sums up my argument. The punctiliousness of honour must be referred to the code of an exclusive and agonistic microsociety; that of honesty to an inclusive, egalitarian macrosociety. Duty, in the first instance, is to those with whom one shares honour. In the second, the un-Greek macrosociety, one's duty is to all fellow citizens or, even further, to fellow humans. Honour is active. Here insecurity and the daily re-evaluation of one's standing breed constant self-assertion and even heroism. The ideals of honesty and equality breed passive conformity and are more congenial to a conception of duty wide in its application, but more accommodating in its expectations.

Pierre Bourdieu

THE SENTIMENT OF HONOUR IN KABYLE SOCIETY

Translated by Philip Sherrard

N. had always been a good eater; he used to make others work for him, taking the best from their fields and houses as by seignorial right. Although he had gone down in the world, he still thought he could do whatever he wanted – could demand anything, say what he liked, insult and even physically attack all who opposed him. It was because of this he was taken to be an *amahbul*. The *amahbul* is not exactly a lunatic; he is a shameless and brazen person who breaks the bounds of normal behaviour, assumes an arbitrary power, and generally acts in a thoroughly unsocial way. They are avoided, these *imahbal* (plural of *amahbul*), since no one wants a dispute with them; for they are without shame, and even if one is in the right one will still turn out to be the victim.

This particular man had a garden wall that needed rebuilding. How was the stone to be found? This was simple. His neighbour had a retaining wall. One day he knocked this wall down and carried the stone off. Here the 'victim' of this arbitrary action was not a weaker person and had ample means of defending himself: he was young and strong, had many brothers and kinsmen, and belonged to a large and powerful family. If he did not take up the challenge, it was not then out of fear. It must have been because public opinion could not see in this abusive action a real challenge, a provocation that touched his honour. In fact, both public opinion and the victimized neighbour pretended to ignore it; and any violent reaction would have been publicly disapproved. For indeed, it is stupid to quarrel with an *amahbul*: 'keep clear of the *amahbul*' – isn't that how the saying goes?

However, the victim sought out the brother of the guilty man, but he, though siding with the complainant, was totally at a loss as to how the *amahbul* could be brought to see reason. He made it clear that he thought the victim had been wrong in not reacting with a similar violence straight away, and he added: 'Who does that waster think he is?' Abashed by this, the victim abruptly changed his attitude, and became angry and indignant: 'Who do you take me for, Si M.? Do you think I'm going to argue with Si N. over a few stones? I came to see you because I know you are sensible and you'll understand what I say. I didn't come to ask payment for the stones (and here he swore upon all the saints, and affirmed that he would never accept any recompense). One must be an *amahbul* to do what Si N. has done, and I'm not going to make myself ridiculous and be put to shame (*adhbahadlagh ruh'iw*)[1] by an *amahbul*. But I'll have you know that it's not by such means that a lawful and just house (*akham necah'*) is built.' And he concluded by saying: 'If you've an *amahbul* in the family, it's up to you to deal with him first, before others do' – meaning by this: 'You are wrong not to accept responsibility with your brother in front of me, even if you reproach him and correct him in my place, which is moreover what I ask of you.'[2] (*Aghbala.**)

In order to understand all the subtlety of this dialogue one must realize that it brought face to face a man who was completely master of the dialectic of challenge and riposte and another Kabyle who, having lived for a long time outside Kabylia and having acquired certain western values, had forgotten the technique and spirit of what he called 'Kabyle rhetoric'. To the latter therefore the incident was one of simple petty theft committed by a brother whom he could disavow in the name of justice and commonsense without the rules of family solidarity being thereby violated. Above all he reasoned essentially in terms of monetary interest: the wall was worth so much and this person must be compensated accordingly. The other, however, refined in his crude way, was astonished that so wise and well-educated a man could be mistaken to this extent about his real intentions.

Once a peasant had his crop stolen by his tenant farmer. The latter was an old hand at this game, but that year he had exceeded himself. Reproaches and threats being fruitless, the matter was brought to the *thajmaâth* – the theft itself was so well known and acknowledged that it was not necessary to prove it. The tenant farmer hadn't a leg to stand on, and he quickly came to seek pardon, as was the custom, though he also had several arguments in his own defence: that he had been cultivating this land for a

* For explanation see Notes pp. 234–41.

very long time; that he considered it as his own property; that the landlord, an absentee, had no need of the crop; that, in order to please him, he was giving him his own figs, which were of better quality, on the understanding that he would later recoup in quantity; that he was poor, that the landlord was rich, rich 'to give to the poor', etc – a whole string of reasons set out with the intention of flattering the landlord. He added that he bowed lower than earth before him and that he was ready to offer any compensation. He uttered the words 'Pardon before God' (*asthughfir Allah*), which according to custom ought to bring all discussion to a close. But he added a formula considered as its equivalent and particularly appropriate – appropriate because a man, even when he makes honourable amends, cannot be absolutely wrong, and in any case cannot attribute all wrongs to himself, and so is always a little in the right just as the other is always a little in the wrong:

'If I have acted well, praise be to God (so much the better)
If I have erred, pardon before God.'

The landlord, a city-dweller who was ignorant of the nuances of 'Kabylian rhetoric', was infuriated by this formula. He wanted a simple 'pardon before God'; he wanted his opponent to acknowledge himself completely and utterly guilty; he demanded unconditional submission. And the other began to call upon those present to bear witness; 'Oh creatures, friends of the saints, what is this? I praise God, and that man there attacks me for it!' and he repeated two or three times the same formula, each time abasing and humbling himself more, and making himself look more wretched. This angered the landlord still further, so much so that in the end the whole village, in spite of its respect for an educated man, 'a stranger' to the country, reluctantly felt it had to blame him for his attitude.

When tempers had died down, the landlord felt ashamed of his intransigence. On the advice of his wife, who was better informed about things than he was, he sought out the *imam* of the village, and elder kinsmen, in order to excuse himself for his conduct and to reinstate himself; he asserted that he had been the victim, and that the other had inflicted upon him *elbahadla* (or *thibhadlith*, the action of *bahdel*), as everyone had realized. (*Les Issers.*)

In a third village a certain incident had pushed to its height the tension between the too moieties (*eçffuf*) which in their modern degenerated form appear more like legues or factions. One of the *eçffuf*, fed up with the situation, went to visit an important member of the opposing moiety, accompanied by a whole train of dignitaries, the *marabouts* of the *douar* and of neighbouring *douars*, the *imam* of the village, all the *t'ulba* (plural of *t'aleb*) from a *thimâamarth* (religious school) nearby – in all by more than forty people whom he had transported, lodged and fed. To everyone except the person who was its object – a Kabyle who'd lived abroad and had little knowledge of local custom – this was a ritual. The custom was that, after kissing the negotiators on the forehead, one accepted their proposals and called for peace. This did not necessarily mean that one would not on some pretext resume hostilities later, and no one would find fault with one if one did.

The dignitaries first announce the purpose of their proceedings: 'the Ath . . . come to seek pardon'. Custom requires that, to start with, they dissociate themselves from the party for whom they have come to intercede. The next to speak, with dignity, are those who ask for pardon 'in the interest of all, and above all in the interest of the poorest in the village, for it is they who suffer from our quarrels: they are quite lost, as you can see, one cannot but pity them, etc (they continue in this strain as far as they can without losing face). Let us make peace, let us forget the past.'

The object of this entreaty is expected to show a certain reluctance and to make one or two reservations; or one part of the moiety, with the tacit complicity of the other, should stiffen its attitude while the other, in order to keep negotiations going, should be more conciliatory. In the midst of the discussion, mediators intervene: their task is to accuse and find fault with the party from whom pardon has been sought, so that a balance may be restored and that the supplicating party may avoid complete humiliation (*elbahadla*). For the mere fact that recourse has been had to the *marabouts*, that one has fed them and come with them, constitutes a sufficient concession in itself; one cannot abase oneself any further.

Moreover, the mediators, being superior to all rivalries and enjoying a prestige which allows them to impose a settlement, can afford to adopt a slight tone of rebuke where the entreated party is concerned: 'Of course, there may be many wrongs on their side, but you, Si X., you have been guilty of this, you should not have done it and today you must forgive them; besides, you both forgive each other and we undertake to sanction the peace you've made, etc.' The wisdom of the dignitaries allows them to administer this skilful dose of rights and wrongs.

In this particular case, however, the entreated party, ignorant of the rules of the game, couldn't accept these diplomatic subtleties. He insisted on having everything out, he reasoned in terms of 'either . . . or'. 'What! If you've come to entreat me, it's because the others are in the wrong, and because they are absolutely in the wrong; it's they you must blame, instead of rebuking me. Or are you defending them because they've fed you and given you money?' No stronger insult could have been given to the assembly of notables. As far as the Kabyle could remember, this was the first time in the whole area that a delegation of such venerable persons had not succeeded in obtaining agreement between the two parties, and the worst curses were predicted for the offender. (*Tizi Hibel.*)

The dialectic of challenge and riposte

A host of similar episodes could be related; but from the analysis of these three stories alone one can distinguish the rules of the game of challenge and riposte. For a challenge to be made, the challenger must consider whoever he challenges to be worthy of it – to be, that is to say, in a position to riposte. This means that he must recognize him as his peer in honour. To issue a challenge to someone is to acknowledge his manliness, an acknowledgement which is the prerequisite of any dialogue as well as of the challenge of honour as the prelude to the dialogue; it is to acknowledge in him also the dignity of a man of honour, since challenge, as such, requires a riposte and consequently is addressed to a man thought capable of playing the game of honour and of playing it well. This presupposes not only that he knows the rules of the game, but also that he possesses those qualities needed to comply with them. Recognition of one's adversary as one's own equal in honour is therefore the basic condition of any challenge.

Because it presupposes recognition of equality in honour, offence is opposed to disdain which is essentially a refusal of the dialogue, because it excludes the possibility of riposte. To disdain, in effect, is to refuse to give one's opponent a chance; it is to enclose him within a fate that is imposed upon him; to refuse the dialogue with him is to deny symbolically that he is equal in humanity. Humiliation corresponds to disdain, and is the situation of the individual confined by his nature to an inferior position, to whom one denies the dignity of being a man to the extent of refusing to enter into a dialogue with him, even by an insult. On the contrary, an offence, by initiating an exchange, gives the offended person his chance and recognizes that he is capable of riposting. Whilst the logic of disdain and humiliation brings together *a* freedom and *a* nature, the dialectic of honour is exercised between two persons who, by their very dialogue, recognize that they are each other's equals in humanity and liberty. What is peculiar to the logic of disdain and humiliation is that the liberty of choice is conferred only upon the one who disdains – either refusing to speak, to give or to challenge, or refusing to reply to what is said, to the gift or to the challenge – and is not conferred at all upon the person who is the object of the disdain.

The vivid Kabyle sense of equality in honour is responsible for many habits and customs and is manifested particularly in the resistance offered to any pretension to superiority: 'I've got a moustache too', is an oft-repeated phrase.[3] The braggart is immediately called to order: 'Only dung swells,' they say. A Kabyle of the Issers tribe who had come back from France with a rifle-stick, was greeted at the cafe where he had gone to show off with the words: 'Welcome to Amar Ajdid', 'Amar the brand-new', the upstart, the newly-rich who has forgotten the past. This nickname stayed with him, as well as with his family (*Les Issers*).

In the village of Tizi Hibel, in Great Kabylia, a rich family built a family tomb in European style, with a wrought-iron gate, a tombstone, and an inscription, thus transgressing the rule which imposes anonymity and uniformity upon tombs. The day after its completion, the ironwork and head-stones disappeared (*Tizi Hibel*). A sense of punctilious egalitarianism sometimes inspires rules of customary law (*qanun*), such as that, widespread in all Kabylia, which obliges the horseman to walk when he comes to a village and when he passes by the *thajmaâth*. To do otherwise would be to offend the honour of the village and to run the risk of being stoned.[4] (*Tizi Hibel.*)

From the principle of the mutual recognition of equality in honour a first corollary follows: the challenge, and even the offence, although it is essentially different from the challenge (*cf.* below, page 216), involve the recognition of honour. 'The man without enemies is a donkey,' say the Kabyles, meaning not so much that he is stupid as that he is over-passive. 'The accomplished man (*argaz elkamel*),' said an old Kabyle, 'must always be on the alert, ready to take up the slightest challenge. He is the guardian of honour (*amh'ajer*), watching over his own honour and over that of his group. There is nothing worse than to pass unnoticed, like a shadow. Thus, not to greet someone, is to treat him like an object, like an animal or a woman. The challenge, on the contrary, is a highlight in the life of the one who receives it.' (*El Kalaa.*) It is the challenge, in fact, which gives one the sense of existing fully as a man, which demonstrates one's manliness (*thirugza*) to others and to oneself.

A second corollary is this: to issue a challenge to a man incapable of riposte – incapable, that is to say, of playing the dialogue through to the end – is to dishonour oneself. There is thus the risk that *elbahadla*, an extreme humiliation inflicted publicly in the presence of others, may fall upon him who provokes it, upon the *amahbul* who does not know how to respect the rules of the game of honour. To take unfair advantage, to crush one's opponent, is to expose oneself to sharing in the humiliation inflicted when some question of honour is really involved; indeed, even the person who deserves *elbahadla* also possesses honour (*nif* and *h'urma*). There is therefore a point beyond which *elbahadla* falls upon the party that inflicts it.

More often than not, rather than inflict *elbahadla* upon someone, one lets him cover himself in shame through his own attitude. In that case the dishonour is irreparable, and one says: he has dishonoured himself *ibahdal imanis* or *ibahdal simanis* (*Aghbala*). For this reason, the party in the stronger position should not push his advantage too far and should moderate his charge. 'Better that he strip himself,' says the proverb, 'than that I should strip him' (*Djemâa-Saharidj*). This is also why an opponent, while making honourable amends, may always try to reverse the situation by forcing his accuser beyond the prescribed limits. The purpose of this, as we saw in the second story, is to rally public opinion to one's side, for a lack of moderation on the part of the accuser is bound to meet with disapproval.

A third corollary is that only a challenge issued (or an offence caused) by one's equal in honour deserves to be taken up; in other words, one only accepts a challenge if one considers the challenger worthy of making it. An affront from an inferior in humanity or honour recoils upon the presumptuous person who makes it and the dialogue is at an end. 'The prudent and circumspect man, the *amah'dhuq*, does not commit himself with the *amahbul*.' Kabyle wisdom teaches: 'Take from the *amah'dhuq* and give to the *amahbul*.' (*Azerou n-Chmini*.) *Elbahadla* would recoil on the head of the wise man who ventured to take up the senseless challenge of the *amahbul*; while if he does not take it up the challenger himself has to bear the penalties of his arbitrary behaviour. Similarly, dishonour is the consequence of sullying oneself in an unworthy revenge – a circumstance which sometimes led the Kabyles to employ 'professionals', those who kill for money (*amekri*, plural *imekriyen*, literally: one whose services are hired). It is therefore the nature of the riposte which confers upon the challenge (or the offence) its meaning, and even determines the fact that it is a challenge (or offence) and not simply a piece of pure aggression.

The Kabyles had an attitude towards the black peoples which illustrates this analysis perfectly. To respond to the insults of a negro, a man of inferior status and bereft of honour, or to fight with him, was to dishonour oneself.[5] A folk tale of Djurdjura relates how a certain tribe, in the course of a war with another tribe, set negroes upon its opponents, who at once laid down their arms. But while the defeated tribe kept its honour, the conquerors were dishonoured in their victory. It is sometimes also said that one had only to link oneself with a black family and one would escape blood vengeance (*thamgert'* or *thimegret'*), though this was such a dishonourable way of behaving that no one would do it, even to save his life. That in fact it was done is none the less indicated by local tradition, according to which the butchers of Ighil or Mechedal, the Ath Chabane, are negroes whose ancestor was a Kabyle who, in order to escape vengeance, turned butcher and whose descendants later could only ally themselves with black peoples. (*Ait Hichem.*)

Rules of honour used to govern fighting also. A sense of solidarity obliged one to protect a kinsman against a non-kinsman, a member of one's own party against a man from another moiety, an inhabitant of the village – even though of a rival party – against a stranger to the village, a member of the tribe against a member of another tribe. At the same time, it was a disgrace for several men to fight against one man alone, so that if one wanted to continue a quarrel one had to find ways and means of taking it upon oneself. Thus the slightest quarrels always threatened to become larger in scope, since the honour of all might be affronted in the honour of the individual and as soon as the incident occurred the moieties were mobilized. These political and warlike leagues pursued their hostilities in the form of a strictly regulated game, of an ordered competition which, far from threatening social order, tended on the contrary to safeguard it by making it possible for the spirit of competition, the point of honour, the *nif*[6], to express itself in prescribed and institutionalized forms.

It was the same with wars between tribes. The fighting some-times took on the form of a proper ritual: insults were exchanged, then blows, and the fighting ceased with the arrival of the mediators. During the fight, the women encouraged the men with their shouts and songs, which exalted the honour and the vigour of the family. One did not seek to kill or crush one's opponent. One tried to show one way or another (and generally through a symbolic act) that one had the upper hand. I was told, for instance, that in Great Kabylia the fighting stopped when one of the two factions had seized possession of the main support beam (*thiyejdith*) and of a flagstone from the enemy's *thajmaâth*. Some-times the incident took a turn for the worse, either because an unlucky blow killed one of the contestants or because the stronger group threatened to burst into the living quarters of the rival faction, the last refuge of honour. Only then did the besieged resort to firearms, and this was often enough to stop the fighting. The mediators, the *marabouts* and the wise men of the tribe asked the aggressors to withdraw and the latter departed under the protection of the pledged word (*leânaya*).[7] No one would molest them, for this would have been to break the *leânaya*, a supremely dishonouring breach of trust (*Djemaa-Saharidj*).

According to an old man of the Ath Mengellat (Great Kabylia), in tribal wars great battles were rare, and only took place after a council had been held by the elders that fixed the day of the action and the objective attributed to each village. Each man fought for himself but shouted advice and encouragement to the others. People from all the villages round about looked on and remarked on the bravery and skill of the contestants. When the stronger group occupied positions from which it could crush its opponent, or when it took possession of a clear symbol of victory, the struggle ceased and each tribe returned home. Sometimes prisoners were taken; placed under the protection (*leânaya*) of whoever had captured them, they were generally well treated. At the end of the conflict they were sent away clad in a brand-new *gandura*, this signifying that the man returning to his village was a dead man in his shroud. A state of war (*fatna*) could last for years. In a certain manner hostilities were permanent, for the conquered tribe always waited for its revenge, and at the first opportunity seized the flocks and shepherds of its enemy; while at the slightest incident at, for example, the weekly market, the fighting would break out again.[8] Under such conditions it was in fact extremely difficult to distinguish between a state of peace and a state of war. Truces between villages and tribes, like protection pacts between families, were sealed and guaranteed by honour, yet to war, the most serious game that honour has invented they put only a temporary end.

It is clear, then, that war had a function and a significance completely different from those in our society. The fighting was a game whose stake is life and whose rules must be obeyed scrupulously if dishonour is to be avoided; rather than being a struggle to the death, it is a competition of merit played out before the tribunal of public opinion, an institutionalized competition in the course of which are affirmed the values that stand at the very basis of the existence of the group and which assure its preservation. That a gulf separates a war aiming at total victory and calling into play all reasonable means available, from a war of honour, an *agôn* or ritual game (within limitations, for an economic interest could both provoke it and profit from it), is clear from the following conversation reported by an old Kabyle: Someone once said to Mohammed Kaci: 'Are you coming to the war?' – 'What's happening?' – 'Well, as soon as a Rumi is seen he's shot at.' – 'Just like that?' – 'How else would you have it?' – 'I thought one should discuss, then insult each other, and finally fight each other!' – 'Not at all; he fires at us and we fire at him. That's it. Are you coming, then?' – 'No, when I am not angry, I can't fire on people.'[9]

But it was not only in war that *nif* could manifest itself. It inspired, for example, rivalries between villages that made it a point of honour to have the highest and most beautiful mosque, the most elaborate fountains, best protected from the public gaze, the most sumptuous feasts, the cleanest streets, and so on. All kinds of institutionalized and ritual competitions also provided a pretext for contests of honour, such as firing at a target, which was practised on the occasion of every joyful event – at the birth of a boy, at a circumcision or marriage. At marriages, an escort composed of men and women entrusted with fetching the bride from a village or a neighbouring tribe, had to win two tests in succession, the first reserved for women, for two to six 'emissaries' renowned for their talents, the second intended for men, eight to twenty good marksmen. The emissaries took part in a poetry contest with the women of the fiancée's family or village, over whom they had to have the last word. It was the prerogative of the fiancée's family to choose the nature and form of the test, which consisted either of riddles or of a poetry competition. The men competed with each other at target shooting. On the morning of the escort's departure for home, while the women prepare the bride and the father is being complimented, the men among the retinue try to shatter with their bullets fresh eggs embedded a long way off in a bank or tree trunk. Elsewhere the eggs are replaced by flat stones. Should they fail, the bridegroom's guard of honour set off again, covered with shame, after passing under the saddle of a donkey and paying a fine. These games, apart from their athletic character, had a ritual and symbolic function, as is demonstrated both by the strict order in which they take place and by the magical practices to which they gave rise.[10] Thus the fights and ritual games constitute the most perfect expression of the logic of honour at the same time as they give to society the opportunity to demonstrate in symbolic form the values and beliefs to which it is most strongly attached.

If every offence is a challenge, every challenge, as will be seen, is not an outrage and an offence. In fact, the competition of honour may be set in a framework of ritual and institutional logic similar to that of the game or wager. What is then at stake is one's *amour propre*, the point of honour, in one word, *nif*, and this stake for the Kabyle is worth more than life itself. *Nif* is also the desire to overcome one's rival in a man-to-man struggle; it is that 'jealous emulation', that struggle for glory of which Hume spoke with reference to Greek cities.[11] Where games are concerned, the good player is he who always supposes that his adversary is able to discern the best strategy and who directs his game accordingly; in the same way, in the game of honour, although unmeasurable stakes are involved, each party must consider the other capable of choosing the best strategy, namely that which consists of playing according to the rules of the code of honour. Both challenge and riposte imply that each adversary chooses to play the game and to respects its rules at the same time as he assumes that his opponent is capable of the same choice. Self-respect, respect for the rule, respect for one's opponent and one's offer to be respected by him – these are inseparable.

Both the challenge itself and the offence are like the gift in that they presuppose the choice of playing a set game in conformity with certain rules. The gift is a challenge which does honour to the one to whom it is addressed, while putting to the test his *amour propre* and his pride (*nif*); consequently, just as to insult someone incapable of riposting is to dishonour oneself, so to make a gift so great that it cannot be reciprocated is also to dishonour oneself. In both cases respect for the person with whom one engages demands that he is given a chance to reply, demands in short that the challenge is a reasonable one. But at the same time the gift or the challenge puts to the test the very point of honour that it recognizes in its adversary. Thus it constitutes a provocation and a provocation to reply. The dialogue has been initiated. He who has received the gift or been offended is inescapably committed to a series of exchanges, and he must choose a line of conduct which, whatever it is, will be a reply (even if he chooses not to reply) to the original act that instigates the dialogue in the first place.[12] He can choose to prolong the dialogue or to break it off (*cf.* plan facing p. 214). If, obeying his *amour propre*, he decides to riposte, his choice is identical with the initial choice of his opponent: he agrees to play the game which can continue unendingly.[13] The riposte is in itself a fresh challenge. Formerly, it is said, vengeance had hardly been taken before the family was rejoicing at the end of dishonour (*thuqdha n-tasa*), that is to say, both at the relief from the pain felt in one's 'liver' because of the offence, and also at the satisfaction of the desire to be revenged. The men let off rifle shots, the women uttered 'you-you' cries. (*Djemaa-Saharidj.*) This was meant to demonstrate to everybody that revenge had been carried out, so that all should be aware how a family of honour was capable of obtaining reparation for an offence and of restoring its own prestige promptly; it was also meant to let the enemy family know the cause of its misfortune as well as to issue it with a challenge. What is the good of revenge if it remains anonymous?

To choose not to reply may have different meanings, even contradictory ones. The offender can, by his physical force, his prestige or the importance and authority of the group to which he belongs, be superior, equal or inferior to the person offended. If the logic of honour presupposes the recognition of an ideal equality in honour between two parties, popular consciousness is nevertheless not unaware of inequalities in fact. He who cries: 'I've got a moustache too!' is answered by the proverb: 'The moustache of the hare is not that of the lion.' In this way a whole casuistry, spontaneous and extremely subtle, may develop. It is this that must now be analysed.

Let us take the case where the offended person is able, ideally at least, to riposte on a basis of equality. If, after giving the appearance of accepting the challenge (whether in the form of a gift or an offence), and consequently the rules of the game which this involves, he then shows himself incapable of playing it, he is tainted with dishonour, as is inevitable in a society dominated by the values of honour, and in which it is inconceivable that one could ever abandon the game. The dialogue in this case is now at an end. The man who, from pusillanimity or weakness, evades or renounces the possibility of riposting, chooses to some extent to be the author of his own dishonour and shame, which are then irremediable (*ibahdal imanis* or *simanis*). He confesses himself defeated in the game, which he should have played in spite of everything.

But non-reply may also be a refusal to reply, an explicit decision not to riposte. The offended person then shows by his attitude that he has chosen not to abide by the rules of honour because the offender himself is completely a stranger to these rules – is, that is to say, an *amahbul*.[14] The offended person refuses to recognize that he has been offended; and by his disdain and scorn, he makes the offence recoil on its perpetrator, who is dishonoured. 'A family is lost, one says, if it doesn't count among its members at least one scoundrel.' The man of honour, who cannot condescend to reply to the insults of an unworthy person, and who is yet unprotected against these offences, particularly in the towns, must be able to pit one scoundrel against another. The professional avenger or killer for money may also be employed in these circumstances. When it is a matter of provoking someone, the scoundrel may again be called on, because he can always be disowned if afterwards an agreement is reached. (Algiers.)

In the same way, where a gift is concerned, the recipient may indicate that he chooses to refuse the exchange either by rejecting the gift or by presenting immediately or after a time an exactly similar counter-gift. In this case again the dialogue is halted. In short, in this logical system, only by outbidding someone, challenge responding to challenge, can one indicate that one chooses to continue the exchange, that one chooses to play the game, according to the rules of challenge and riposte, both of which are continually being renewed.

Let us now take the case in which the offender is clearly superior to the offended person. The code of honour, and public opinion charged with the duty of seeing that it is conformed to, demand nothing from the offended person except that he agrees to play the game. To draw back from the challenge is the only blamable attitude. At the same time, the offended person need not triumph over the offender in order to be rehabilitated in the eyes of public opinion. A defeated person who has done his duty is not blamed; indeed, although he is defeated according to the laws of combat, he is the victor according to the laws of honour. To have taken up the challenge at all is already to have won a victory. But there is something more: *elbahadla*, dishonour, falls on the offender who thus doubly abuses his superiority, first in issuing the challenge to start with, and then in defeating his inferior opponent.

The offended party can also cause *elbahadla* to fall upon the offender without having recourse to riposte. To do this it is sufficient for him to adopt an attitude of humility, which, by emphasizing his weakness, makes apparent the arbitrary, unfair and immoderate character of the offence. Consciously or unconsciously, in the eyes of public opinion he merely invokes, by his whole attitude, the second corollary of the principle of equality in honour, according to which he who offends a person incapable of taking up the challenge thereby dishonours himself.[15] This line of conduct is of course only admissible on condition that in the eyes of the group there is no doubt about the inequality of the opponents. This inequality is normal among those who are recognized by society as weak individuals, clients (*yadh isumthen*, those who are dependent) or members of a small family (*itaâfanen*, the lean ones, the feeble ones). (*Aghbala*.)

Lastly, let us take the case where the offender is inferior to the offended person. The latter can riposte, thus transgressing the third corollary of the principle of equality in honour; but if he uses his advantage unfairly he exposes himself to the dishonour which would normally have fallen upon the offender who, inconsiderate and immoderate, is a despised and presumptuous person (*ameh'qur*), unconscious of the nature of his actions. The wiser course for him in this case is to abstain from any riposte and to act as though he disdained his offender. He must, as they say, 'let him bark until he grows weary of it', he must 'refuse to compete with him'. Since the failure to riposte cannot be imputed to cowardice or weakness, the dishonour recoils upon the head of the presumptuous offender.

Although each of the cases examined can be illustrated by a host of observations or stories, it nevertheless remains a fact that usually the differences are less clear-cut, so that everyone, with the complicity of public opinion, can play on the ambiguities and equivocalities of conduct; thus the gap separating the non-reply out of fear and the refusal to reply as a sign of scorn is often minute, so that disdain can always serve as a mask for pusillanimity. Every Kabyle however is a past master in this casuistry, and the court of public opinion can always discern the true facts of the case.

The motive force in the dialectic of honour is thus *nif*, which tends always to choose to riposte. But is this choice absolutely free where the person who takes it is concerned? In practice, apart from the fact that, in a society in which honour is the keystone of the system of values, any choice other than that imposed by the code of honour is unthinkable, it is at the moment when the choice is being made that the pressure of the group is exerted most forcibly. First, there is pressure from members of the family, who, should the challenged kinsman default, are ready to take his place, since honour, like land, is indivisible and the infamy of one of their number taints all the others. Then there is pressure from the community of the clan or village as a whole, prompt to blame and condemn cowardice or complacency. When a man is under an obligation to avenge an offence, those about him carefully avoid reminding him of the fact. But everyone observes his slightest gesture and tries to guess his intentions. His kinsmen are uneasy until before a family council, assembled at his request or at the request of its eldest member, he outlines his plan of action. Generally aid is offered him, either in the form of money to pay a professional killer, or by volunteering to accompany him if he insists on avenging himself by his own hand. Custom decrees that he must reject this assistance and only demand that, in case of failure, another person should continue his interrupted task. Indeed, honour prescribes that all members of the family, united like the fingers of the hand, should successively, in order of closeness of relationship, undertake to carry out the revenge if the need arises. When the offended person shows less determination and when, without publicly renouncing vengeance, he continually defers carrying it out, the members of the family begin to grow anxious; the wisest among them consult together, and one of them is asked to remind their defaulting kinsman of his duty, summoning him to act, and calling upon him to avenge himself. Should this fresh call to duty have no effect, they resort to threats. Another person will carry out the vengeance instead of the offended person, who, though dishonoured in everyone's eyes, will still be held responsible by his enemy's family, and thus threatened in his turn by *thamgart'* (blood vengeance). Realizing that he lays himself open to the consequences of both cowardice and vengeance, he can only comply 'half-heartedly', as is said, or choose exile.[16] (*Ait Hichem.*)

The sentiment of honour is lived out openly before other people. *Nif* is above all in the action of defending, cost what it may, a certain public image of oneself. 'The man of quality

HONOUR			DISHONOUR			SACRED
Point of honour	*Honour*	*Respectability*	*Action of dishonouring*	*State of dishonour*	*Shame crime against honour*	
nif	elâardh	esser	bahdel	h'achma	elâar	elh'urma
if	lah'ya	nur	echuwah	thibhadlith	elâib	elh'aram
anzaren	riya	thaqbaylith	h'achem	thimâayrith	elkhazzwa (arab)	
thirzi nennif	elh'achma	thirugza	afdah'	chuha	or tikhzi	
	amesrur (adj.)	thirujla	nouns of action:	elfadh'a	lah'ram	
	amah'ruz	chiâa	abahdel or	itswâayar		
	nesser		elbahadla (arab)	(rad. âar)		
	elâali		âayer	ineh'chem		
			amâayer	itswah'chem		
			ah'achem			
			tuksa nesser			
			tuksa laqdhar			
			tirzi laqdhar			
			tirzi el h'urma			

(*argaz elâali*) must continually be on his guard; he must watch his words, which, "like bullets fired from the gun, don't return" '; and this is all the more important because each of his acts and each of his words involve his whole group. 'If animals are tied by their paws, men bind themselves by their tongue.' The man of little worth is on the contrary one of whom it is said: 'he is in the habit of forgetting' (*ithetsu*). He forgets his word (*awal*), that is to say his pledges, his debts of honour, and his duties. 'A man of the Ilmayen once said that he would like to have a neck as long as the camel's; so his words, proceeding from his heart, would have a long way to go before reaching his tongue, and this would give him time to reflect.' The metaphor indicates all the importance bestowed on the word one has given and on one's sworn pledge. 'The man who forgets,' says the proverb, 'is not a man.' He forgets and he also forgets himself (*ithetsu imanis*); he forgets his ancestors and the respect he owes them; and he forgets the respect he owes himself in order to be worthy of them. (*Les Issers.*)

A man lacking in self-respect (*mebla, elâardh, lah'ya, riya, elh'achma*) is a man who exposes his inner self with all its errors and weaknesses. The wise man (*argaz elâali*), on the other hand, is the man who knows how to keep a secret, who constantly proves his prudence and discretion (*amesrur, amah'ruz nesser,* who jealously keeps a secret). Constant watchfulness over oneself is indispensable if one is to obey that fundamental precept of social morality which prohibits one from making an exhibition of oneself, which demands that, so far as is possible, the innermost personality, with its uniqueness and individuality, is concealed beneath a veil of modesty and discretion. 'Only the devil (*Chit'an*) says "I" '; 'only the *Chit'an* begins with himself'; 'the assembly (*thajmaâth*) is the assembly; only the Jew is alone'. All these sayings express the same imperative: one which demands the sacrifice and negation of the inner self and which is achieved as much in the self-effacement required by solidarity and mutual assistance as in the discretion and modesty imposed by convention. The man who, incapable of preserving his dignity, grows impatient or angry, speaks at random or laughs without reason, is precipitate or uncontrolled, acts without thinking, throws his weight about, shouts, vociferates (*ah'amaq*), in short, abandons himself to his first impulse, such a man is unfaithful to himself, and falls short of the ideals of dignity and distinction, of modesty and shame, which are summed up in the one word, *elh'achma*. The man of honour, on the contrary, is essentially faithful to himself (*constantia sibi*, as the Romans said), and this is revealed in the care he takes to be worthy of a certain ideal image of himself. Level-headed, prudent, restrained in his speech, he always weighs the pros and cons (*amiyaz* in contrast to *aferfar*, the 'light' man who flits, or in contrast to *achet't'ah'*, the man who dances), he pledges his word frankly and does not evade his responsibilities by a '*wissen*', 'perhaps', 'who knows?', a reply that is fitting only for women. He is the person who keeps his word, to others and to himself, the one of whom it is said, 'He is one man, and of one word' (*argaz, edwawal*). (*El Kalaa.*)

The point of honour is the basis of the moral code of an individual who sees himself always through the eyes of others, who has need of others for his existence, because the image he has of himself is indistinguishable from that presented to him by other people. 'Man is man through men; God alone', the proverb runs, 'is God through himself.' (*Argaz sirgazen*; *Rabbi imanis.*) The man of honour (*aâardhi*) is both the virtuous man and the man who enjoys a good reputation. Respectability, the reverse of shame, is the characteristic of a person who needs other people in order to grasp his own identity and whose conscience is a kind of interiorization of others, since these fulfil for him the role of witness and judge. Defined essentially by its social dimension, respectability must be conquered and defended in the face of everyone; boldness and generosity (*elh'enna*) are the supreme values, while evil lurks in weakness and pusillanimity, in the fact of daring to do little, of suffering the offence without demanding reparation. An insult sullies both the picture of himself that the individual intends to project, and that which he imagines to be his.

Hence it is that the dynamics of exchanges of honour are based essentially on the pressure of opinion. The person who fails to take revenge ceases to exist for other people. This is why even the most worthless man has always enough *h'achma* (shame, modesty), however little it may be, to avenge himself. The formulas employed when speaking of dishonour are significant: 'How shall I be able to appear before (*qabel*) people?'; 'I can no longer open my mouth in front of others.' 'Will not the earth swallow me up?'; 'My clothes have slipped from my body'; 'My life is over!' (*Aghbala*). The fear of collective reprobation and shame (*elâar, lah'ya, elâib ulayermedden*), the negative aspect of the point of honour, is such that it compels a man most lacking in self-esteem to conform, with constraint and of necessity, to the dictates of honour.[17] This is because the accomplished man, the true man, cannot be other than the man of honour. A man's honour is his own honour. In him, existence and honour are one. He who has lost his honour no longer exists. He ceases to exist for other people, and at the same time he ceases to exist for himself.

Perhaps the conclusion is that the important position accorded to sentiment of honour is a characteristic of 'primary' societies in which the relationship with others, through its intensity, intimacy and continuity, takes precedence over the relationship one has with oneself; in which the individual learns the truth about himself through the intermediary of others; and in which the being and the truth about a person are identical with the being and truth that others acknowledge in him. In groups whose members are well-known to each other, such as the Kabyle clan or village, the control of public opinion is exercised at every moment, and community feeling is experienced with the highest possible intensity. Penned inside this enclosed microcosm in which everybody knows everybody, condemned without the possibility of escape or relief to live with others, beneath the gaze of others, every individual experiences deep anxiety about 'people's words' (*awal medden*), 'weighty, cruel and inexorable' (*Les Issers*). And how could it be otherwise? It is the all-powerful force of opinion that judges the reality and gravity of an offence; it is this which, acting in a sovereign capacity, insists that reparation should be made. For example, the thief who breaks into a house that is inhabited, as distinct from the one who steals cereals or animals left outside, exposes himself to blood vengeance; and this because people will at once insinuate that the honour of the womenfolk has not been respected. Thus the fascinated attention paid to the conduct of others, coupled with the almost haunting preoccupation with their judgement, render unthinkable or despicable any attempt to free oneself from the dictates of honour.

Considered as an act of communication, the challenge or the gift is defined by the riposte or counter-gift in which it is completed and in which it realizes its full significance. Perhaps every exchange carries in itself a challenge more or less dissimulated, so that the logic of challenge and riposte may only be the extreme limit towards which every communication tends, especially where the exchange of gifts is concerned. But the temptation to challenge someone and to get the better of him by putting him in some difficulty, is counterbalanced by the need to communicate. To submit the other party to an over-difficult test is to risk seeing the exchange interrupted. Thus communication is effected in a compromise between contract and conflict. The generous exchange tends towards an attack on generosity; the most ample gift is also that which is most liable to cast dishonour on the recipient, for it makes it impossible for him to make any gift in return. Thus the *tawsa*, the gift made by the guests on the occasion of great family feasts, and one publicly proclaimed, often provokes competitions of honour and ruinous attempts to be the most lavish donor. In order to avoid this, agreement may be reached as to the maximum value of the gifts. In the same way, at marriages and circumcisions, the families make it a point of honour to give feasts as sumptuous as possible, even running the danger of ruining themselves. This is particularly so when a girl marries outside her village: 'then,' it is said, 'one must be particularly attentive to *nif*, because those she'll have to face are strangers.' Such competition even plays a part between members of the same family, for example, between the women (sisters-in-law, mother) at the marriage of a daughter. It was reported to me that in 1938 a man of the tribe of the *Ath Ughlis* spent on the occasion of the first confinement of his daughter more than 3,000 francs in gifts, that is to say 1,400 eggs, 15 head of poultry, 300 francs value of mutton, 20 kgs of salted meat, 20 kgs of fat, oil, coffee, semolina, 25 garments, etc. Another man of the same tribe sold the only field he still possessed, in order to do honour to his daughter on a similar occasion (*Azerou n-chmini*). But there is general agreement in denouncing 'the devil's point of honour', *nif nech-chit'an*, or the foolish point of honour, *thihuzzith* (from *elhaz*, the foolish), which angers one or leads one to take offence over trifles, to commit one's honour in futilities or to drift into ruinous attempts to outbid others. 'None incurs shame,' it is said, 'if he must lose by it' (if he must ruin himself for the sake of vainglory).

Thus an exchange, by involving the point of honour, naturally tends always to lead to competition. But if in the exchange there is always implicit this virtual conflict, the conflict of honour still remains an exchange, as is seen by the very clear distinction which is made between the stranger and the enemy. Only prudent reflection makes it possible for the communication to go on – a continued creation, a continued miracle – while being always exposed to the danger of breaking down. By the very fact that it tends to sacrifice the wish to 'exchange' with others to the wish to surpass them, the point of honour carries always with it the risk of the exchange failing; but at the same time this compels one to continue the dialogue in an attempt to have the last word.

If offence does not necessarily involve dishonour, this is because it allows the possibility of riposte, a possibility affirmed and recognized by the very act of giving offence. Dishonour remains virtual as long as the possibility of riposte remains; but it becomes more and more real the longer vengeance is delayed. Thus honour requires that the time lapse between the offence and its reparation should be as short as possible. *Nif* is asserted in the promptness and strength of the reply. Doubtless the reply is sometimes delayed for a very long time. It is said that Djeha, a legendary character, replied to someone who asked him when he had avenged his father: 'After a hundred years had gone by.' Another story tells of a lion who always walked at a measured pace: 'I don't know where my prey is,' he said. 'If it's in front of me, one day I'll reach it; if it's behind me, it'll catch up with me.' But revenge taken after a long delay is only praised in retrospect: before taken, it is all the more doubtful and uncertain; once it is taken, it is all the more meritorious. A large family has indeed sufficient members and courage not to delay for too long. Known for its *nif*, its sensitivity, and its resoluteness, it is even protected from all offence; by the threat it always presents to any potential aggressor, it appears that it is capable of riposting simultaneously with the offence. To express the respect that a good family inspires, the Kabyles say that it can 'sleep and leave the door open', or that 'its women can walk alone, with a golden crown on their head, without anyone dreaming of attacking them'.

The man of honour, he of whom it is said that he fulfils 'his role as a man' (*thirugza*), is always on his guard. Consequently he is immune from any attack, including the most ill-judged, and 'even when he is absent, there is someone in his house' (*El Kalaa*).

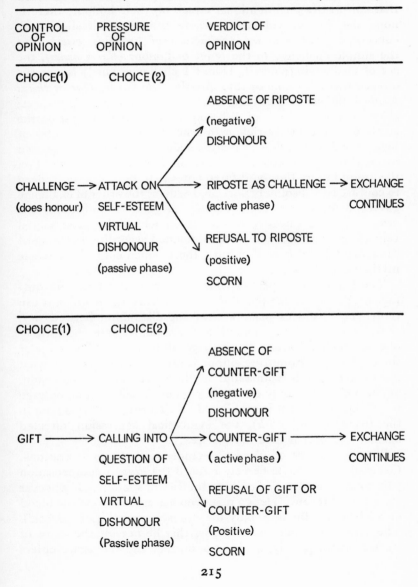

Point of honour and honour: NIF *and* H'URMA

If certain families and individuals are protected from offence that constitutes an intentional attack on their honour, there is none that is not vulnerable where unintentional slights are concerned (*thuksa nesser*, the action of breaking *esser*). But the simple challenge to the point of honour (*thirzi nennif*, the act of challenging; *sennif*, Done! I challenge you!) is not the offence that calls honour into question (*thuksa laqdhar* or *thirzi laqdhar*, the act of depriving one of or shattering one's respect; *thirzi elh'urma*, the act of dishonouring). Ridicule is cast on the attitude of the newly-rich man who, ignorant of the rules of honour and attempting to redress a slur upon *h'urma*, reposted by challenging his offender to beat him in a race, or to lay out on the ground more thousand franc notes than he. This was indeed to confuse two absolutely unrelated orders: the order of challenge governed by its own logic, namely *the game* of outbidding the other; and the category of offence in which the most sacred values are involved, and which is planned according to the most fundamental divisions of culture, those which control the whole mythico-ritual system.

The honour of respect of which the group is a target for outrage is opposed to the point of honour according to which it can reply. The Kabyles make a clear-cut distinction between *nif*, self-esteem or point of honour, and *h'urma*, honour, the entirety of that which is *h'aram*, that is to say all that is prohibited under the penalty of committing sin, or is sacred. Consequently, what makes the group vulnerable is its most sacred possession. While a challenge only casts a slur on one's self-esteem, outrage is a violation of what is prohibited, is a sacrilege. This is seen in the insult (*thimâayrith*), the symbolical aggression directed against whatever is held most sacred.

Thus a slur cast on *h'urma* precludes settlements or evasions. Generally the Kabyle fiercely refused the *diya*, a compensation paid by the murderer's family to the victim's family. Of whoever accepts it, it is said: 'He is a man who has agreed to eat the blood of his brother; for him, only his stomach counts' (*Ain Aghbel*). The *diya* is only accepted in cases that lie outside the scope of *h'urma*. Consequently, the logic of outrage and vengeance differs profoundly from the dialectic of challenge and riposte. Witness and judge, public opinion is the sovereign arbiter both of the gravity of the offence and of the appropriate vengeance. In the case of a slur upon *h'urma*, whether committed indirectly or inadvertently, the pressure of public opinion is such that any other way out save that of vengeance is excluded.[18] If this is not executed, there remains, for the coward bereft of *nif*, only dishonour and exile. *Nif*, honour in so far as I am attached to it, therefore obliges me to avenge any slur upon *h'urma*, honour in so far as it is attached to me. Indeed, if *h'urma* is defined as something which may be lost (*thuksa elh'urma*, the fact of taking away *h'urma*), in short as virtual dishonour, *nif*, while is does not protect *h'urma* from any slur cast upon it, yet makes it possible to restore its integrity. Thus the integrity of *h'urma* depends on the integrity of *nif*, the person lacking in *nif* being particularly exposed to seeing his *h'urma* impugned by the offence and to losing it entirely if he lacks sufficient courage to defend it. Honour is thus defined by the indissoluble link between *nif* and *h'urma*.

CONTROL AND VERIFICATION OF OPINION	CONSTRAINT OF OPINION	SANCTION OF OPINION
Outrage, slur on h'urma → (Honour in so far as it is attached to oneself)	*Riposte of nif* → (Honour in so far as I am attached to it)	*Honour restored, h'urma or esser* (esteem)
	Absence of riposte (Lack of nif) →	*Dishonour* social death *Exile*

Only the punctilious and active vigilance of the *point of honour* (*nif*) can guarantee the integrity of *honour* (*h'urma*) (which, being sacred, is naturally exposed to sacriligious outrage) and procure the *esteem and respectability* conferred by society upon whoever possesses sufficient point of honour to protect his honour from all offences.

Honour in the sense of esteem is termed *esser*. *Esser* is the secret, the prestige, the radiance, the 'glory', the 'presence'.

It is said of someone that '*esser* follows and radiates around him', or that he is protected by 'the barrier of *esser*' (*zarb nesser*). *Esser* is the protection of *nif*, by virtue of the fact that it protects whoever possesses it from being challenged.[19] To cast shame upon someone is 'to remove *esser*' (one also says 'to take away *lah'ya*', respect). *Esser*, that indefinable thing which makes a man of honour, is as fragile and vulnerable as it is imponderable. 'The *burnous* garment of *esser*,' say the Kabyles, 'is not tied on', and again, '*esser* is a turnip seed'.[20] (*Azerou n-Chmini*.)

H'URMA – H'ARAM *Honour* (honour in so far as it is attached to me) Capable of being lost, sacred and secret	NIF *Point of honour* (honour in so far as I am attached to it) Capable of defending *h'urma*, public
H'URMA or ESSER Esteem, honour, glory, respectability, is acquired, conquered and defended before other people	

H'urma, in the sense of something sacred (*h'aram*), *nif* and *h'urma* in the sense of respectability, constitute three inseparable aspects of a single total reality, each being a function of the other two. Thus, the greater a family's vulnerability, the more *nif* it must possess to defend its sacred values and the greater are the merit and esteem that public opinion accords it. This is why poverty, far from being considered a hindrance to respectability, makes doubly meritorious the person who, although he is particularly prone to outrage, succeeds in spite of everything in imposing respect, by respecting himself and through faithfulness to himself.[21]

Conversely, the point of honour only has significance and function for a man for whom sacred things exist, things which are worth defending. A person for whom nothing is sacred (for example, the bachelor) could dispense with the point of honour because in a certain way he would be invulnerable. In short, if the sacred (*h'urma-h'aram*) exists only through the sense of honour (*nif*) that defends it, the sentiment of honour exists by virtue of the sense that certain things are sacred.

How can one define these sacred things (*h'urma-h'aram*) that honour must defend and protect? Kabyle wisdom replies to this question: 'One's home, one's wife, one's rifles.' The polarity of the sexes, so strongly discernible in this society of patrilinear descent, is expressed in the division of the system of representations and values into two complimentary but opposing principles.[22] What is *h'aram* (namely, taboo, in the exact sense), is essentially the sacred of the 'left-hand', namely the intimate life, and more precisely, the feminine world, the world of the secret, enclosed space of the household, in contrast to the open world of the public square (*thajmaâth*), reserved for men.

The category of sacredness indeed applies very naturally to space. It is objectified in the form of spatial contrasts, by isolating from total space certain areas in order to make them sacred – as for example the home as the refuge of *h'aram*. The opposition between outside and inside, a special form of the opposition between masculine and feminine, appears as one of the fundamental dichotomies of Kabyle thought. But inside and outside are not situated side by side, each one constituting a separate domain; indeed, on the contrary, they are reflected in each other, and it is only by this opposition and this complementary nature that they reveal their true meaning.

The sacred of the 'right-hand' is essentially 'the rifles', that is to say the group of agnates, 'sons of the paternal uncle', all those whose death must be avenged by blood and all those who are bound to carry out blood vengeance. The rifle is the symbolical embodiment of the *nif* of the agnatic group, of *nif* defined as that which can be challenged and that which allows one to take up a challenge.[23] Thus, to the passivity of *h'urma*, continually threatened, and to the vulnerability of *h'aram*, of a feminine nature, is to be opposed the active susceptibility of *nif*, of a manly nature. If *h'urma* is identified with the sacred of the 'left-hand', that is to say essentially with what is feminine, *nif* is pre-eminently the manly virtue.

The opposition between these two aspects of sacredness, like the opposition between *h'aram* and *nif*, does not in any way exclude their complementary nature. It is indeed the respect for the sacred of the 'right-hand', for the name and good repute of the agnatic family, which motivates the riposte to any offence against the sacred of the 'left-hand'. Thus one must take care not to confuse a sacred value and an affective one. *H'urma* is not only what possesses value, is precious and cherished (*elâazz*); it is more precious than what is most precious, for it is cherished absolutely. The duty of defending what is sacred is imposed upon one as a categorical imperative, whether it is 'the sacred of the right hand', such as a male member of the group, or 'the sacred of the left hand', such as a woman, weak, impure, and malicious. If a Kabyle avenges his honour which has been impugned through his wife, this does not necessarily mean that he is impelled by jealousy or love; even if he was without either of these feelings he should nevertheless carry out his duty, and in so doing he would increase his merit. The attitude of the father who, disdaining his own feelings, killed his guilty daughter was praised and put forward as an example. Animated by love of honour more than by love itself, jealous of his honour rather than of his love, a Kabyle may wreak vengeance and wipe out the insult even by scorning his deepest feelings, and he will receive by so doing the complete approbation of the group. It is respect for the sacred of the right hand, for, that is to say, the honour of the agnatic family, which impels one to avenge the offence done to the sacred of the left hand, to the weaker party, through which the group is vulnerable.

Nif is therefore the love of the honour of the family, a love of *h'urma* in the sense of respectability and esteem, a love for the good name and renown of one's ancestors, a love of the ancestral lineage, which must remain pure and unsullied, and must be protected from offence as much as from misalliance.[24] It is *nif* that impelled the Kabyle to avenge pitilessly and intransigently any attack on the ancestral lineage itself, such as the murder of a blood-relation, as well as any attack on the weakest point of the family, namely on his wife or on those women to whom he is allied through women. Thus, *nif* is above all *amour-propre*, that is to say, in a society in which the individual exists only through the group, the respect and the love of the group.

Nif, the cardinal virtue, the basis of the whole patrilinear system, is indeed essentially a respect for one's lineage, of which one is proud, and of which one intends to be worthy. The greater the bravery or virtue of one's ancestors, the more one is justified in being proud and consequently the more one must be punctilious in honour in order to match that bravery and virtue. Thus birth, however important it may be, does not necessarily confer nobility; this can be acquired also by virtue and merit. The character of honour, no less than purity of lineage, imposes duties rather than bestows privileges. 'When there is damage to a great ship,' said an old man, 'it sinks; if it is a small boat one can always stop up the hole with one's hand.' (*Les Issers.*) Those who possess a name, those of good stock (*ath laâradh*), have no excuses.

The opposition between *h'aram* and *nif*, between the sacred of the right hand and the sacred of the left hand, is expressed in different proportional oppositions: the opposition between woman, burdened with powers that are harmful and impure, destructive and formidable, and man, invested with powers that are beneficent, fecund and protective; the opposition between magic, which is the exclusive affair of women and is concealed from men, and religion, which is essentially masculine; opposition between feminine sexuality, guilty and shameful, and virility, symbol of strength and prestige.[25] The opposition between the inside and the outside, a form of the opposition between the sacred of the left hand and the sacred of the right hand, is concretely expressed in the clear-cut distinction between the feminine area, the house and its garden, pre-eminently the place for *h'aram*,[26] an enclosed space, secret and protected, sheltered from intrusion and from the gaze of others, and the masculine area, the *thajmaâth*, the place of assembly, the mosque, the café, the fields or the market-place.[27] The opposition is between the secrecy of intimate life, entirely veiled in modesty, and the open area of social relationships, of religious and political life; between the life of the senses and feeling and the life of man-to-man relationships, of the dialogue and exchanges. In the Kabyle village the two areas are distinctly separate; the path that leads to the fountain avoids the domain of the men. In the urban world in which male and female areas overlap, claustration and the veil ensure the protection of the intimate life. Most frequently each clan (*thakharrubth* or *adhrum*) has its own fountain, situated in its own quarter or in the neighbourhood of its quarter, so that the women can go to it without running the risk of being seen by a man who is a stranger to the group[28] (*Ait Hichem*).

When this is not the case, the women go to the fountain at certain hours, at nightfall, for example, and a poor view would be taken of a man who went to watch them. The fountain is to the women what the *thajmaâth* is to the men. It is there that they exchange news and carry on their gossip which centres essentially on each other's private lives, on all the intimate affairs of which the men could not speak among themselves without incurring dishonour and of which they are informed only through their wives. It is commonly assumed that in North African society the woman is shut up in the house. In fact, this is completely untrue, because the peasant woman always works out of doors. Moreover, it should be remembered that, the house being the domain of women, the men are to some degree excluded from it. The place of the man is out of doors, in the fields or in the assembly, among other men. This is something taught very early to the young boy. Men who remain too much in the house during the daytime are suspect. The respectable man must allow himself to be seen, to show himself and place himself continually under the gaze of others, to face up to them (*qabal*). Hence a saying re-

H'URMA – H'ARAM	NIF
SACRED OF THE LEFT HAND	SACRED OF THE RIGHT HAND
Feminine, femininity	Masculine, virility
Woman, the possessor of harmful and impure powers	Man, the possessor of beneficent, fertilizing and protecting powers
Left, twisted. Vulnerability, nakedness	Right, straight. Protection, enclosure, clothing
INSIDE	OUTSIDE
The preserve of women: house, garden	The preserve of men: assembly, mosque, fields, market-place
Enclosed and secret world of the intimate life: food, sexuality	Open world of public life, of social and political activities. Exchanges
Magic	Religion
DAMP, WATER, etc.	DRY, FIRE, etc.

peated by women, and implying that the man is ignorant of much that goes on in the house: 'O man, you poor wretch, all day in the fields like a donkey in the pasture!' (*Ait Hichem*).

These proportional oppositions provided by the mythico-ritual system constitute the fundamental postulates of the system of values (cf. plan p. 222). From these postulates derive a certain number of rules of conduct.

The principal imperative is to conceal the whole domain of intimacy. Internal dissensions, failures, and insufficiencies must on no account be displayed before a stranger to the group. The house is the first small world of secrecy in the sub-clan or clan; the sub-clan or clan is a similar world in regard to the village, and the village is locked in its own secrecy in relationship to other villages. Thus there are as many concentric zones of secrecy as there are interlocking collectivities: family secrecy before a member of the clan; clan secrecy before a member of the village; village secrecy before a stranger to the village.

In this way it is natural that the moral code of woman, centre of this enclosed world, should be made up essentially of negative injunctions. 'Your tomb is your house', a maxim says. 'The woman owes faithfulness to her husband; her household must be well kept; she must watch over the good education of her children. But above all she must preserve the secrecy of the family's intimate life; she must never belittle her husband or shame him (even if she has every reason to do so, and all the necessary evidence), either in her intimate life or before strangers; for such action would force him to repudiate her. She must show herself satisfied, even if, for example, her husband is too poor to bring back something from the market; she must not interfere in the discussions between men. She must have confidence in her husband, must not disbelieve him, or seek to prove anything against him' (*El Kalaa*). In short, since she is always 'the daughter of so and so' or 'the wife of so and so', her honour, the woman's 'glory' are none other than the honour of the group of agnates to which she belongs. She must therefore be on her guard against acting in any way that might prejudice the prestige and reputation of the group.[29] She is the guardian of *esser*.[30]

The man, for his part, must above all protect and cast a veil (*esther*) over the secrecy of his house and his intimate life. Intimacy is connected first of all with one's wife, who is never referred to in this way, still less by her forename, but always by periphrases such as 'the daughter of so and so', 'the mother of my children' or even 'my house' (*akhamiw*). In the house the husband never addresses her in the presence of others; he calls her by beckoning, by a grunt or by the name of his eldest daughter, and never shows in any way his affection for her, above all in the presence of his father or his eldest brother. To pronounce the name of his wife in public would be a dishonour. It is often said that men going to report a birth at the registry office have sometimes stubbornly refused to give the name of their wife. In the same way convention ordains that one never speaks to a man about his wife or sister. This is because woman is one of those shameful things about which one never speaks without excusing oneself and adding 'saving your presence' (*h'achak*).[31] It is also because woman is for man the most sacred thing of all, as is shown by the expressions customarily used in oaths: 'May my wife be unlawful (if I do not do such and such a thing) (*thah'ram etmet't'uthiw*)', or 'May my house be unlawful for me!' (*ikhrem ukhamiw*).

Also belonging to the sphere of intimacy are what may be described as the natural aspects of life: the body and all its organic functions, the self and its passions, sentiments and affections. Honour commands that a veil is cast over these things. Any allusion to these subjects, and particularly to one's own sexual life, is not only forbidden, but almost inconceivable. For several days before and after his wedding, the young man takes refuge in a kind of retreat in order to avoid finding himself in his father's presence, a situation that would cause both of them unbearable embarrassment. In the same way, the young girl who has reached the age of puberty ties up her breasts tightly in a sort of corset that is buttoned up and lined; moreover, in the presence of her father and her elder brother, she stands with her arms folded over her chest[32] (*Azerou n-Chmini*). A man would not speak to his father or his elder brother about a girl or a woman that was a stranger to the family; consequently, when the father wishes to consult his son about his marriage, he has recourse to a relation or friend who serves as an intermediary. A Kabyle cannot enter a café where his father or elder brother are already sitting (and here the converse also applies); nor can he stand with them and listen to one of those wandering singers who recite licentious poems. The relationships between members of the family are all hedged in with similar prohibitions, the chief intention of which is always to conceal and cast a veil over the whole of this natural side of life.

Food must not be spoken of. One never wishes anyone 'good appetite', but only that they may eat their fill. Politeness requires that the host should continually invite his guest to help himself to more, whilst the guest should eat as discreetly as possible. To eat in the street is indecorous and immodest. When a Kabyle wishes to eat at midday in the market, he withdraws to a secluded corner; if the young boy nibbles at his cake before having left the market, his father makes him put it immediately into the hood of his garment. A Kabyle carrying away meat keeps it concealed in a sack or under his clothing. In the meal itself, the essential point is not to feed oneself, but to eat in common, to share the bread and salt, the symbol of alliance; eating at the same table is above all a communication and a communion.

Extreme modesty is the rule also in the expression of the feelings, even in the family circle, between husband and wife, between parents and children. A Kabyle told me that when he was still a child his mother used to send him to the assembly of men in order to fetch his father; he used to go up to him and silently press himself against him, and in this way his father understood that he was expected at home (*Tizi Hibel*). The expression of the feelings is always carefully controlled, restrained and reserved. Generally it is seemly to dissimulate and keep silent about the natural side of life, the inner world, the affections, emotions and feelings. *H'achma* (or even *lah'ya*), the modesty which governs all relationships between persons, even within the family circle, is essentially a protection for *h'aram*, for the sacred and the secret (*esser*). He who speaks about himself is unseemly or a boaster; he is incapable of submitting to the anonymity of the group, the essential principle of convention, which enjoins the use of the polite 'we' form or of the impersonal form, the context showing that one is talking of oneself.

Other principles also proceed from the system of complementary oppositions. These determine the divisions of labour between the sexes, and, more particularly, the division between the differing lines of conduct held to be honourable or dishonouring to men and women. In general, most tasks performed by women are held to be dishonouring for a man. But are they dishonouring because they are feminine or feminine because they are dishonouring? Or should one seek the basis for the division of labour between the sexes in a simple technical and economic differentiation, the industrial occupations devolving upon women, and the non-industrial tasks upon men? This, however, is clearly to question round in a circle. Is what determines the allocation of tasks their degree of hardship and difficulty? Yet a good number of feminine tasks are as laborious as those performed by men. In fact, it is once again the logic of the mythico-ritual system that furnishes the fundamental principles from which the system of values of honour has developed its own logic. Thus the Berbers of *Chenoua* cannot touch eggs or chickens save in the presence of people who are strangers to the family. They are forbidden to carry them to the market to sell them, since this is a matter for children or women. To ask a man whether he has any eggs to sell is to insult him. The men are allowed to slit the throat of chickens and to eat eggs so long as they are within their family.[33] The same customs are to be found, altered to a greater or lesser degree, in Kabylia. Similarly, the wife can ride on a mule with her husband holding the bridle rein; on the other hand, to ride on a donkey is shameful. Daughters who dishonour their family are sometimes led around publicly riding on a donkey, and there is a saying that 'Only the *Gabliyat* (women of the south) ride on donkeys.' Again, it is dishonouring for a man to carry a load of dung, since this is a woman's task, just as to carry water in earthenware jars, or wood for heating purposes, is also a woman's task (*Ait Hichem*). All these imperatives of the morality of honour which individually seem arbitrary and gratuitous, and whose non-fulfilment is regarded as barbaric, yet appear necessary if they are seen as a whole within the framework of the mythico-ritual system. And certainly one of the fundamental categories of this sytem is the division of the world into complementary and opposing principles, masculine and feminine; and of these principles, the oppositions between the sacred of the right hand and the sacred of the left hand, the outside and the inside, fire and water, dryness and dampness, constitute special facets.

That this is so is due to the fact that the same system of values dominates all early education. As soon as the boy has been given a name, he is considered, and must consider himself, as a responsible representative of the group. I was told that in a village of Great Kabylia a young boy some ten years old, the last male of his family, went to funerals even in distant villages and was present at ceremonies with adults (*Tizi Hibel*). The whole attitude of grown-ups, all the ceremonies and rites of initiation or passage from one state to another, tend to indicate to the boy his state as a man as well as the duties and responsibilities linked with it. The actions of childhood are very quickly evaluated in terms of the ideals of honour. The education imparted by the father or the paternal uncle tends to develop *nif* in the child, as well as all the manly virtues which are connected with it – the warlike spirit, boldness, vigour and endurance. In this education given by men and designed to mould men, the stress is laid on the paternal lineage, on the values that have been handed down by the male ancestors and of which every male member of the group must be the preserver and defender.

There is no doubt that the same mythico-ritual categories are the basis of the logic of matrimonial exchanges. This may be indicated briefly here. The reason for early marriage is obvious when one recalls that woman, who is bad by nature, has to be placed as soon as possible under the beneficial protection of man. 'Shame is a young girl' (*alâar, thaqchichth*), and the son-in-law is termed *setar laâyub*, 'the veil cast over shame'. The Arabs of Algeria sometimes call women 'the cows of Satan' or 'the devil's nets', thus signifying that they are the initiators of evil. 'The straightest woman,' says a proverb, 'is as twisted as a sickle'. Woman is like a young shoot which bends to the left; man is the guardian who sets it straight again. Woman cannot be straight, but only straightened by the beneficial protection of man.[34]

Without claiming here to grasp in all its depth the logic of marriage with one's parallel cousin, one may nevertheless note that the norms that regulate matrimonial exchanges and the rationalizations that are used most often to justify their form, are formulated in a language completely dominated by the categories that have been described above. Is it not said in Great Kabylia: 'It is better to protect one's *nif* than to give it over to others?' (*Djemaa-Saharidj*.) 'He has protected her' (*isethrits*) one says about a young man who has married his parallel cousin. He has acted in such a way that the secret of family intimacy is safe. (*Aghbala*.) One often hears it said that he who marries into his own family is certain that his wife will try to safeguard the honour of her husband, that she will keep secret the family disputes and will not go complaining to her parents. 'A woman who is a stranger to your family will disdain you. She will think that she belongs to a family nobler than your own; your cousin, on the contrary, who has the same paternal grandfather as yourself, will not be able to curse your ancestors' (*Ain Aghbel*). Marriage with a woman who is a stranger is feared as if it were an intrusion; it creates a breach in the protective barrier which surrounds the intimacy of the family.

The ethos of honour

The ethos of honour is fundamentally opposed to a universal and formal morality which affirms the equality in dignity of all men and consequently the equality of their rights and duties. Not only do the rules imposed upon men differ from those imposed upon women, and the duties towards men differ from those towards women, but also the dictates of honour, directly applied to the individual case and varying according to the situation, are in no way capable of being made universal. It is the same code which lays down opposing modes of conduct according to the social sphere. This is so much the case that a single system of values of honour establishes two opposing sets of rules of conduct – on the one hand that which governs relationships between kinsmen, and in general all personal relationships that conform to the same pattern as those between kinsmen; and on the other hand, that which is valid in one's relationships with strangers. This duality of attitudes proceeds logically from the fundamental principle, established previously, according to which the modes of conduct of honour apply only to those who are worthy of them.

It is because of this that a theft was only to be condemned when it was committed within the group. Carried out to the detriment of the enemy group – a rival tribe, for example – it was, on the contrary, held to be a feat of arms (*Ain Aghbel*). In the same way, the occupation of professional killer was considered an honourable one. To sell short weight, to deceive anyone as to the quantity, quality or kind of goods, to cheat at gambling, to bear false witness: these were actions to which no dishonour was attached, provided that one was dealing with strangers, that is to say, with people towards whom one had no duties of honour. On such an occasion, the rules of conduct required only that one should outwit one's opponent. The victim, wounded in his *amour-propre* and humiliated at having proved himself less adroit, accepted the trickery as an insult and plotted to avenge it, sometimes by violence. Once a very rich man, renowned for his sumptuous hospitality, was told by someone who was jealous of him: 'Guests should not be offered *couscous* of corn and mutton. The prostitute living at the corner has a pot as well filled as your own. To have a pot full of meat and lots of money is easy. It's not this that makes a man. What makes a man is for him to go to the market with very little money in his pocket and return with a pair of oxen' (*El Kalaa*). Although commercial and financial occupations like horse-dealing, and still more moneylending, were not regarded highly, theft or fraud were held to be reprehensible in themselves – so long as it was evident that they had been carried out with skill and craft – only when they were committed within the group.

Honour, when it concerns kinsmen or those to whom one is allied, imposes a completely different line of conduct, but one that derives from the same principles: 'Help your own kinsmen,' runs the proverb, 'whether they are right or wrong.' The values of honour are part of the atmosphere breathed by the closely-knit group, the clan or village; thus the precepts of the morality of honour are obligatory in all aspects of private and public life. If no distinction is made between the various spheres that our own society treats as autonomous, that is to say, subjected to principles and governed by a logic of their own – namely, law, politics and economics as such – this is because the personal relationships established within clan or village communities are conceived on the pattern of kinship relationships.

It is for this reason that values of honour constitute the true basis of the Kabyle political order. That such a system can function is due to the fact that compliance with the injunctions of the community is ensured by the feeling of clan solidarity which in its turn derives from the feeling of brotherhood that grows from living together. Consequently, social rules do not appear as a constraining force, for they both objectify the feelings of each individual and sustain the living reality of custom.

229

Respect for the injunctions of the collectivity is founded on respect for oneself, on, that is, the sentiment of honour.

The assembly of the clan or village is hardly a tribunal in the sense of a specialized organism entrusted with the task of pronouncing decisions in conformity with a system of formal, rational and explicit legal norms. It is rather an arbitrating council or can be a family council. Collective opinion constitutes the law, the tribunal and the executive power. The *thajmaâth* in which all the families are represented embodies public opinion, whose feelings and values it tests and expresses, and from which it derives all its moral force, since its condemnation casts shame upon the guilty. The punishment most feared is to be put under a ban or to be banished. Those sentenced in this way are excluded from the communal distribution of meat, from the assembly and from all community activities – in short, condemned to a sort of symbolic death. The *qanun*, a collection of customs peculiar to each village, consists mainly of an enumeration of particular crimes and of their corresponding penalties. Thus, for example, the *qanun* of Agouni-n-Tesellent, a village of the Ath Akbil tribe, numbers, out of a total of 249 articles, 219 'repressive' laws (in the sense employed by Durkheim) – *ie* 88 per cent – and 25 'restitutory' laws – *ie* 10 per cent – and 5 articles concerning the fundamentals of the political system. Customary regulation, derived from a jurisprudence directly applied to the particular case and not from the application of a general rule to a particular case, exists before it is formally framed. Indeed the basis of justice is not a formal, rational and explicit code, but a living sense of honour and a system of unformulated values. Its essence – the totality of the values and principles that the community asserts simply through its existence and on which its acts of jurisprudence rest – is itself unquestioned and unquestionable. 'What is forbidden by honour,' said Montesquieu, 'is even more forbidden when the laws do not forbid it; and what honour prescribes, is even more obligatory when the laws do not demand it.'

Economic relationships are also not considered as such, as relationships governed, that is to say, by the law of self-interest. They always remain, as it were, concealed beneath a veil of prestige and honour relationships. Everything takes place as if this society refused to face up to economic reality, to conceive it as governed by laws that are different from those regulating impersonal and family relationships. The result is a permanent ambivalence: by a kind of self-deceit one is continually acting both within an ambit of self-interest, which must not be admitted, and of honour, which is proclaimed. Is the logic of giving not a way of overcoming or concealing the calculations of self-interest? If a gift, like the granting of credit, entails the duty of giving back more, this obligation of honour, however categoric it may be, remains tacit and secret. If the counter-gift is deferred, does not the generous exchange, as opposed to a commercial one, tend to veil a transaction of undeclared self-interest by situating it in the temporal order, by substituting for the uninterrupted series of gifts followed by counter-gifts a discontinuous series of gifts with apparently nothing in return? Another example may be given. It is customary that the seller, after an important transaction such as the sale of an ox, ostensibly gives back to the buyer a portion of the sum of money he has just received 'so that the latter may buy meat for his children'. And the father of the bride does the same when he receives the bridewealth (*Ait Hichem*). The more considerable the share given back, the greater the honour accruing to the giver. Everything takes place as if the clinching of what is often a hotly argued bargain by a generous gesture is an attempt to cover the whole commercial nature of the transaction, and to make it look like an honourable exchange. Anxious to remain faithful to that picture of himself with which the community present him, the Kabyle strives to confer upon the actions and relationships of production a symbolic significance.

The sentiment of honour is the common and intimate code with reference to which the Kabyle judges his actions and those of others. But are the values of honour really the ideal norms that everyone accepts and feels bound to respect? Or are they on the contrary unconscious models of behaviour that govern one's conduct and regulate one's attitudes without clearly rising to consciousness, and which colour one's attitudes without ever being formulated? In practice, the system of the values of honour is lived rather than clearly conceived. Thus, when they spontaneously believe that such and such a mode of conduct is dishonouring or ridiculous, the Kabyles are like someone who

picks out an error of language without being in command of
the syntactical order which it infringes. Perhaps the essential
point is that the norms, felt and experienced so deeply that they
do not need to be formulated, have their roots in the system of
the most fundamental cultural categories, those which define the
mythical vision of the world. Consequently, nothing is more
difficult or can be more futile than to attempt to distinguish
between the area directly and clearly perceived by the consciousness and the area buried in the unconscious.

One example is sufficient to illustrate this. The man of honour
is the man who confronts others (*qabel*), who looks them in the
face; *qabel* also means to receive someone who arrives and to
receive him well, to do him honour. The word *leqbayel* (masculine plural) designates the Kabyles.[35] *Thaqbaylith*, the feminine
of the noun *aqbayli*, a Kabyle, designates the Kabyle woman, the
Kabyle language and also, if one can so express it, the quiddity
of the Kabyle, what makes a Kabyle a Kabyle, what he could not
cease to be without ceasing to be Kabyle, that is to say, the Kabyle
spirit, the Kabyle honour and the Kabyle pride. But *qabel* also
means to face the East, *elqabla* (feminine), and the future, *qabel*
(the next year). In the Kabyle mythico-ritual system, the East
has a homological connexion with the High, the Future, the
Day, the Masculine, the Good, the Right-hand, the Dry, etc,
and is opposed to the West, and at the same time to the Low, the
Past, the Night, the Feminine, Evil, the Left-hand, the Humid,
etc. All informants spontaneously assert that the essential
characteristic of the man of honour is the fact that he 'faces one',
qabel; it can be seen that the explicit norms of behaviour meet
and overlay the deepest categories of the culture.

The history of common and individual consciousnesses
demonstrates an unceasing movement towards a clarification in
which models, acted and lived without being stated thematically,
become norms and values explicitly recognized. Doubtless a
diachronic analysis would discern a reverse movement. If social
equilibrium requires a minimum of conformity between models
and norms, the existence of distance and disharmony revealed
by the mere act of clarification or rationalization saves society
from that immobility which over-perfect coherence, resulting
from complete identity with itself, must otherwise impose on it.
Perhaps it is this disharmony which gives societies and their

structures a history. A culture, like visible objects themselves, can only be apprehended in a series of profiles. The person who lives this culture can grasp it, not in its totality, but only through successive and partial views. The constant movement whereby the profile of a particular aspect of the whole appears for a moment at the centre of conscious vision, while the profiles of other aspects that may soon in their turn come to the fore are temporarily thrown into the background. This constant movement seems to be the essential characteristic of the way in which a subject perceives his culture.[36]

NOTES

Conditions and purpose of the enquiry

The analyses set out here are based on information and observations gleaned in the course of several enquiries carried out in different places in Kabylia between 1957 and 1961. In order, the principal places of enquiry were: Ait Hichem, a village of 800 inhabitants, belonging to the Ath Yahia tribe, situated 4 kilometres from Michelet; Aghbala, a village of 2,500 inhabitants, belonging to the Beni Jellil tribe and situated 25 kilometres from Sidi Aïch; Aïn Aghbel, a *Zriba* (clan) of 500 inhabitants, belonging to the tribe of the Beni Išaq, and situated 15 kilometres from Collo; Djemâa Saharidj, a village of 3,000 inhabitants (5,000, some months later, after the resettlements) belonging to the Ath Frawsen tribe. Other documentary evidence collected indirectly from informants residing in Algiers, concerns the villages of Taka, Tizi Hibel, in Great Kabylia, Les Issers in Little Kabylia, El Kalaâ among the Beni Abbas and Azerou n-Chmini among the Ath Ughlis in Little Kabylia. Certain information concerning a more distant period has been extracted from written sources that have been checked, as far as possible, by direct enquiry. This for example applies to the information concerning tribal wars, that was given by the *Bulletin pour l'Enseignement des Indigènes de l'Académie d'Alger*, and verified in 1960 through a centenarian of the *Zriba* of Aïn Aghbel. As, at every stage of the enquiry, the information was

H*

collected from different persons, and as the same information was, in most cases, checked in different places, it has seemed preferable to indicate in each case only the principal source of information in the form of the place of the enquiry.*

These different enquiries have given us many opportunities of determining how much the system of the values of honour as it has been described here has been changed and disturbed by the impact of different factors, among which not the least important are, first, the emergence of new models of behaviour determined by contact with European society, and, second, the war with its train of violence suffered and compulsory renunciations. However, it was not possible to examine within the framework of this study the extent, form and logic of these changes.†

1 *Bahdel*, means to dominate someone completely, to 'beat him hollow', to mock him, in short, to push victory beyond all bounds. *Bahdel* is more or less reprehensible according to one's opponent and above all according to what he is blamed for. Where *amahbul* is concerned, one does not say: 'I am afraid that he may mock (*bahdel*) me', but: 'I am not going to mock (*adhbahadlegh* – reflexive form – *ruh'iw* – my mind) myself with him.'

2 'He who strips his brother,' says the proverb, 'strips himself.' 'He insults himself (that is to say, his brother or his family), the donkey is worth more than he is: *Itsâayer imanis, deghyul akhiris.*' *Aayer* (verb) means: designate, point out (with one's finger), to call to account, to reveal, to denude, the *âar* of someone (*âar*, vulnerability, weak point, that by which one gives cause for dishonour), to insult; *âayer* designates the symbolic or ritual insults that women cast at one another (*lamâayrath*). Examples of *lamâayrath*: 'Your father is a stealer of chickens'; 'Your mother goes begging in the mills'. As an unfounded accusation the action of *âayer* is permitted to women, and of no consequence – not so for men. Whilst *âayer* demands a reply, at least on the same level – insult replying to insult – to parry it in the intention of leaving the other without any reply, *achuwah* is irreparable. *Achuwah* is to cause to lose face, above all among members of one's own group, by a clumsy and involuntary action, for example, by revealing a shameful secret in the presence of members of another group, or throwing into confusion the members

---

* For the names of places, the spelling of the General Staff maps has been preserved.

† *cf.* P. Bourdieu et A. Sayad, *Le déracinement* (Paris 1964).

of his own group. *Achuwah* is more permissible in a man than *âayer* (the opposite is true for a woman). The one who suffers *achuwah* confesses to it more readily than the one who suffers *âayer*.

3 The moustache is a symbol of virility, an essential component of *nif*; so too is, and was, the beard, especially in earlier times. To illustrate profound outrage, one said: 'So and so has shaved off my beard (or my moustache).' A popular song recalls in these terms the conquest and submission of the Djurdjura, which was offered to General Beauprêtre by a Si Djoudi, considered as a traitor among his own people:

> 'What a trick was played by El Djudi
> On the mountain of the Zwawa!
> He clipped their beard
> And shaved off their moustache.
> And the haughty mountain
> He lowered to the level of the Nezliwas!'

4 This custom was still in force about 1952. None would have risked breaking it, with the exception of the old men or sick people who were tacitly authorized to do so by the assembly.

5 Of a man who does not care much about his honour it is said: 'He is a negro.' The negroes do not have honour and need not have it. They were excluded from public affairs; although they could take part in certain collective affairs, they were not allowed to speak at the meetings of the assembly; in certain places they were even forbidden to be present. To listen to the opinions of a 'negro' would have been to cover oneself with shame in the eyes of other tribes. Kept outside the community or kept as clients of great families, they practised professions considered degrading, acting as butcher, skin merchant or itinerant musician and so on (*Ait Hichem*).

6 *Nif* is, literally the nose, and then the point of honour, one's *amour-propre*; *tinzarin* (or *enzaren*, according to the region), the plural of *tinzert*, the nostril, the nose, is also used in the same sense (*cf. elghir*, the point of honour).

7 The social function of the *marabouts* is evident. They find the way out, the 'door' (*thabburth*) as the Kabyles say, and sanction the ending of a fight without dishonour and shame recoiling on either of the contestants. Society, by a kind of self-deception indispensable in maintaining its existence, provides commands of honour as well as indirect ways by which they can be evaded without being violated, at least in appearance.

8 An old man of the village of Aïn Aghbel, in the Collo region, recently gave me (summer 1960) a description similar in all respects.

9 'Souvenirs d'un vieux Kabyle – lorsqu'on se battait en Kabylie' – *Bulletin de l'Enseignement des Indigènes de l'Académie d'Alger* Jan.–Dec. 1934, pp. 12–13.

10 By different processes the old witches charmed the eggs so that they remained 'virgin'. To break the charm the eggs were pierced with a needle (*cf.* Slimane Rahmani, 'Le Tir à la cible et le *nif* en Kabylie', *Revue Africaine* T. 93, 1er et 2ème trimestre, 1949, pp. 126–32). In the logic of the ritual system, the rifle and the rifle shot (like the needle) are associated with sexual virility. *Nif* is inseparable from virility, as we shall see later.

11 'On Balance of Power' quoted by R. Aron *Paix et Guerre entre les Nations* (Calmann-Lèvy 1962) p. 83.

12 One of the fundamental paradoxes of the phenomena of communication is that one must still communicate in order to indicate that one is stopping or refusing to communicate, as may be seen simply in the fact that one must speak in order to say: 'I am no longer speaking with you'; and every civilization invents a veritable symbolical system of non-communication. Among the Kabyles it is essentially the action of turning one's back, as opposed to *confronting face to face* (*qabel*), which is the distinguishing mark of the man of honour.

13 At Djemâa-Saharidj they still remember a *thamgerth* that lasted roughly from 1931 to 1945, in the tribe of the Ath Khellili (Ath Zellal). 'It had begun like this: two brothers had killed two brothers of another family. In order to make it look as if they had been attacked, one of the two brothers had wounded the other. They were sentenced, the one to eight years imprisonment, the other to a little less. When the second (the most influential in the family) was released, he was always glancing behind him, always on watch, always on his guard. He was assassinated by a professional killer. A third brother, who was a soldier, smashed the head of a member of the other family with a stone. The two families threatened to exterminate each other. There had already been eight victims (among them the four that have been mentioned). The *marabouts* were commissioned to try to settle the dispute. In spite of all their efforts to reach a settlement, the third brother, the soldier, would not hear a word of it. It was decided to maintain and prolong the struggle. The mediation of a notable of a neighbouring tribe, who had been a *caïd* and who was universally respected, was called for. The *Caïd* went to see the reluctant soldier and gave him a good talking to: "Your head is already in the *delu*" (the funnel through which the grain passes to the millstone). "Next time your head will go under the millstone." The young man had a kind of nervous breakdown; he offered his own head. He was asked to declare solemnly that he agreed to put a stop to the extermination. The *fatiha* was pronounced.

In the presence of the assembled village, an ox was sacrificed. The young soldier offered money to the *marabouts* and *couscous* was eaten in common.' (The story is told by one of the protagonists.) It can be seen that the intervention of the group is essential when the sub-groups are threatened with destruction. By virtue of the fact that the logic of challenge and riposte would entail the endless prolonging of the exchange, it was vital, in any case, to find an honourable way out of the dispute, a 'door' (*thabburth*), that is to say a solution which does not cast dishonour on either party and which without violating the dictates of honour, sanctions their suspension in the particular circumstances. The task of conciliation fell always on the major group or on 'neutrals', strangers or the families of *marabouts*. Thus, so long as the difference is situated within the framework of the greater family, the wise men dictate the line of conduct and settle the conflict. Sometimes they impose a penalty on the refractory party. When the conflict arises between two great families, the other families of the same *adhrum* attempt to settle it. In short, the logic of conciliation is the same as the logic of conflict between sections of the same lineage, whose first principle is contained in the proverb: 'I hate my brother, but I hate the one who hates him.' (*Cf.* Pierre Bourdieu, *The Algerians*, Beacon Press, pp. 100–1, September 1962). When one of the two factions was of *marabout* origin, it was other *marabouts*, who were strangers, that came to invite them to make peace. The wars between the two moieties were subject to the same logic as revenge. This can be understood when it is realized that revenge is never, properly speaking, individual, the perpetrator of vengeance being always the agent of the sub-group of which he is a member. The *nefra* could sometimes be prolonged for decades. 'My grandmother related to me,' recounts an informant from Djemâa-Saharidj, 'that the çuff *ufella* (moiety of high) spent twenty years away from home, in the valley of Hamrawa. What had happened was that the defeated *çuff* had had to take flight with its women and children. In general, the antagonism between the *eçffuf* was so rigid and strict that marriages were impossible. However, sometimes, to set the seal on peace between two families or two *eçfuff*, a marriage was effected between two influential families. The marriage guaranteed the end of the struggle. In this case it was no dishonour, to seal the peace; after a *nefra*, the two *eçfuff* met together. The heads of the two factions brought with them a little gunpowder; this was put into reeds that were exchanged. This was *aman*, peace.'

14 *Cf.* the first story, pp. 1–3.
15 *Cf.* the second story, pp. 4–5.
16 The cousin of a complacent husband (called '*radi*', the consenting

or '*mustaâlem*', the one who knows) said to somebody one day: 'What can you do? When you have a brother who has no *nif*, you can't stick a *nif* of earth on him!' And he continued: 'If my cousin was an invalid it would be normal for me to avenge him; and if he had no money, it would be normal that I pay to avenge him. But he sits back, takes it and doesn't care. I'm not going off to Devil's Island or going to ruin myself for his sake!' (*El Kalaa*). The fear of French justice, the weakening of the sentiment of family solidarity and the contagious effect of another system of values have often caused the Kabyles to give up the ancient code of honour. In former society, honour was indivisible, like the family land. Alongside the tendency to break up the indivisibility of the family possessions which has manifested itself ever more and more strongly in the last twenty years, the feeling has developed that the defending of one's honour is a matter that concerns the individual alone.

17 In the Béarn one says of a man who delays doing his duty: he will have to do it 'out of shame or out of honour'; in other words, the fear of shame will impose on him what the sense of honour cannot inspire in him.

18 *H'urma*, being in a certain respect identifiable with *h'aram*, with what is objectively sacred, can be violated inadvertently. It has been seen, for example, that theft from an inhabited house was particularly serious and required vengeance because it constituted a slur on *h'urma*; theft or fraud on the market-place merely constitutes a challenge and a slur on the *amour-propre* of the victim. The village has also its *h'urma*, which can be violated, for example, when a stranger comes to make a scandal.

19 *Esser*, charm, grace (speaking of a woman), nobility, strength, authority, power, magical power acting in favour of the one who possesses it, predisposing men and nature in his favour, protecting him against assaults on his honour and against dangers. *Esser* paralyses the offender through its mysterious influence. '*Adhidum Rebbi esser*: May God cause *esser* to stay with you always.' *Esser* is the secret, the intimacy, what a man does not wish to reveal, his thoughts, his body, his past, what is most personal to him, most irreplaceable, that which cannot be displayed in public, that which is not expressed, mystery, the ineffable. The wife must always protect the *esser* of her husband. It is said: 'Weave for him a blanket (or *djelaba*) of *esser*' (*cf. elhiba*, moral authority; *nur*, light, radiance; *elâardh*, width, volume; by extension, what is imposing; desire not to weaken that by which one is imposing; honour, self-respect, dignity, restraint (*aârdhi*, the man of honour); *thaqbaylith*, the fact of being Kabyle, Kabyle honour; *thirugza* or *thirujla*, the fact of being a man (*argaz* or *rajel*); *chiâa*, decoration, insignia, the

action of performing a brilliant feat by which one leaves one's mark.)

20 The turnip seed, minute and round, is extremely slippery.

21 The following narration, given by an old Kabyle of the Ath Âidel who had heard it from his father, gives the portrait of the man of honour, a portrait in every way identical to the one drawn for me by a man of the tribe of the Issers, which leads one to believe that it concerns a mythical and exemplary person whose adventures are each time situated against a familiar background. There was once a man of Illulen who was called Belkacem u Aïssa and who, despite his ignorance, was respected for his wisdom and virtue. His influence extended over several tribes. Each time there was a dispute or fight, he served as mediator and settled the conflict. The Ben Ali Cherif, a great family of the region, were jealous of his influence and prestige, all the more so because he refused to pay them homage. One day the tribesmen decided to attempt to reconcile them. They invited the eldest member of the Ben Ali Cherif family, as well as Belkacem u Aïssa. When the latter entered, the old man, who was already sitting down, said to him ironically: 'How fine your *arkasen* (plural of *arkas*, the country footwear of a ploughman) are!' Belkacem replied: 'Custom demands that men look others in the face – in the face and not at the feet. It is the face, the honour of a man, that counts.' To strangers who asked him how he had acquired his influence in the region, Belkacem replied: 'I first gained the respect of my wife, then of my children, then of my brothers and my relatives, then of my locality, then of my village: the rest merely followed.'

22 This bipartite division appears indeed as one of the fundamental categories of Kabyle thought, and especially of the mythico-ritual system. Everything takes place as if this system had provided the fundamental postulates (the impure nature of woman, for example) from which the system of values may have developed its own logic. The mythico-ritual system in all its aspects cannot be studied within the framework of this paper. At the risk of appearing to proceed by begging the question, we will do no more here than recall the meanings, the knowledge of which is indispensable for an understanding of the system of values, because they constitute, if they may be so termed, its axioms and postulates.

23 Formerly, in certain regions of Great Kabylia, the *thajmaâth* (assembly) obliged the tribesmen, under the threat of paying a penalty, to buy a rifle in order to be able to defend their own honour, and that of the group. He who failed to comply, in spite of the penalty, was banned, scorned by all, and considered to be 'a woman', the supreme dishonour.

24 Matrimonial alliances with stranger groups always run the risk of

239

diluting the purity of the blood and compromising the integrity of the group of agnates. The desire to preserve the purity of the blood and the family honour unchanged is the reason invoked most frequently to justify marriage with a parallel cousin. Among the gravest insults is the one that calls into question the purity of the lineage: *ammis Bu Winathen*, 'son of so and so'.

25 The connection between *nif* and virility is particularly revealed in ritual games, such as target shooting, which is practised at the birth of a boy, at a circumcision and a marriage. We have indicated above other significant relations between the needle, the rifle and the rod, between the rifle shot or casting of a stone, and the sexual act.

26 The threshold, the point of meeting between two hostile worlds, is the site of multitudinous rites, and completely hedged round by prohibitions. In certain regions of Kabylia, only relatives can cross the threshold, because the house is the place of family secrecy. In any case, one could not enter without being invited to do so. The visitor makes known his presence by a shout, as in the South of France, or by coughing and shuffling his feet. According to custom in certain regions (El Kseur, Sidi Aïch) the distant relative or relative on the female side (for example, the wife's brother), who is introduced into the house for the first time, hands over a symbolic offering called 'the sight' (*thizri*). The village is also a sacred area; one only enters it on foot.

27 Formerly, it is related, the women went to the market alone, but they were so talkative that the market dragged out until the market of the following week. Then one day the men swooped down on them armed with sticks and put an end to the idle chatter of their womenfolk. It can be seen that the present apportionment of space and tasks is explained by the myth which invokes the 'evil nature' of women. To indicate that the world is topsy turvy, it is said that 'the women are going to the market'.

28 Each lineage, even at the lowest level, constitutes a virtual social unit. In case of dispute, the political organization is redefined on each occasion, according to the relative genealogical position of the persons concerned. Consequently, by the same logic very extensive groupings can be constituted, namely all the descendants of an ancestor to the fourth or fifth generation, or even of a mythical ancestor, for example, of the tribe, as well as extremely closely knit groupings, such as the wider or narrower family. It is, evidently, just the same whether the conflicts are between individuals or between groups, since whether one belongs to such and such a group, or such and such a genealogical degree, is defined in relation to the nature of the opponent group. The *thakharrubth* or *adhrum* may be defined as the sum total of people who owe to each other

blood vengeance and between whom there is no blood vengeance, and also as those who are on the same side in case of a dispute.

29 Everything occurs as if the woman could not really increase the honour of the agnates, but only preserve it intact by her good conduct and respectability, or destroy it (*ekkes elâardh*, take away one's reputation) by her misconduct. Only alliance by marriage with the male relatives of the wife can increase the honour of the group.

30 *Cf. supra*, p. 239, note 21, in the portrait of the man of honour: 'I first gained the respect of my wife . . .'

31 The Arabs say '*lamra âara*', 'woman is shame'.

32 The taboo against nakedness is absolute, even in sexual relationships. Moreover, as one knows, dishonour is described in popular expressions as being placed in a state of nudity: *ijayi âaryan* (from *âerri*, to bare, to strip naked), he has left me naked; *amin iyiksen âaryan*, as if he had stripped me; *ţuwaârragh yer elghachi*, I have been unclothed in everybody's presence; *ikseyi lah'wayej*, he has taken away my garments.

33 *Cf.* Laoust *Etude sur le dialecte berbère du Chenoua comparé avec celui des Beni Menacer et des Beni Salah* (Paris, Leroux, 1912) p. 15.

34 'The dignity of the daughter,' runs an Arab proverb, 'exists only when she is with her father.'

35 *Cf.* A. Picard *Textes berbères dans le parler des Irjen* (Kabylia, Algeria) Alger 1961.

36 If the whole of the analyses set out in this study constantly cause the Western reader to refer to his own experience or his own cultural tradition, the differences must not be minimized. This is why we have made it a rule to avoid suggesting comparisons for fear of encouraging ethnocentric identifications. In our society the modes of conduct that stem from the logic of challenge and riposte are rather a function of individual inclinations (although their institutional aspect is never completely absent). In Kabyle society, these modes of conduct have a totally different meaning, because essentially they regulate relationships between groups (since relations between individuals always affect the groups), and because they obey institutionalized rules approved by the whole group even when the system of which they form a part is not in itself one of which they are conscious. Finally, the modes of honourable behaviour form part of a mythico-ritual system from which, in the last analysis, they derive their sense. Thus the relation between person and object can be defined with reference to very different contexts, theft being interpreted, according to the case, as a mere act of aggression, as a challenge, or as an offence.

Abou A. M. Zeid

HONOUR AND SHAME AMONG THE BEDOUINS OF EGYPT

Of all the value concepts employed by the Bedouins of the Western Desert of Egypt, those of 'honour' and 'shame' are the most vague, most complicated and most difficult to grasp and to analyse. For both words are used very freely in daily parlance in reference to a large variety of modes of behaviour. A man is considered 'a man of honour' if he displays honesty in his personal dealings and contacts, if he keeps his promises and sticks to his word, if he revolts against injustices and declines to comply with any form of oppression, and if he shows sufficient eagerness and readiness in defending his own interests as well as those of his kin-group and his neighbours. Shame, on the other hand, is ascribed to those who fail to observe the rules of good manners in general: the unreliable, the treacherous, the spiteful and the unfaithful to both their spouses and their friends.

The Arabic word *sharaf* (honour) comes from a root verb which implies 'highness' both in physical position and in social standing. All good achievements, whether realized by personal endeavour or by the laborious efforts of other members of the kin-group to which a man belongs, build up his *sharaf* or at least contribute to it. Thus, a man's share of honour is largely determined by his own personal behaviour and by the behaviour of his kinsmen, particularly his near agnatic kin. The kin-group as a whole has its specific *sharaf* which is acquired mainly, but not entirely, by the achievements of its own living members and their good deeds. That is the main reason why the different groups of kin which belong to one and the same clan enjoy different 'levels' or 'degrees' of *sharaf*. *Sharaf* can thus be described as 'honour' which is acquired either by personal achievements or through belonging to a certain kin-group whose members, living or deceased, have succeeded in attaining, for themselves and by honest means, a minimum of prestige in their community. In this sense, *sharaf* can be subject to increase or decrease, to development or deterioration, according to the conduct of the person and his kin. Heroic raids on hostile camps enhance the prestige of the raiding group and augment their *sharaf*, whereas defeat and hesitation to take reprisal eradicate the *sharaf* and bring shame.

The two concepts are in fact more complicated and more confused than they may seem to be. The same attribute or action may bring honour or shame on the performer and his kinsmen according to the particular situation or context. Shyness, for example, is generally appreciated in the woman and is taken as a sign of fine breeding and good manners. It is also a sign of solid character in the man in his dealings with women. But it is shameful for a man to be shy in the society of men. Bedouin society which admires, and in fact encourages, attacks on the camps of strong and powerful clans considers it a most shameful action to violate the rights of the poor and the weak. Daring raids on large hostile camps which result in killing a number of men and driving away their camels are highly praised and deeply admired. In certain clans, a girl may ask her young man, as a condition to her consent to marriage, to bring her as part of the bridewealth a camel which he himself has seized during a raid on a hostile camp. This is still regarded as a most daring action of chivalry and heroism which enhances the prestige of the young man and his group. To seize any lesser animal, such as a sheep or a goat, is usually looked upon as a rather mean action, as mean as the seized animal itself, and is likely to arouse pity.

However, it should be noted that not all bad deeds are equally shameful and not all good deeds are equally honourable. Different shameful or honourable actions bring different kinds of shame or honour and provoke different reactions. Thus although all shameful actions raise the indignation and disapproval of society, this shame may in some cases befall the performer only and in certain other cases his group as well, requiring communal action against them. In the first case, for example, if a woman should wear short clothes, the action is called *'aib*. In the second case an action, such as adultery or rape, is called *'ar* and brings *'ar*. Actions of *'aib* do not usually require severe intervention on the part of society as a whole and any response is usually directed against the wrongdoer himself. Such response takes a mild form. The wrongdoer may be blamed or mocked and ridiculed or simply taken as a joke. Actions of '*ar* are treated differently, for they usually bring shame not only on the performer but also on his kin, as well as on the victim and his kin. Here different groups of people are involved, and the action threatens the social equilibrium.

The same principle applies to the concept of honour, but with much more confusion, since the Bedouins (who use the word *sharaf* to refer to the 'honour' of both individual and group) have a separate word for the honour of woman. This exclusive term, '*ird*, is rather difficult to translate, for it is used only in connection with female chastity, prudence and continence. We shall discuss the concept of '*ird* later in detail. But it should be borne in mind that the Bedouins distinguish between the 'individualistic' and the 'communal' connotations of 'honour' and 'shame', *io*, between the honour or the shame of the person as an individual and that of the group, *vis à vis* other similar groups within the community. This distinction may sound rather arbitrary, for the good or bad behaviour of the individual affects the prestige of his kin-group, while, on the other hand, the individual acquires much of his social standing from his kinsmen. Yet the distinction does exist, is recognized and has far-reaching effects.

This essay will be concerned mainly with 'honour' and 'shame' in their communal connotations and only as far as they have a bearing on the whole of social life. Thus, it will not deal with the concept of '*aib* or with the *sharaf* of the individual; whenever the word 'shame' is used, it will mean '*ar*, while 'honour' will invariably mean the *sharaf* of the group. It will nevertheless be necessary to examine, in detail, the term '*ird*. Only in this usage have the two concepts a clear structural meaning and only here do they express a solid body of values which control the patterns of behaviour in Bedouin society and act as an effective check on social relations. With these limits and restrictions borne in mind, let us go on to analyse the two concepts among the Bedouins of the Western Desert of Egypt, and in particular, those sections of the Awlad Ali clans in the Sallum area, near the Egyptian-Libyan frontiers.

I

We need not go into detail about the tribal structure of the Awlad Ali. Only the essential facts will be given here. The Awlad Ali clans who comprise the majority of the inhabitants of the Western Desert are an offshoot of the famous Sa'adi tribes of Cyrenaica. They were driven out of Libya and forced to take asylum in Egypt after their defeat in some tribal war, but nevertheless they still maintain strong links with their Cyrenaican cousins, especially the 'Ebeidat who live near the Egyptian border. Descending from a common ancestor, they soon bifurcated into two major branches known as Awlad Ali El-Ahmar (the Reds) and Awlad Ali El-Abiad (the Whites). Each branch has since segmented into smaller sections all of which, perhaps with the exception of the smallest, are invariably called 'tribe'.

Besides the Arab Awlad Ali, there also exist a few Morabiteen clans of Berber origin who occupy an inferior political position, although they enjoy a certain degree of social prestige acquired from their unique position as the religious leaders of the community. The Morabiteen are generally regarded as the 'People of God', for they mediate between disputing parties and restore friendship between hostile clans. Nevertheless, their social status is in general lower than that of the Cyrenaican Morabiteen because the Egyptian Bedouins, especially the younger generation, have grave doubts about their piety and religious sincerity and are inclined to overlook them in their disputes. They claim to be the descendants of the original inhabitants who lived in the Western Desert and North Africa long before the Arabs came. But although this is a source of pride to them, they increasingly tend to attach themselves to the more powerful Sa'adi even to be grafted on to one or another Arab clan.

Both Sa'adi and Morabiteen clans display the same general structural principles, especially in regard to their segmentation. The smallest kinship unit is the *beit* (*ie* the people of the tent) which is the basis of all social organization. One seldom comes across a single tent standing alone. More frequent is the *nag'a* or camp which comprises anything from four to thirty tents, inhabited by cousins descending from a common ancestor usually three or four generations back. In the larger camps some of the tents are occupied by the herdsmen, or perhaps the agricultural labourers, who herd the flocks or till the land of the original members of the *nag'a*.

The economic activities of the Sa'adi and Morabiteen are generally determined by the prevailing physical conditions. Livestock husbandry is the main and most honourable occupation, although it is always supplemented by a little barley cultivation along the coast. The life of the people and their activities follow therefore a dual pattern which entails two different structural relationships. In the wet winter season they move south after sowing their barley. The search for pasture compels them to spread widely in the desert, with the result that the clan divides into a large number of small grazing bands. With the coming of spring and the dry summer, these small bands move slowly back to the north and gather gradually round the water holes in larger clusters. But it is very seldom indeed for all the members of one clan, or even one lineage, to come together for a long period.

This brief and rather sketchy account should be enough to bring out the two central points round which most of the Bedouin values concerning honour and shame revolve, *ie*, kinship and livestock. A man feels proud of the size of his kin-group in the same way that he feels proud of the size of his flock and he defends both his kinsmen and his herds with the same zeal. Both kinsmen and livestock are important in regard to political power and social security. In spite of the increasing drift, especially among the younger generation, to settled agricultural life and to wage labour, it is usual to invest savings in animals, particularly in sheep. A man who does not own livestock is regarded as rootless and is not considered a real member of the community. In fact, the wealth of a person is always measured by the number of animals he owns regardless of his other possessions. This means that his prestige and his social standing, which are constituent parts of his personal honour, are actually determined by the size of his herd. This is especially so because land is generally regarded as owned exclusively by the State which grants only the rights of usufruct to the people. Wells also are owned either by the clan or a clan-segment as a whole but never by an individual. It is the livestock which constitutes the object *par excellence* of private ownership and although people may speak about the flocks of a certain lineage or clan, a distinction is clearly and neatly made between the animals owned by the different members of that group. The role which livestock plays in determining the political power of a person or group is shown in the fact that a wealthy man, *ie* a man with a large number of animals, is likely to be invited to look into disputes and to settle quarrels. He is also likely to offer hospitality to others, thus rallying adherents and clients both round himself and round his kin-group. It is a fact that generosity and hospitality have always been accorded a supreme value in Bedouin society and many persons have established their fame and prestige, and consequently those of their respective groups, by lavish generosity and nothing less than reckless hospitality.

In the same way, considerations of kinship control the behaviour and attitudes of the people and determine their social standing. The migration of the young men from their traditional tribal land in search of new wage jobs has certainly weakened the bonds of kinship, but it has not severed them completely. In fact, the traditional social obligations are to a great extent still observed. Kinship bonds are traced with great precision over a number of generations, and the exact relationship between a man and other members of his clan are usually common knowledge. But although a man owes his loyalty and allegiance in the first place to his immediate lineage and kin, he always regards himself and his lineage as part of a larger kin-group from which they both derive much of their prestige, social standing and 'honour'. Similarly, a man feels responsible in the first place for maintaining and defending the honour of his immediate kin, but at the same time he bears responsibilities towards other members of his clan which vary according to the place which his own lineage occupies in the total kinship structure. In this sense it can be said that a study of honour and shame among the Bedouin is, to a great extent, a study of the bonds and values of kinship.

2

In a society like that of the Bedouins of the Western Desert where most people descend from a single ancestor, it is difficult to attribute differentiated honour to origin or race. Racial differences amount to no more than the large, but rather vague, distinction between the Sa'adi who are of Arab origin and the few Morabiteen who come from Berber stock. All the Sa'adi descend from one or other of the two brothers, Ali El-Ahmer and Ali El-Abiad, and all give much weight to their Arabian origin in contrast to the Berber origin of the Morabiteen. The Awlad Ali may, however, boast among themselves about the purity of the Arabian blood in their veins since marriages with Berber women and women from the Nile Valley take place from time to time and lead to mixed blood in various degrees. It is honourable to have pure Arabian blood without the slightest trace of Berber or 'peasant' blood. We shall come back to this point later.

Kinship affects the honour of the lineage and the clan in certain other ways. In the first place, the size of the lineage is relevant. A man usually takes pride in the number of his offspring, for this is a simple and obvious token of his sexual virility and masculinity. The size of the lineage is also a determining factor in political and military affairs which, in Bedouin society, hinge upon the opposition, and sometimes bitter strife and overt struggle, between lineal groups with conflicting interests. A large lineage is a potential guarantee against injustice and maltreatment and in general a deterrent against aggression of any kind. It is also a potential striking force which can be used in raiding hostile groups. We have already noted the Bedouin ideals of military strength and courage in offensive raids. The hero dies gun in hand here and each clan has its own 'poet' and 'orator' to praise the heroic achievements of the members of the clan throughout the ages. These poems are recited in the camp at night and are learnt by heart as a precious heritage. Thus the living can celebrate the actions of their dead ancestors who contributed so greatly to their honour.

Such feats could hardly be achieved without a numerous clan. So the importance of numbers for acquiring and maintaining honour is clearly recognized. But mere numbers would not mean much unaccompanied by social, military and political dominance. The importance of number as a factor in honour manifests itself in various ways. A man usually regards himself as a member of a kinship unit larger than the small *beit* to which he belongs. For although the *beit* is the effective social and economic unit in day-to-day life, it does not by itself confer enough honour. A man takes pride in his particular *beit* only on the occasion of an outstanding achievement of a fellow-member. The other kin-groups related to it then hasten to associate themselves to that particular *beit* on the assumption that it is their undisputed right to share in the prestige and honour acquired by it. Thus honour usually spreads beyond the limits of the particular group which achieves it. It is the heritage of the whole lineage or the whole clan according to the circumstances. Hence the tendency of individuals to attach themselves by one means or another to the group which has gained such honour. Hence also the complementary tendency to drop from their consideration the less important and less famous ancestors as well as the less significant clan segments which have not acquired high prestige. These tendencies lead one into great confusion when one tries to trace the kinship relationships in any Bedouin clan. Yet they illustrate the importance of kinship in the field of honour.

3

Membership of a certain clan or lineage imposes on its members certain well-defined obligations and responsibilities towards one another. The higher the status of the kin-group in the community, the more rigorous and binding are these obligations and responsibilities. This appears not only in the patterns of behaviour which should be followed or in the rules which control daily contacts and dealings, but also and more particularly, in the duties which a man should feel constrained to perform towards his kin especially in times of social, economic and political crisis. Thus it is a man's responsibility to help the needy, to defend the weak and to protect and support the oppressed within his own lineage and to a lesser degree his clan. Failing to comply with these binding duties brings shame on him and on his immediate *beit*. These responsibilities vary, nevertheless, according to the nature and degree of the kinship links and although a man is generally expected to protect the good name of his clan as a whole, his responsibility is greater in the case of his immediate *beit*. Good deeds and right actions enhance initially the prestige of the *beit* and subsequently that of the lineage and the clan. Similarly, a man who commits a shameful blunder brings shame initially on himself and on his *beit* and subsequently tarnishes the honour of his clan as a whole. For the *beit* is the nuclear unit on which all social organization is based and although it derives much of its prestige and honour from the lineage or clan of which it forms a part, it contributes in turn to that honour (or reduces it) by the behaviour of its members.

In Bedouin usage, the word *beit* covers both the tent and its occupants who always form one family. A tent, as has been said, seldom, if ever, stands alone. More frequently a number of tents, forming a large family or a lineage segment, cluster together and act as one solidary economic, kinship and political unit. In this dual sense the *beit* is regarded with tremendous respect and jealousy and even with awe. It is often referred to as the *ḥărăm* (sanctuary) and is regarded in this sense as a sacred thing. It is also *ḥarām* (taboo) and thus strangers are forbidden to come near it without the permission of its members. For the *beit* is, in the first place, the abode of the *ḥ'aram* (womenfolk), a word which, misunderstood and abused, acquired a derogatory meaning outside Bedouin society. Contrary to the prevalent idea, the woman, who occupies a secondary position in relation to man, is always regarded as something sacred and to be protected from desecration. In fact, much of the honour of the *beit* and the lineage depends on observing this sanctity and in this sense a woman plays a vital and unique role in preserving the honour of her people. This role is connected in the first place with her nature as a female, subject to sexual desires and temptations. The reputation of a woman and her people thus depends mainly on her willingness to observe the rigid and severe rules governing sexual relationships and on her ability to preserve her chastity. It is a most humiliating and destructive blow to the honour of the lineage if a woman is discovered to have yielded to her sexual impulses outside marriage. Thus the main contribution a woman makes to the honour of the lineage is through this passive role of preserving her chastity and purity. We shall return to this point in the following section. Gossip may spread about a woman who does not keep strictly to the conventional rules of behaviour and her relatives may be taunted for this. In such cases, it is the duty of her agnatic kin to get rid of her. But on the other hand, if the accusation turns out to be false, the slanderers are held responsible for whatever may have happened to the innocent woman. In any case, tribal customary law permits the killing of a man who has committed a sexual offence against a woman, or kidnapped her, as used to happen before the authority of the government reached the nomadic groups in the heart of the desert. If the offender escapes, his kinsmen are held responsible for his action and retaliation may be exacted from any one of them. Sometimes the two parties reach an agreement with regard to the payment of honour compensation which varies according to the nature of the damage and the status, married or single, of the woman. Nevertheless, the payment of compensation does not prevent her kinsmen, in most cases, from killing her, if it is known that sexual intercourse took place with her consent. Sometimes, the girl is killed even if she were raped. It may be significant that the Bedouins before Islam practised female infanticide as a safeguard against a girl's future misbehaviour or kidnap. It may also be significant that the way of ending a long feud is for the aggressors to give one of their girls in marriage to the wronged party, not as compensation but as a sign of good faith, manifest in the act of entrusting them with such a precious 'part' and symbol of their honour.

Indeed the concept of the *haram* implies immunity not only to the original members of the *beit*, but also to all strangers who may be staying in the tent. Any attack on such persons is automatically taken as a direct assault on the members of the *beit* themselves and an insult to and infringement of their honour. Consequently the responsibility for protecting and defending these strangers and the obligation to avenge any injury done them falls on the *beit*. This principle has led to the emergence of a number of rules which take the form of absolute rights and which control people's behaviour in regard to the *beit* and its occupants.

Perhaps the most important of these rights bearing on the honour of the *beit* is what is generally known as the 'right of refuge'. According to this right a man pursued by enemies for a crime may enter any tent and claim asylum. It is the duty of the head of the *beit* and all his kinsmen to protect the fugitive and take him after a certain length of stay either to another *beit* to receive the same treatment for the same period or to arrange his escape. During the period the fugitive spends in any *beit* he enjoys complete immunity and his pursuers refrain from harming him as their action would be regarded as an assault on the honour of his protectors who would then retaliate. It is also the responsibility of the protectors to seek ways and means of settling the dispute between the parties concerned and to reach an agreement on compensation.

The 'right of refuge' is pushed one step further in what is called the 'right of the *wajh*' (face), which displays in a more striking way the relation between the concept of the *ḥ'aram* and the honour of the group. Initially, this right states that immunity should be guaranteed for an enemy who surrenders to his foes in wars or raids. By analogy a culprit, especially a murderer whose blood and life are sought in retaliation, can go to the *beit* of his own victim and claim immunity. It is the binding duty of the people of the *beit* to accept him as a fugitive and as a *protégé* and to grant him the immunity he asks for. Tolerating the culprit, who now becomes their guest, certainly requires a high degree of self-control on their part, for it involves 'swallowing' their grudges and suppressing their feelings. In fact, it is also their responsibility to convince the other branches of the lineage to forget their injury and to accept the blood compensation. Their reward is the sublime honour they acquire by behaving in such an honourable way. Needless to say, failure to comply with these rules brings shame and disgrace on the whole lineage.

In fact, the rules and principles attached to the *ḥ'aram* extend far beyond the limits of the material *beit* to encompass strangers from other clans who, for one reason or another, come to live in the vicinity of a certain *beit* in a tribal area not their own. Here also the members of the *beit* are obliged to extend to them their hospitality and protection as defined by the 'rights of neighbourhood'. They have also to provide them with all the necessary facilities for making their livelihood, and may go to the extent of allotting them a patch of land to cultivate and allowing them to graze animals on their pasture-land and use their wells. Besides acquiring prestige by extending this sort of hospitality, such a generous action secures for them potential clients and political allies in tribal disputes. The honour of a lineage is much enhanced by the number of clients who gather round it and who may in time be grafted on to it. 'Neighbours' in this sense usually enjoy the same right to be protected and avenged as the real members of the *beit*. It is noteworthy that if the 'rights of neighbourhood' are withheld from a man for any reason and he suffers loss or harm as a result, the people of the *beit* who refused him these rights are held responsible.

4

In a paternalistic society like the Bedouins' where the male occupies a dominant social position in all aspects and activities of life, it is only natural that the honour of the group is determined primarily by the behaviour and achievements of the men rather than the women. Nevertheless, the woman can, and indeed does play a conspicuous role in determining the honour of her family and lineage in an unique and decisive way that cannot be ignored or minimized. Apart from the important concept of the *ḥ'aram* which is conceptually linked with the woman, the woman's own conduct in daily life bears heavily on the honour of her people. As has been noted, this is clearest with regard to her sexual activities and especially her chastity. The Bedouins do not impose sexual segregation but they do respect severe rules for the behaviour of one sex towards the other. Deviation from these rules results in the murder of the offenders. Thus a girl with a bad reputation may disappear suddenly from the camp. Everyone guesses what has happened to her, but no one speaks about it, let alone approaches the authorities. Rape on the other hand is considered a more humiliating offence than homicide. The offender himself is usually killed in retaliation, but retribution is not exacted from any of his kinsmen unless he escapes beyond reach. Yet this is not regarded as sufficient to wipe out the shame. The girl herself is therefore killed, especially if it is thought that intercourse took place with her consent and her disgraced kinsmen usually desert their traditional homeland and migrate in a voluntary exile to a region where no one knows about their *'ar*. Sexual offences, however slight they may be, are offences against that particular and more specific kind of honour which is called *'ird*. As has already been said, *'ird* is affected only by the conduct of the woman and in this respect it differs from the more general concept of *sharaf*. *'Ird* differs also from *sharaf* in that *sharaf* can be acquired and augmented through right behaviour and great achievements, whereas *'ird* can only be lost by the misconduct of the woman. And once lost, it cannot be regained.

The responsibility for retaliation in cases of offences inflicted against *'ird* falls on the shoulders of the near kin of the girl and more particularly on her *ibn 'amm* (father's brother's son) who stands in a unique position in relation to her, especially as far as her sexual life is concerned. The husband of the adulterous woman cannot impose any punishment on her, apart from divorcing her and recovering the bridewealth. Her shameful action does not affect the *'ird* of his lineage in the least. Thus if he kills her for adultery he will be subject to retaliation or the payment of bloodwealth to her kinsmen. Marriage does not sever the bonds which link a woman with her own agnatic group. The *ibn 'amm* on the other hand is always regarded in Bedouin society as a potential, and in fact a preferred, husband to his *bint 'amm* (father's brother's daughter). He is the closest relative permitted to marry her and he is considered the best man to look after her and thus to protect the *'ird* of the lineage. She cannot get married unless he consents to the marriage and states that he does not desire her as a wife. If a girl marries without the consent and approval of her *ibn 'amm* he is entitled by tradition to kill her, while her father and brothers are severely reprimanded for violating custom and tribal law. It is because of these functions and privileges that the *ibn 'amm* is regarded as the person responsible for retaliation for the stain on their collective *'ird*.

But although the woman does not affect the *'ird* of her husband's lineage, she certainly affects the honour of her sons and their descendants, not only through her behaviour or her lineage's social position, but also through her so-called origin or race. As has been said, the Bedouins give much weight to the question of the purity of their Arab blood and consider it important to their honour. A man usually boasts of having Arab ancestors and ancestresses on both sides. This does not mean that it is shameful to have a Berber or an Egyptian (peasant) mother, but somehow Berber or Egyptian blood puts a man into a lower grade as far as honour is concerned. This distinction is made even between the descendants of half-brothers born of an Arab and a non-Arab mother. Thus, patrilineality among the Bedouins does not entirely eliminate the matrilateral elements supplementing the prestige of the paternal and patrilocal lineages and defining their social position.

5

From the above account of the concepts of honour and shame, the main points can be summed up and new light shed on a few others.

(a) Honour, in the wide sense of the word, is regarded as a matter of compliance with the traditional patterns of behaviour. In this sense, honour is almost tantamount to 'goodness' or 'virtue' and a man of honour is simply a 'good' or 'virtuous' man. Honour is here attained, or rather maintained, by simple and sincere conformity to the prevailing social norms. This is a rather passive way of acquiring honour.

(b) In the narrower and more precise sense, honour requires more than the mere acceptance of the established social norms. It depends rather on the achievement of superiority and distinction. Social ideals can be realized in daily life in ways which contribute in various degrees to the reputation and prestige of both the individual and the group. In most cases the realization of the ideal (and the means to this) and consequently the attainment of honour are influenced by the behaviour of others. This appears clearly in the action which a group takes, for example, to rebuff a raid or to reply to an offence. Honour here is gained and maintained by wiping out the shame which befalls a group as a result of the behaviour of others. Sometimes, the social ideal can only be realized at the expense of another person or another group. Here also, raids on hostile camps and groups serve as an example. For, in such cases, the raiders do not acquire honour merely because they have raided the camps of their enemies and shown daring courage, but also because in doing this they have tarnished their honour and disgraced them. Unsuccessful raids bring only shame on the attacking party regardless of the courage or the military ability they may have shown. The highest grade of honour, however, is attained when the ideal can only be realized at the expense of the performer himself. The best example of this is the obligation to grant sanctuary to an enemy when he asks for it. In such cases a man gives practical proof that in his consideration honour is larger than life.

(c) The excessive and uncontrolled desire to realize the ideal may sometimes bring the opposite results. Thus an unchecked passion for raiding and wars does not necessarily raise the prestige of raiders nor enhance their social standing. On the contrary, it is always regarded with dismay and considered as shameful rashness. Even generosity and hospitality, which are generally admired, may bring shame when carried to excess. It is difficult to say where exactly lies the line at which honourable deeds may find their sense reversed and become a source of disgrace, but the line does exist and society knows how to evaluate the same action in different contexts.

(d) In the segmentary society of the Bedouins of the Western Desert, which have only recently been submitted to a strong governmental authority, honour has played, and still plays, a most vital role in the field of social control, besides providing an effective code of morality. As in all segmentary societies of this type, social and political relationships among the Bedouins depend largely on maintaining a balance between opposed segments and the various kinship groups. A disturbance in this delicate balance usually results in bitter strife and leads to long and bloody feuds. A slight offence inflicted against a lineage or a lineage-segment is taken as an unforgivable humiliation requiring immediate retaliation to wipe out the shame, regain honour and restore the same relations as formerly between the groups. This strict defence of honour stands as a guarantee against misconduct and unjustified aggression. The fear that the offended group will retaliate with violence is an effective check on the behaviour of individuals and groups alike. On the other hand, the shame which strikes an aggressor or a culprit and the consequent humiliation he brings on himself as well as on his kin-group is an additional factor in regulating social behaviour. Thus, it is clear that honour and shame which are usually attributed to a certain individual or a certain kinship group have in fact a bearing on the total social structure, since most acts involving honour or shame are likely to affect the existing social equilibrium between the different kinship units which constitute at the same time political entities in which this society is ordered.

I*

Index